COMING HOME

A Guide to Dying
at Home
with Dignity

The medical, health and supportive procedures in this book are based on the training, personal experiences and research of the author and on recommendations of responsible medical and nursing sources. But because each person and situation is unique, author and publisher urge the reader to check with a qualified health professional before using any procedure where there is any question as to its appropriateness.

The publisher does not advocate the use of any particular healing technique or practice but believes the information presented in this book should be available to the public.

Because some risks may be involved, the author and publisher assume no responsibility for any adverse effects or consequences resulting from the use of any of the suggestions, preparations or procedures in this book. Please do not use the book if you are unwilling to assume those risks. Feel free to consult a physician or other qualified health professional. It is a sign of wisdom, not timidity or cowardice, to seek a second or third opinion.

This book may be quoted up to one full page without written permission, provided credit is given including the name of this book, the author, and Aurora Press.

Published by Aurora Press Inc.
205 Third Ave 2A
New York, NY 10003

Library of Congress Catalogue Card No. 87-0713
ISBN: 0-943358-31-0

COMING HOME

A Guide to Dying
at Home
with Dignity

DEBORAH DUDA

AURORA PRESS
205 Third Ave. 2A New York, N.Y. 10003

To Mom and Dad, Judy and Suzy,
Auntie Thelma, Ben and Joshua
for giving me so much love that I could
look at things I was afraid of.

TABLE OF CONTENTS

Chapter 9:
LIVING FULLY WITH DYING—OUR FEELINGS

ABOUT THE AUTHOR

Deborah Duda was raised in a small town in England and traveled around the U.S. and the world in a military family. After graduating from Miami University in Oxford, Ohio, she worked in the National Gallery of Art, in Washington, D.C., studied art in Europe, and lived for many years sailing on a boat in the Mediterranean Sea. Concerned about the war in Vietnam and U.S. foreign policy in general, she returned to the U.S. and joined the U.S. Foreign Service. She served as an Ambassador's protocol aide, and vice consul and cultural attaché in the U.S. embassy in Santiago, Chile.

Dismayed with U.S. policy in that country at the time of the election of President Salvador Allende, she resigned and moved to Paris. There she helped a Brazilian exile leader write an exposé of the torture in Brazil, the first presented to the Human Rights Committee of the United Nations.

She came to believe that political solutions for human problems are useless until individual people change and began an inner journey. She moved to San Miguel de Allende, Mexico where she studied the world's spiritual teachings, painted and was a successful fashion designer. She spent time in a Zen Buddhist and a Tibetan Buddhist monastery and a Hindu Temple in Nepal and India.

After meeting Mother Teresa, she returned to the U.S., studied alternative healing and began her work with the dying. At 39 she completed an MA with Goddard College.

"I did it so people would believe I knew what I already knew." For the last ten years she has been actively involved in helping people accept dying and death as a natural part of life.

She is learning and helping others to learn to release the addiction to pain and the addiction to running away from it taught by our culture so we can live joyfully which she believes is our birthright. She is currently writing on this topic.

Her home is on Kauai, Hawaii.

Deborah Duda

ACKNOWLEDGEMENTS

I give again the thanks I've already given many times in my heart to John Muir, Mary Conley, Dad and all the others who shared with me the incredible gift of their dyings and deaths. And to all the families and friends with the courage to make their dying at home possible, particularly my Mom, Craig Conley and Jean Pallares, and Eve Muir. Thank you, dear Eve, for also caring enough about the book to spend so much time helping me make my vision understandable to others.

Each person who helped with the book cared in his or her own way that there be less fear in the world and a greater acceptance of life including death. The caring of each increased the light in the world. A loving thanks to each friend, advisor, supporter, teacher and inspirer along the way: Ken and Barbara Luboff, Leigh Peacocke, Gathanna Parmenas, Carolyn Silver, Robert Waterman, Elisabeth Kubler-Ross, Mother Teresa and to myself.

I give love and gratitude to my publisher, Barbara Somerfield, for our shared vision.

Thank you fellow typists and dear friends, Jim Sinclair, John Midgley, Carolyn Elliot and Joan Griffiths. And again thanks to Ken Luboff for very graciously returning the book rights to me.

3

In the Beginning there was Life. And Life seemed to be without form. It was indistinguishable. So Death was created to give form to Life. And then people began to become attached to Life as the enemy, the place of suffering, and Death, the friend.

And now we come to a place where we see that both are One.

So those of us who made an enemy of Death, must make of Death a friend. And those who made an enemy of Life, must make of Life a friend.

INTRODUCTION

Ten years ago I was wandering around the world looking outside myself for some teacher or teaching to help me understand what my life was all about. I decided to return to the clarity I remembered in a small village at the foot of Mount Machupuchere, in Nepal.

In Pokkara, I found a Sherpa guide who volunteered to act as interpreter and go with me to the village to find a house. The next day two Tibetan women carried my bags up the mountain trails to the tiny mud house we had found and I set up housekeeping. I quit trying to figure "it" all out and just lived contentedly with the villagers, taking photographs and recording the sounds and music of village life.

After a few weeks I began to have nightmares, I or someone in my family was dying. Each day I was afraid of what the next night might bring. One day a few months later, a Sherpa stopped by with a valentine from Mom and Dad and a copy of *Newsweek* magazine with Mother Teresa's picture on the cover. That night I dreamed about her. The next morning I decided the only way to overcome my fear of death was to put myself in the middle of it. I would go to Calcutta and ask Mother Teresa if I could work in a *Hydray House*, one of the homes she created for people dying on the streets. *Hydray* is Sanscrit for "heart".

By the time I arrived in Calcutta, I was so sick with dysentery and worms that getting out of bed to call Mother Teresa was a great effort. When I did, I found her easy to talk with. I told her about my dreams and asked if I could see her. Very lovingly she said, "Come right over, my child."

I dragged myself to the main convent in Calcutta and asked her my crucial question, "Can I work for a few months in one of your homes for the dying?"

She answered, "No, my child. Go home. There is sadness and suffering right around you at home."

Then, feeling desperate and lonely, I asked, "Can I adopt a child from the orphanage?"

Again she answered, "No, my child. Go home and work with the sadness and loneliness around you."

And I did—first with the fear, sadness and loneliness in myself. And the key has been *hydray*, the heart—transforming the fear that keeps hearts closed.

I began writing this book after two friends I love very much were cared for at home until they died. Then I worked with terminally ill patients and their families at our local hospital and with some who chose to die at home. While I was doing the final editing on this book, my father died at home.

Before the deaths of my two friends, when I thought of dying I felt stupid, which made me afraid or angry—so I

Introduction

pretended indifference. As a teenager, a gray squirrel on a country road was the only living thing I'd seen die. I shuddered as I watched its death dance in the rearview mirror. A public road! It's out of place, unnatural. Everyone knows animals go away to die in hidden places. For three days I kept off the road while trying to figure out where this death fit into the scheme of things. Later in life I shot a few deer, and blanked that out. I saw my grandfather dead but didn't see how he got that way.

Not until past thirty did I really become aware that people were dying around me all the time; that I was dying all the time, parts of me, old cells, old ideas, old ways of being. Death was hidden out of sight in hospitals, in statistics, in a compartment of my being I didn't look at. I saw a friend lonely and isolated because fear kept friends from talking with her about the most important thing happening in her life—her dying.

Then I was angry, truly angry—anger born from awareness of my own ignorance and fear. I felt cheated. Most of us are cheated out of the fullness of life by fear and embarrassment. We experience the pain and joy of birth and life and then many of us deny ourselves our death, the closure of a circle. Denial comes from fear . . . our fear, doctors' fear, loved ones' fear, our whole culture's fear.

As I began to accept dying and death as part of my life, my fear was transformed into love, my anger into compassion, my depression into joy. The quality of my relationship with myself and with others improved. After working with dying people and the deaths and rebirths within myself, I feel more profoundly my kinship with all of life.

The book has grown from a sense of our wholeness (holiness). It covers the practical information needed to

7

help alleviate many of our fears. "Practical" includes not only the "what-to-do and how-to-do-it" of physical care, but also mental, emotional and spiritual support. Once the needs for comfort and relief from pain are met, spiritual food can be more nourishing than a glass of carrot juice or a hamburger. Supporting a home-dying is a wonderful opportunity to learn that spiritual support can be practical and physical care can be spiritual.

The book, then, is a synthesis of my psychological and spiritual understandings and the basic information on physical care needed to support someone who lives at home until he or she dies. It includes things to keep in mind when making the decision where to die. And, if home is the choice, what to do about family morale, pacing yourself, pain relief, calling a doctor, giving injections, taking care of your feelings, etc. Although the book is directed principally to the family and friends, much of it can be shared with the dying person as well.

I share with you my reality, my vision at this time in my life. Your reality, including your spiritual understanding and approach to death may be different. Use this book as a tool to help find the answers in yourself. If I use words that are not your words, let's move deeper than the word level . . . to the heart.

Trust yourself! We learn by having the courage to enter another's reality without seeing it as a threat and we can do this only if we trust ourselves. Sometimes seeing ideas in print convinces us that someone "out there" is the expert who knows more than we do about our experience. Anyone outside of ourselves can only be a provider of information or inspiration. You're the only expert on your reality. The appropriate way to support someone who is dying is the way the dying person and you choose. And if some of your choices are different from theirs, you can do it your way when it's your turn.

Dying is the process of the life forces withdrawing from the body and death the moment of withdrawal. We often hear that life and death are opposites. To me, the opposites are birth and death. One describes entering into form, the other leaving form. Which is which depends on your perspective. Either way, life continues without end. In this book "dying", "death", and "died" refer only to change in form and do not mean "the end," "the final disaster", or the "uncontrollable enemy." I see death as a friend on our way home to more life.

I believe at some level of our being we decide when we're going to die. After that our only choices are our attitude about dying and sometimes, where it will take place. Both affect the quality of the time we have, and the latter may affect the quantity.

Accepting death is a process of surrender, of letting go and accepting life as it *is* rather than how we think it *should* be. Exquisite beauty and meaning can be present in dying when we and the dying person accept in our hearts that life is following its natural course, and when we cooperate with life instead of fighting against it. When we do, we no longer feel separate from each other and from life: we experience the underlying unity of everything.

Love makes being alive worthwhile. Love transforms fear. Caring for a dying person is an opportunity to increase our capacity to love by decreasing our fear. Within each of us is love, a lover, and a beloved — so we can't really lack love, someone to love, or someone to love us. But fear keeps hearts closed, which prevents us from experiencing this.

Fear prevents surrendering and makes us feel separate and alone.

Fear projects awful things that may happen, especially while someone is dying. I've never encountered anything awful in all the home dyings I've been involved with. Before I worked with dying people I seemed to be the ideal candidate for *not* being able to handle dying. I had a long history of passing out in health class, at the sight of blood, or just visiting a friend in the hospital. I was terrified each time I got a shot and on more than one occasion, threw up when someone near me did.

To be afraid of death is to be afraid of life. This book is about acknowledging our fears, while at the same time moving through them toward greater love, joy and freedom as we experience dying.

One way our culture teaches fear of death (life) is by making security a goal. Total security is, of course, an illusion. Life is a process of change and inherent in change are vulnerability and risk. At any moment our plans for the future can disintegrate. Holding on to security or chasing after it creates more insecurity and fear. And do we really want it anyway? Maximum security is prison, not life.

We break the circle of fear and insecurity when we live each moment as it comes. You can do this right now with this "dying" you're living.

Peace is possible in this moment. It's not out there somewhere in the future. The future never really comes, anyway. By the time it gets to us, it's the present.

Focusing on life as a process instead of as a goal has helped me accept death. I accept that at any point in time a process is complete up until that moment. At each moment each of us is complete and whole. No one dies before the

Introduction

purpose of his or her life is fulfilled even if we cannot understand that purpose. I believe that a child who dies young or someone who dies unexpectedly dies complete. Perhaps some of their projects aren't complete but who we are is not our unfinished work, projects or goals. The purpose of goals is just to give us a sense of direction.

When a life is seen as a process and not a goal, death loses much of its sting and,

Today is a good day to die for all the things of my life are here.

— Chief Crazy Horse

Dying, like living, has its share of sadness and joy. The sadness of letting go of a person we love is tempered if we remember to hold everyone lightly, knowing they are "just on loan." When someone we love is dying, we tend to focus on sadness, not on joy. But it's a choice. We can allow joy into this often most painful experience of our lives; the quiet joy of sharing love and caring, of seeing a loved one content, of touching into timelessness.

If we live each moment of each day fully, we transcend time. Each moment then becomes an eternity and we have all the time in the universe to share with this dying person we love. It doesn't matter how long we live, only *how* we live the time we have. It's possible to create of this experience a beautiful time in your life.

The increased love and compassion we can learn while caring for someone who dies at home will help us through our initial loneliness. If the death has not been sudden, there's been time between smoothing sheets, emptying bedpans, holding hands and talking of what may come, for grieving and resolving any unclarity with the dying person. There's been time to begin a gradual adjustment to earthly life without this person.

Because dying is living intensified, the qualities most needed to support someone dying are the same ones needed for living fully: love, compassion, courage, serenity, patience, humor, humility and right use of will — allowing others to live or die as they choose as long as they take responsibility for their choices.

By taking responsibility for dying, we reclaim responsibility for living and regain the personal power we'd given away. One way to take responsibility is to stop playing victim to our culture's pressure to go away quietly and die in the sterility of a nursing home or hospital. Who wants to be seen as a forthcoming vacancy! We can die *right here* amidst the people and things we love, the kids, the dog, the garden, our favorite chair.

As you live this dying, be gentle with yourself and love yourself. There's no need to judge or blame yourself or feel guilty. Our lives are a learning process in which we outgrow some old thoughts and feelings as we increase in wisdom. Blame or guilt about the past is punishing ourselves for learning! Keep forgiving yourself for being so hard on yourself, and remember: What we're accustomed to calling "mistakes" are really experiences to learn from.

In this book I use the phrases "dying person", "sick person" and "patient" to save more convoluted wording. Inherent in these phrases are notions that hold us to old patterns. **We're all dying.** I don't believe there is such a thing as a "sick person" — only people with imbalances between their bodies, minds, feelings and souls. "Patient" has an impersonal quality which denies our uniqueness and

Introduction

humanness and promotes the illusion that a dying person's experience is separate from ours. Our experiences aren't separate. **We aren't separate.**

CHAPTER 1

THREE EXPERIENCES
WITH DYING AT HOME

I'd like to share with you my first two experiences with friends who died at home and my dad's death. Perhaps after reading about them, dying at home won't seem like walking into the unknown. At least their stories will give you an idea of what it can be like. Their deaths and each home death I have been privileged to share were unique. And each was a song of love.

JOHN

John Muir was best known for his book, *How to Keep Your Volkswagen Alive, A Manual of Step-by-Step Procedures for the Compleat Idiot.* I remember his love, generosity and heckling to remind me to live in the *present*.

I met John and his wife, Eve, eleven years ago in a colonial town and artist colony high in the mountains of Mexico. The big treat in San Miguel was Thursday afternoons at John and Eve's. There we soaked in the hot pool and talked and talked about our projects and dreams. John had a gift for sharing love and money to help his friends make their dreams come true without undermining their dignity or initiative.

Over the years, a loving family of friends grew, that supported each of us in being and doing whatever we chose. Some wanted and needed a patriarch and John allowed himself to be it. And he was a delightful one. He loved all the attention and had fun with the power. At the same time, he encouraged us to take responsibility for ourselves and tried to teach us that "Humans have evolved to where leaders are no longer necessary."

If a 'hero' is someone who's true to his or her beliefs and inspires others, John was a hero. Physically he looked the part. He was a huge, lion-like, tawny-colored being with blue eyes that saw deeper than appearances. John did and thought what he wanted . . . which ranged from unique to outrageous. Without regard for the traditional value of job security, at various times he was a musician, sailor, mechanic, welder, structural engineer, builder, and author; also beatnik, hippie, philosopher, lover, husband and father. He traveled the U.S. and Mexico in a converted 33-passenger army bus and sailed a Chinese junk until it sank in a hurricane off Cape Hatteras.

When no publisher wanted the "Volkswagen Idiot Book", John and Eve had enough faith in it to sell a house and start their own publishing company. They made a reasonable fortune and shared it. Each January, John held a business meeting/party at a beach in Mexico and paid expenses for friends who otherwise couldn't have come to share their ideas and manuscripts.

John had an incessant curiosity about life. His second book, *The Velvet Monkey Wrench*, was a blueprint for a society based on agreement among people to respect each other and the land. John and I became closer amidst yelling, steaming and reasoning as I helped edit it. Later, after trekking through Nepal together, John continued to work on a book about the energy that gives life to matter, sometimes called "the life force."

John loved women and there were generally lots around him. He felt we held a clue about this illusive life force. He knew it was connected to the balance of male and female energy in the universe. In his last couple of years, John was obsessed by his search to understand it. A number of friends asked him to take a break away from the book because it seemed to be making him sick. John wouldn't let go.

One hot June morning in Oregon, he stood up feeling dizzy after his usual three-minute headstand and fell. The dizziness continued and couldn't be diagnosed — a CAT Scan showed nothing; his ears and eyes were perfect. He asked Eve, seemingly out of the blue, "Is this just an inconvenience or is this death?"

By late August the dizziness was worse and his handwriting was shaky. A second CAT Scan showed a growth on the brain. He decided on an operation which verified a fast-growing malignant tumor, an offshoot of one in his lungs. The doctors said, "Two months to two years." John was fifty-nine.

Coming Home

He recovered quickly from the operation and refused radiation therapy, joking, "If I'm wrong will you dance on my grave?" Then he and Eve searched for alternative treatments and went camping in their favorite spots in the Southwest. Armed with laetrile, at that time considered by some as a hopeful alternative treatment, they headed to Santa Fe, New Mexico. There, John tried acupuncture again, but found it too painful. Except for occasional forays into ice cream, he stuck to a vegetable diet — a major change for a "meat and potatoes man". He denied having cancer and told us not to mention it. Every morning he dictated his life force ideas into a tape recorder.

One day in mid-October John woke up with a terrific headache. Pressure from the growing tumor was causing fluid to collect in his head. He agreed to have the fluid drained. This supposedly *simple* procedure impaired his speech. To a man who loved to talk, slurring his words was a kind of death. Blessedly his thinking remained clear.

The doctors said if he stayed in the hospital he'd be hooked up to life support systems. After an exuberant session playing guitars and singing around his hospital bed, it was obvious that his friends were too many and too noisy for a hospital. He wanted out. We wanted him out. Elizabeth, his friend and former wife, spoke for us all, "The quality of life is more important than the quantity."

John and Eve didn't own a home in Santa Fe, so a friend loaned them a large, empty adobe. In the four hours before the ambulance arrived with John, we made the house a home . . . rugs, pillows, wall hangings, rented TV and hospital bed, a complete kitchen, and a schedule for cooking and sitting with John in two-hour shifts. No one in particular directed. Each person sensed the needs and went about fulfilling them.

Three Experiences with Dying at Home

It was a glorious Autumn afternoon in the mountains when the ambulance pulled up. John was carried on a stretcher through the open garden gate and down the stone path. The sun shone on him through golden aspen leaves. After we tucked him in bed next to a window partially opened to the fresh mountain air, he seemed relieved and content. Some of us fussed with food; others gathered around the fireplace and played guitars. Often someone tiptoed in to see John sleeping, not because he needed checking, just for the joy of seeing him *at home.*

That evening friends were called all over the country. "If you need to say goodbye to John in person, it's time to come." Already fifteen or twenty of us had gathered, eight lived in or camped around the house.

John orchestrated his dying as he did his living. Rusty, a nurse and masseur friend from Mexico, became coordinator for his needs. Some family members still had ideas about saving his body and the first morning home John said, "Let the kids test their theories." He believed actions are things to learn from. There are no mistakes, no being wrong. If we do nothing, we learn nothing.

In fairness to the different treatments tried—diet, laetrile, poultices, acupuncture, etc.—they were tested, I believe, after John had already decided at some level to die.

My concern was his preparation for the soul voyage rather than the attempts to save his body. I gave him Bach Flowers, tinctures of flower essences that work on an energetic principle which many believe help integrate the personality and the soul. (See Appendix B)

Day by day I watched John and Eve as they decided what he did and did not want. He continued to take laetrile and although he was very uncomfortable he did not have severe pain. Perhaps the laetrile and Bach Flowers had positive benefits in terms of pain control. It's hard to say, though, because doctors estimate that up to fifty percent of terminal cancer patients don't have pain.

Within the family, loving factions developed over diet. Was it best to maintain an extreme cleansing diet or was it too late? John wanted ice cream, not wheatgrass juice and raw vegetables. Seemed reasonable to me. Ice cream and cigarettes were sneaked to him to protect the feelings of friends not yet ready for him to die.

Time seemed to stand still as we shared those last few weeks together. When we weren't massaging, bathing, feeding or just being with him, we sat around the fire, reminisced about shared experiences, and caught up on current news. In the evening some made a circle of power for healing around him, some chanted. An Indian medicine man was called and made a "helping the spirit to leave ceremony." A minister from the Native American Church who married John and Eve ten years earlier, came to give his blessings. An oncologist, two unconventional MDs and a homeopath came in and out.

Having friends to share this dying experience was very supportive and not all roses. Two couples who weren't speaking to each other, gracefully and with difficulty, laid aside their grievances. Several of us had opportunities to examine jealousy or irritation as we imagined that so-and-so was 'more important' or 'taking over'.

One night a friend of John and Eve's brought her drunk and suicidal brother to the house and left him there while she went dancing. I was outraged. "How can anyone be so thoughtless? John is dying in the next room." Eve didn't seem bothered. Without words she helped me understand that there was enough love for everyone. It was an important lesson for me about operating out of the belief in plenty instead of scarcity. And it still took me a while to let go of my anger.

Then there was the afternoon two friends put a clay poultice on John's neck and left him to play with a video camera in the living room. Everyone was making so much noise that no one heard John's bellow for help until after the poultice burned him. He was furious and hollered, "I want to see ALL of you with one of these on."

We all wondered what the family would be like without John. We wondered why he was dying when he seemed to live with such joy and enthusiasm. Our theories about his death told more about our relationship with him and about our own beliefs than about the actual reasons for his death. I believed John and I had the same "dis-ease" — an attachment to being in control and resistance to surrendering. We were both stubborn and we were both looking for answers outside of ourselves.

It seems to me now that dying was John's ultimate lesson in surrender. Without surrender, the feminine principle, he couldn't complete his ideas on the life force. If we haven't learned it earlier, dying can teach us surrender. When we surrender, we open to the life force which is always within us. Perhaps John wanted the answer to his question so much that he created his dying to get the answer.

It's been nearly as tough for me to let go of fantasies about the patriarch as it was for the patriarch to let go.

After it seemed obvious to us that saving his body was impossible, John seemed to be deciding whether to fight or surrender to death. Some of us were reading Elisabeth Kübler-Ross's description of the stages of dying — denial and isolation, anger, bargaining, depression and acceptance. John moved back and forth between all of them.

Most of the time John denied he was dying; this left him in control but unable to find ways to heal himself. He bargained, "Let me just finish the book" or "Oh, OK, if Eve and I can just take a trip to Hawaii first." Off and on he was depressed. He said, "I was always afraid of being hurt and now I hurt."

It was difficult to talk with John about dying because he hadn't accepted it was happening to him. He'd often said, "Death is the greatest adventure of them all. I'll see what it's like when I get there." Now, he was angry at dying. Yet being angry and fighting seemed to clear the air so he could finally accept *his* dying. Once he did, it took him only a day and a half to die.

Occasionally now images come to me of Eve's graceful calm and humour; the oncologist in suit and tie crossing paths in John's room with a medicine man in a black feathered hat; Eve lifting cupped hands of new fallen snow to John so he could enjoy the first snowfall; the two of them cuddled in the narrow hospital bed; Eve and John's former wife working side by side bathing him; John and I watching Walter Cronkite report the news while Eve was off dancing; his telling everyone who brought up business, "Look, my will's in order and if you don't leave me alone, I'll put Star and Craig in charge of everything." Both sons were eighteen. Earlier he'd said he wanted the "60 peso funeral," the cheapest in Mexico!

The last weekend there were fewer people and we all stayed overnight in our Victoria Street home. The whisperings in the kitchen subsided. It was quiet and peaceful. John was tending to dying and each of us to finishing our 'business' with him.

The day before he died, John asked Dr. Greg if there was any way for him to live. Greg gave the medical answer, "No, we can only make you as comfortable as possible without making you unconscious." John said, "I'm too uncomfortable to go on living anyway."

As Greg left the room, John said to me, "Deborah, you've got to stop your compulsive lying."

That stopped me in my tracks. John still had a knack for getting someone's attention by using something they were attached to . . . like my image of myself as an honest person.

At first I thought he was referring to my saying "nobody dies" because the doctor had just told him he was going to die. But that wasn't it. I was stunned. I felt like I'd been kicked in the gut. I asked him to repeat what he said and he did. Choked and teary I demanded, "Don't you dare die without explaining to me what you mean. It's not fair to leave a ghost like that." He continued, "Stop saying you're going to quit smoking or *going* to do anything in the *future*." What I understood from his slurred words was that he was trying to help me stop setting booby-traps for myself. Often enough he'd heard me project something I *might* do in the future, then feel I'd failed when I didn't do it. One of his last gifts to me was again trying to help me live in the *present*.

That night none of us expected John to live until the morning. We held our last healing circle. This time the healing was for John, not for his body. He seemed to finally accept that we loved *him*, not just the part of him that helped us out or made our lives happier. We loved him whether or not he finished his book.

After the healing circle he said, "Eve, I love you . . . such good friends." And someone said, "You've been a wonderful friend to us." John did not speak again.

We scheduled ourselves by twos every two hours to help him sit up and cough. Now his breathing had an unnerving rattling sound. He couldn't swallow and we kept moistening his parched lips. It was terrible to watch helplessly as he suffered. Only later did I understand that his soul, or consciousness, was already out of the body. The body was suffering but John was not suffering.

The shifts shortened to one hour, then to half an hour. When not on shift, we cuddled together like children and slept on mattresses covering the living room floor. I remember looking down on my sleeping partners and feeling how much I loved them.

John's body labored all night, coughing and struggling for air. The body seemed to have a life of its own and it hung on.

In the morning I went to my construction job, plastering. Rough to get the walls smooth when my heart and mind were with John and the family. Each time I called home, John was still alive. After work I stopped by the most expensive grocery store in Santa Fe and bought two baskets of fresh raspberries and a Toblerone chocolate bar. Perhaps outer nourishment might ease the inner loss! I ate one whole basket on the way home and saved the other for Eve.

When I got home, John was weaker and Eve was away. She'd gone out in her car to scream, yell and cry. This, along with dancing, usually helped her remain calm. This time she came back mad. "John has pulled us into a terrible sadness

24

trip. He said death is the greatest adventure – he might as well relax and enjoy it!" Gently she repeated this to John. He relaxed and breathed easier. Maybe he'd been waiting to hear from *her* that it was OK to let go.

She left the room and we sat there and ate the Toblerone. A few minutes later Rusty motioned me to get her. She came and held John's hand. At three o'clock in the afternoon, John stopped breathing. The six of us there chanted OM as he left his body. (Om, or Aum, is understood by many as the Primal Sound or the sound that connects us to everything. It's used particularly by Hindus and Buddhists.)

Tears of sadness, relief and joy rolled down our waiting faces. We held each other and prayed, each in his or her own way, for his soul to move quickly on. Candles and incense were lighted. Then we dressed him in his favorite blue flannel shirt and a pair of Eve's drawstring pants. His own were now too big. Eve put an *Ojo de Dios* (God's Eye) at his head and a child's pinwheel in his hand. Rusty shaved him. John's face seemed to fill out – all signs of pain and struggle gone. His real nobility of heart again came through the old familiar face.

That night we cried and laughed and told stories. I'd be talking with someone with tears running down my face and the next minute we'd both be laughing as we greeted others. Someone on her way to the house when John died said she saw him whooping up and down the foothills on a roller coaster laughing his head off. Friends phoned and were phoned. Eve called Wavy Gravy, a clown, and told him about John's death. His reply was, "Well . . . it was Patrick Henry's second choice!"

Two friends went off with a bottle of Scotch to build a coffin and hammer a thumb. The burial laws in New Mexico are very humane. You may bury someone on private property within twenty-four hours of death if the site is at least fifty feet from water. You file a burial certificate and get a body transfer permit, a one-stop operation. Later you note the burial site on the land deed so a highway or something isn't built over the grave. Friends offered a weedy little field by their house as a burial site. We decided to plant an orchard there.

The next morning, waiting for the coffin to arrive, many of us felt a little unfocused, like the day after Christmas. We wanted to bury him quickly. We'd had plenty of time to 'clear' with John and it was time to move on. I went to buy a cherry tree and a Jonathan apple for the new orchard and flowers for the grave. We arranged for a truck; a hearse didn't feel right. Our impression that John was a giant of a man manifested in a ridiculously large coffin, 9' x 4'. We placed John's body on a faded red *serape*. It was a relief to be outside. The body had begun to smell which wasn't as noticeable outside. (I learned later that the smell was probably from body fluids released after death.)

We followed the truck with the coffin over to Ken and Barb's field. Sawhorses were set up under a clear, early winter sky. People came and looked and cried. Some put treasures in the box they wanted to send with John's body; copies of his two books, a piece of jade, a bit of lapis lazuli, a Tibetan mandala, dancing shoes. Another writer put his pen in John's shirt pocket. "You can't put an author away without a pen."

We dug a great hole in the earth, much deeper than needed. Nearly everyone wanted a turn digging. I watched a friend with tears running down his face work with a pick and shovel until he was exhausted. "This is the last thing I can do for him," he said. It was great therapy to be out in the fresh air using our bodies. I wondered later why people let professionals take this therapy away from them.

We made a large circle, some sixty people, joining hands around the coffin. Whoever wanted to could speak. Eve had asked a friend to read a passage from *The Velvet Monkey Wrench*:

> Imitating someone else's style just because they are stronger, richer, fatter, or hipper is a stone drag. Picking our very own lifestyle is not a process of copying.

Not many of us trusted that if we opened our mouths words would come. Instead we sang *When the Saints Come Marching In*, and two women sat on a knoll playing a french horn and a fiddle. Eve tossed a yellow rose on top of the box for an absent friend as it was lowered into the earth. We shoveled in the earth and planted and watered a Jonathan apple tree.

A friend was free. A new orchard begun. A great day to celebrate . . . feasting, talking, dancing, crying, holding and being held. Someone asked, "Why aren't we this close all the time?"

John's last gift was giving us an opportunity to learn that "Dying is OK."

*   *   *   *   *

In many ways, John's experience and ours with him was unusual, but the feelings and situations we encountered are common.

In case you're beginning to feel hopeless and think you can't handle someone's dying without a squadron of friends, buckets of money, an extra house and endless supporters, take a break . . . then read on.

MARY

My next experience with dying came while we were still discussing writing a book about the last one. What we'd learned with John seemed useful to share.

Mary Conley's dying was very different from John's. Cancer was about the only thing they had in common. Mary had few close friends and almost no money. Her wealth was faith that death is a doorway to more life. The richness of our shared faith, my experience with John, and fewer people to orchestrate made her dying much easier for me.

There were four of us; Mary, her twenty-one-year-old son Craig, myself and later Craig's friend Jean. At first we felt alone, a tiny island tending to dying in a world going about business as usual. Our combined resources at the time were $200 and a house with one month's rent paid. Neither Craig nor Jean had been in close contact with someone dying, although Mary's husband (Craig's father) died ten years earlier of cancer. A daughter in Mexico had already done what she could and wasn't with us. That seemed OK. Each person has to decide what's right for them when someone's dying; not everyone has to be or can be present.

Mary and I met in San Miguel about the same time I met John and Eve and became close and beloved spiritual sisters. After her husband died, she traveled with her chil-

28

dren and continued to study astrology and the underlying laws of life. When we met she was a doting young grandmother often caring for her baby granddaughter by herself while writing a book on the Tarot. The Tarot is an ancient card system that uses universal archetypal symbols to bring to the conscious mind what the unconscious mind already knows.

When I was especially happy or depressed, I'd head down the cobblestone alleys to Mary's tiny adobe house at the bottom of the hill. No matter what state I arrived in, I left feeling better and seeing my life more clearly. Many others can say the same. Mary shared herself and her wisdom with whomever arrived on her doorstep and wanted to receive them.

For two years almost no one knew Mary had cancer. The last year of that time, she was housemother in a home for pregnant teenagers. Mary was the one who held a rejected girl's hand as she went through labor. Her love and guidance helped at least thirty young girls live through and learn from a potentially fearful experience. And at the same time she worked on healing her own dis-ease.

Mary knew cancer was her teacher and looked for the lessons it offered. She understood life as a spiral of births into flesh and deaths into spirit, moving closer each time to one's God-Self. Cancer was helping her learn something she needed to understand for this journey home. Mary believed it was about fear and the unworthiness she felt as a parent-less child.

Since childhood, she'd struggled between two parts of her personality she called Pitiful Pearl and Mary C. Pitiful Pearl was always afraid and felt she didn't deserve anything good from life. Mary C, on the other hand, was wise and courageous and manifested strongly when she was house-mother. Mary thought that as Mary C. got stronger, Pitiful Pearl felt threatened and expressed herself by creating ill-ness. It seemed to me that not expressing her sadness nor loving herself as generously as she loved others were impor-tant factors in her illness. Until the last five months, she seemed to have eliminated the cancer.

For me, Mary's dying began with a phone call I received at my parents' home in Texas. Craig said he and Mary were alone in her tiny second-story apartment in Albuquerque and both feeling crazy with the confinement and summer heat. They'd just returned from trips to a clinic in Mexico and to a psychic healer in Costa Rica and Mary was in terrible shape.

"OK", I told Craig, "I'm coming. We'll go to my house in Santa Fe." After I said it, my "Fearful One" did a terrific dance. "How can I care for her and work on my M.A. thesis *and* make enough money to survive?" "What if she's in terri-ble pain and I can't help?" "Where will I move if I have to leave my house because the echoes of her pain haunt me?"

In Albuquerque, I found a tiny, shriveled being who couldn't move or eat alone. When I'd last seen Mary five months earlier she was a very attractive, peppery red-haired woman of fifty who looked forty. Now she appeared a gray, skeletal eighty. My initial joy at seeing her changed to shock and pain. My chest felt like it was pushed against my spine. Knowing I needed time and space to grieve, I suggested I go to Santa Fe, clean house, then return for her.

During the hour's drive home, I yelled from as deep in my gut as I could. Yelling relieved the pressure; I was free to race around preparing the four small rooms. I chose the living room for Mary because afternoon sun illuminates it and the mountains, and I needed the nourishing morning light of my bedroom. I moved furniture, hung a wind chime and birdfeeder outside her windows, bought a bedpan and straws that bent, washed and ironed peach silk nightgowns, rented a wheelchair and potty chair and chose music she might like.

We couldn't afford an ambulance so we decided to bring Mary to Santa Fe in my pickup truck. Craig called the Fire Department Rescue Squad to carry her down the steep stairs of her apartment. They helped Mary onto the foam mattress in the pickup and we wedged her in with quilts and pillows. Because Craig's truck was threatening to break down, I followed him slowly up the valley between the *Jemez* and the *Sangre de Christo* (Blood of Christ) mountains. The trip was horrendous but Mary, with her usual grace, said, "Oh, it was just fine. Thank God to be home in the mountains."

Somehow we got her from the pickup to the house to the bed. She couldn't raise her arms so nightgowns, silk or not, were out! I felt again the blessed relief I'd felt when John came home. Now Mary was *home* and comfortable and had two people who loved her to do whatever was needed. The house was peaceful — filled with loving new energy and enormous bouquets of wild gold sunflowers.

Craig was exhausted. He'd dropped out the last quarter of his senior year of college to be with his mother. For six weeks he'd single-handedly fed, bathed and moved her everywhere (even between countries), and had helped her with whatever she needed including enemas. Knowing he could sleep soundly for the first time in months was deeply satisfying to me. He had to sleep on a sheepskin rug in the prayer room, but at least there was someone else to take a turn.

Coming Home

Because we had almost no money, we set about phoning everyone in town we could think of for help. If an agency or office couldn't help, we asked if they knew who could. We followed every lead. In a few days we had laetrile and two offers of wheelchairs to replace the rented one. We found a Visiting Nurse Service which had a grant from HEW to help the terminally ill. They supported our decision to be at home, and sent gentle competent nurses to visit twice a week and said we could call them any time.

I knew of another group, Open Hands, who visit with the elderly, disabled and terminally ill and provide counseling and other services like running errands, bathing, cooking or just being there to talk. They'd take over for us if we needed it. We found that Mary was eligible for Social Security and applied (although the money came after she died). We found a County Emergency Medical Fund that would pay any hospital expenses. Shanti, a volunteer counseling group, was willing to send a counselor. The nurse friend who gave John his laetrile shots didn't charge to give Mary hers.

Doctor Greg visited Mary and took care of her the night she went to the hospital and never sent a bill. He even took me to dinner one night when I *had* to get away. Another friend co-signed a bank loan so I could splurge on a color TV. With a TV Mary could have some variety and diversion when she wanted and I felt freer to do what I wanted. I went to a flower shop, told the florist that my friend was dying and that I wanted to surround her with beauty and didn't have much money. He let me scruffle through the trash cans where the imperfect flowers are tossed and I'd go home happily with bouquets of yellow roses and delicate white baby's breath.

Three Experiences with Dying at Home

Our day-to-day supporters were each other, God and Gathanna. The Quimby Center in Alamogordo, New Mexico, and the White Lodge in England, sent spiritual healing and support. One friend came with food, massages, love and recipes. One of my biggest fears had been what to cook. Another friend gave me energy by calling to check on how *I* was doing. Craig's relatives sent love and money and I sold antique clothing off the back porch.

I was surprised how much joy I could find in that little house with my friend dying in the living room. For a few minutes each morning before getting out of bed I meditated on joy and imagined myself as the "joyful servant." I put a sign JOY on the refrigerator door and over my bed to remind me of it throughout the day. As I nurtured my joyful servant, I experienced more and more what a privilege it was to share this opportunity to learn with Mary.

I joyed in our talks, watching the birds, daubing on Tea Rose perfume, hearing the wind chime, and massaging her. There was joy in our jokes about our spiritual interests or my using her as an excuse to get out of meetings I didn't want to go to—and in waltzing. When Mary couldn't walk alone anymore, I held her up under her arms. I'd ask, "Madame, may I have this waltz?" Our silliness let her know she wasn't a burden and helped her release some of the frustration of no longer being able to walk alone.

I took time for myself—for Tai Chi, jogging, paperwork and gardening—and encouraged Craig to do the same. He and Jean went camping for two days and visited with old friends. At twenty-one, Craig and Jean seemed young to be going through this. I would have felt motherly, except they were so sensitive and capable.

Coming Home

When Mary came to my house, she was denying that she would die. The denial continued for about three weeks. Maybe if she took more enzymes, she would throw off the cancer! Maybe a piece of stool was blocking her intestines and not a tumor! Maybe we should put poultices on the huge lump on her leg and open and drain it so it wouldn't poison her body! She needed hope.

One day Mary decided she wanted to take a coffee enema to detoxify her liver, which would eliminate the cancer. (Coffee enemas are sometimes used in alternative cancer treatments to help detoxify the liver, but must be part of a larger healing program.) The plan was to build a bench in my white prayer room and give her the enemas there, close to the bathroom. I hit the wall! I couldn't stand the idea of my sanctuary being messed up, and I felt guilty for it. "Deborah, how can you be so persnickety! Those enemas might help Mary live . . . at least they'd support her trying to help herself!" I wasn't compassionate enough with myself to think, "There's something important to me about this prayer room that gives me the strength to support her through this experience."

To assuage my guilt about my 'selfishness', I suggested an alternative plan, a liver flush commonly used in holistic healing. It's a cocktail of cayenne, garlic, ginger, olive oil and lemon juice mixed in orange juice to help it down. I mixed one up, a little heavy on the cayenne, and gave it to Mary. She took two sips, gagged and said, "It's awful!" and in five minutes she was shaking, sweating and delirious. I jumped into the bed and held her, thinking, "Deborah, she's going to die. You've killed her." Fortunately *for me* she didn't die but I felt guilty anyway. I hadn't yet graduated from the school of guilt.

34

Three Experiences with Dying at Home

About a week before Mary died, lumps sprouted all over her body. It was obvious she was dying, yet she was still denying it. Craig often felt disgusted and angry with his mother's lack of acceptance. "She's denying everything she ever taught me." He wished it were already over and felt guilty for wishing it. He didn't know that many people, living with someone they love who is dying slowly, have similar feelings. I suggested it was perfectly natural; his guilt was unnecessary. It's possible to feel "I wish it were over" and have compassion at the same time. Sometimes I was fed up and wanted Mary to be somewhere she wasn't: already accepting her death. But my nonacceptance was my problem, not hers.

Dealing with our frustrations was more difficult than physically caring for Mary. We'd sit on the back porch watching the chipmunks play and talk things out that bothered us. Sharing our fear, sadness and frustration, helped release them.

After one back porch discussion, Craig and I decided to tell Mary what we thought about her condition. We were frustrated with the attempts to save her. Doctor Greg wasn't around to do the talking for us so I told Mary, "We feel it would take a miracle to save your body. We believe in miracles, and it would have to be a big one . . . soon." This left *some* room for hope and gave her a clear picture of what *we* thought was happening.

But, she decided on a trip to the hospital to find out if some physical or mechanical obstruction, other than a cancerous tumor, prevented her from eating and eliminating. Although we didn't think much of the idea, it wasn't *our* life so we arranged it. This time we had to use an ambulance. The four of us spent one night in the hospital.

Coming Home

When we came home, Mary had to decide whether or not to continue the intravenous feedings that kept her body from dehydrating. Doctor Greg told her what he knew about dehydration. She decided not to continue the IVs, a decision that took great courage. In saying "no," she was also saying "I know I'm going to die." She chose, in effect, to die of dehydration instead of cancer. It's not a bad way to go. You slip slowly into unconsciousness and the main discomfort is dryness in the mouth.

About five days before she died, Mary accepted she was dying. That ended her depression and we could talk about death and what her work might be on the other side. If possible, she would report to us. We decided to use sunflowers as a sign for communicating after her death. If we were meditating and saw a sunflower, whatever we heard would be from Mary. I've since had a couple of sunflower messages.

Mary told us, "Get ready for Sunday. I'll be leaving." One part of me was irritated. For months I'd planned a retreat in the mountains that weekend with Patricia Sun, a well known spiritual teacher and healer. It took a while for me to realize that the most important spiritual teaching for me was going on in my own home. We started to get ready.

I suggested that Craig talk with his mother about anything unclear in their relationship so he wouldn't be left with the "I-wish-I-hads." Mary's daughter called from Mexico. I held the phone. It was a privilege to share that conversation: a mother saying goodbye to a daughter with whom the relationship had not been easy, expressing her love and her understanding of her daughter's absence.

Craig had Mary's land transferred to his name to avoid lawyers later. Mary had few other material possessions and

36

told Craig what to do with them. She gave me the perfect reminder of our common commitment, a little gold Florentine box with The Prayer of Saint Francis — the same prayer Mother Teresa later sent me.

I've often wondered how Craig felt as he went to the lumber yard to buy pine boards and quietly set about building a box for his mother on the back porch. He put his heart and hands into making the best box he could, using screws instead of nails so Mary wouldn't hear the hammering. I became the 'interior decorator' and for our sake made the inside of the box beautiful with old hand-sewn quilts.

Saturday and Sunday we let out the stops . . . no more pacing ourselves. At night we slept lightly in my room, with the door open so we could hear her calls or changes in breathing. During the day we were with her constantly. Seven or eight times daily we massaged her back, hands and feet. Touching was among the few things she still enjoyed. It was important for her to know that she was still a person to us and that we weren't too repulsed to touch her lump-covered body. We continued to wash her teeth, bathe her and comb her hair. To alleviate the dryness in her mouth, we used ice chips or held a wet washcloth for her to suck on.

Sunday, while we were practicing sliding a suction tube down the throat of the visiting nurse in case we'd need this procedure, Mary's breathing became very heavy and labored. I thought she was leaving and suggested she move toward the Light and practice letting go. After hardly speaking for two days she managed to get out. "You're rushing me!"

We broke up laughing and joked about the rebellion on our hands. Who is to know God's timetable or what unfinished work she had to do on a level beyond our understanding? From that point on she was in and out of consciousness.

She mumbled or mimed to us to turn her in bed about every twenty minutes, which was tiring because she couldn't help at all. Because she couldn't move, eat or drink and her skin was raw, she was in extreme discomfort. We asked if she wanted a shot of Demerol that had been prescribed, and she nodded. Earlier we'd practiced in the kitchen giving shots to a helpless orange. Jean was elected to give Mary the first one because of her greater experience – giving shots to mice in a biology lab. Because Jean and Craig were willing, I didn't have to face my fear of shots . . . this time.

In the beginning we'd been afraid that we might not know what to do for Mary, but as each situation arose, we found we could handle it, which increased our confidence for the next. Taking care of things ourselves seemed preferable to waiting for a nurse.

Demerol was the first pain medication Mary took since way back when she could swallow an occasional Tylenol. In the hospital, doctors and nurses were amazed she wasn't in pain. Perhaps color therapy, Bach Flowers and laetrile helped prevent the intense pain one might expect with tumors throughout the body and with the vital organs barely functioning.

Monday evening Dr. Greg stopped by and said, "You know she could go on breathing like this for a couple of days." I crumbled. A few nights earlier he had gently and sensitively repeated the now familiar words, "We can't save your body, but we'll make you as comfortable as possible." Because we'd stopped pacing ourselves, I was exhausted and didn't know if I could keep going as long as she could. We decided I'd go to dinner with Greg and the next morning Craig and Jean would go for a walk in the hills.

As much as I needed to get away, I didn't enjoy it. I felt divided; half of me wanted to be with Mary. When I got home after midnight, Craig and Jean were just lying down on the floor to rest. "How's it going?" I asked. "We just sat quietly with Mom all evening. She's the same." I went in to see her. She was still breathing but looked already dead. I said offhandedly, "She looks macabre," and went into the bathroom. Craig called and she was gone before I got back to her room. I think she'd been waiting for me to get home so Craig and Jean wouldn't be alone.

We stood shocked for a bit by death, the event we'd been anticipating. While it was sinking in, I distracted myself by phoning Greg to tell him Mary was dead and to remember the death certificate. Calmed, I went back to her room. We lit candles, said prayers for her to be on her way, and held each other. Then we dressed her in a favorite peach silk and lace nightgown. I tied a scarf under her chin to the top of her head (as if she had a toothache) so her mouth would set closed.

With the focus of our energy suddenly gone, we felt shaky, uncertain. Holding each other and praying helped steady us. We all thought of food at the same time and left the body to go rummage through the refrigerator. How surprising to be hungry! We talked a while, then fell into our sleeping places feeling we could sleep forever.

No. Greg woke us at 6:00 AM to certify her dead. I could easily have waited till 9:00 to have the obvious made official. We lifted Mary's body into the coffin which, after all my warnings about John's absurdly big one, seemed to me a little snug. Craig still maintains it was "just right".

Coming Home

After putting in her Tarot deck, Craig hammered down the top of the box, and he and a childhood friend, Joey, loaded the heavy coffin into my pickup. We were to meet Greg at the Office of Vital Statistics to fill out the death certificate and body transferral form. Mary wanted to be buried on her land in the mountains three hours north of Santa Fe.

Greg thought our digging crew was understaffed and volunteered to help, but not without breakfast. So while Craig, Joey and Jean set off with borrowed picks and shovels, I had breakfast with Greg. The young doctor said, "I hope if I help enough folks, there'll be people around to give me a good burial some day."

On the way, I stopped at my usual gas station. When the owner asked "What ya up to today," I answered, "I'm off to the mountains to bury my friend," and motioned toward the back of the truck. The look on his face when he saw the coffin delighted me. Our relationship was different after that day—he took a special interest in what I carried in the back of my truck.

It was an exquisite late summer day. The high desert country was covered with purple asters, golden chamisa and silver Indian sage. We chose a spot called The Meadow overlooking valleys and more mountains. "Meadow" in the Southwest generally means "open", not green and grassy. This one was covered with gray, weathered wood, sculpted like driftwood. As we dug, Greg took the role of "the one who knows." I let go and was silly . . . and how I needed to be silly.

I shoveled a little, but mostly walked in the wind and felt the joy of being free in the mountains after so many days indoors. The others joked and told stories; dug and rested; ate and drank beer. The hole seemed to get shallower instead of deeper. I kept singing "Bury me **four** feet deep in the lone prairie"! Craig wanted the standard "six feet deep". "The hole has to be deep enough so animals can't dig her up." Unlikely. And his need needed to be respected.

When the sun began to set and we were still digging, I was worried. I was due back in town for a lecture I was co-sponsoring. There was nothing to do now but let go and trust that someone would handle it. We finished digging in the headlight beams of the pickups with the moon already up.

I lashed together a cross of four equal arms and placed it in a circle of stones. As a handful of earth ran through my fingers, the sense of loss of a sister caught up with me. I cried. Greg squatted beside me and repeated a Navajo prayer,

> May it be beautiful before me.
> May it be beautiful behind me.
> May it be beautiful below me.
> May it be beautiful above me.
> May it be beautiful all around me.
> In beauty it is finished.

DAD

Throughout the writing of this book, I knew my father was dying. My friends' deaths and writing this book were part of my preparation to accept his death.

Coming Home

My family is a family like many others—perhaps extraordinary in the amount of love and loyalty among us. Each of us would tell a different story about my father's death. This is mine.

When we found out *we* had cancer, it was not seen as Dad's alone but as the concern of us all.

It was Eastertime and the bluebonnets were blooming when we gathered in San Antonio, Texas, to be with him for his first surgery. We were frightened. When hours and more hours passed and we were still sitting in a waiting room at the VA hospital, we knew the cancer must be more extensive than the surgeons had thought.

Dad came out of surgery into a ward with exceptionally overworked nurses, which made them appear incompetent and unloving. The ward he shared with three other men was like a TV M.A.S.H. unit. The humor in the situation saved us. We were all in the same leaky life boat together!

The chief instigator, a man named Dolph, wore a panama hat with his pajamas, sneaked cigarettes and drank hot coffee right before his temperature was taken. Anything the men needed except pain medication, we had to do or find. We'd go off "midnight requisitioning," looking through closets for pajamas, sheets, towels, ice, and lemon swabs— the most appetizing items available.

The camaraderie of the four men—a Navy admiral's steward, an Army master sergeant, a warrant officer, and my father, a colonel—helped us adjust to his situation. At times we laughed so hard that Dad had to hold his stitches to keep them from bursting. And the laughter opened our hearts and released some of the pain and fear.

After surgery, Dad's way to treat cancer of the colon was chemotherapy. That was not my way. I'd studied and worked with natural healing and had seen friends heal themselves of cancer without drugs and surgery. Choosing chemotherapy seemed to me like signing a death warrant because it severely damages the body's immune system. I knew Dad had to do it his own way and I didn't want him to die! I gave him all the information I had on alternative healing and his response was, "I don't want to be the world's greatest expert on cancer." He had faith in the medical system he grew up with and in a young Dr. Page at the VA hospital. The VA hospital was connected with the University of Texas Medical School and to research programs around the country. One week each month he stayed in the hospital for chemotherapy.

I returned to Santa Fe furious with the medical establishment, which admitted it didn't have the answer but insinuated that its way was the only way. I was furious with the Army for sending human beings, including my father, to be guinea pigs at the nuclear bomb tests in Nevada in the 1950's. I was angry with everything and I hurt. There were lots of summer mornings when I sat on my back porch eating breakfast with tears rolling into my cereal. Slowly, very slowly, what I knew in my head entered my heart. Each of us has to die in our own way. I began to take interest in my work again.

I thought of Dad often that summer as I worked on this book. I remembered him as a father. I remembered he and Mother tucking the twins, Judy and Suzy, and me into bed every night; his singing a song to wake us up for school; his taking me alone to Holland and braiding my pigtails and letting me pick as many tulips as I wanted; teaching us to shoot and hunt; taking us exploring on the weekends, even when we didn't want to go. I remember now his face as I looked up from a wheelchair when he met me and my sheep dog in Mexico the time I came home sick from the diplomatic service in Chile. I remember his voice when I phoned from Mexico to say I'd broken my back, then he and Mother taking turns visiting me twice a day in the hospital in San Antonio—his walking me up and down the halls as I learned to walk again. I remember his wanting to go to New England with Mom to help Suzy when her Joshua was born and instead staying home to take care of my sheep dog. He loved, trusted and was proud of us. The only real gripe I remember was when he said, "Do it right or don't do it at all"—and "right" meant "his way".

Who was this man I loved so much? He was my mother's husband for forty-three years. But that's her story. What I know is that the light from their marriage gave other people strength.

Col. Edward Duda was an army officer for thirty years. (My friends would say, "But how can an army officer be so mellow?") What was it like for him after he retired and instead of his telling twenty thousand men when to jump, Mother would tell him, "Put your dishes on the *left* side of the sink?" Who was this quiet, charming man who reminded some of Jimmy Stewart, which secretly delighted me? I'd watch him and wonder . . . He once even said, "I wish you wouldn't watch me so much."

Dad was born a few years after his parents came steerage class on a boat from Poland; they worked hard to make it in a new country. Ethnic groups weren't fashionable at the time and Dad wanted to be an American, not a Pollack kid. He grew up proving a Duda was as good as a Johnson, Jones or Smith. Because the American culture values doing and achieving, he set out to achieve—editor of the yearbook, captain of the track team, the fastest runner ("The Irvington Flash"), senior class president, the Zippity Duda who worked his way through college and graduated with honors. First the Depression, then World War II, made Dad and nearly everyone else think of security. He was called into the army a day after I was born, liked it and stayed. He wanted to be a general. But the army, like every company, has its politics, and he didn't make it. We were proud of him anyway, but I know it hurt.

Why the cancer? Why him?

One evening we recorded Dad's life story up to his high school years. One of the first things he remembered was an accident when he was seven. He was relaxed and having fun when a kid hit him in the eye with a baseball bat. "From then on," he said, "my vision was distorted." Later he related.

"When I was a boy, I believed the most important thing was being in control; if I wasn't, I got hurt. My family got upset when I was hurt. I grew up believing that my being hurt made others suffer . . . so when I hurt, I kept it to myself. I kept swallowing the hurt. When I was older, I didn't hurt anymore . . . I wouldn't let myself. But things still happened that made me hurt and it just sat inside. I picked up the radiation in Nevada but without all that hurt, it wouldn't have affected me. The hurt was a weakness the radiation could attach itself to . . . the hurt became the cancer."

As a little girl I saw the hurt and decided I had to be Dad's protectress; and now he had cancer and I couldn't protect him. Part of me still wanted to and part of me realized this was his opportunity to learn.

45

Coming Home

That summer and fall, everything went along fairly smoothly. Mom sent out Christmas cards that said, "We have cancer and we're doing fine." We all wondered if this was the last year Dad would put the angel we'd had for thirty-five years on top of the tree.

One morning four months later, I woke up in Mexico knowing something was wrong at home and phoned. Mom was crying, Dad was in the hospital again. They'd found a huge tumor in his liver and spots on his lungs and were planning to operate. She'd been sitting up all night alone in the house with my dying sheep dog Benjy, and had just taken him to be put to sleep.

After a series of painful tests, the doctors decided Dad's tumor was inoperable. They decided to insert a tube into the liver so chemotherapy drugs could be fed directly into it, "a minor operation." Mom was holding together pretty well. She'd always said, "I can do anything I have to."

I arrived home in time for surgery. In the waiting room Mom played cards, I meditated and sent love to Dad and we picknicked on chicken. The ward room held a strange fascination for me. I watched deserted old and young soldiers sitting in wheel chairs, connected to tubes, many with mechanical voice boxes, watching TV quiz shows while life slowly drained out of them. I remembered Mother Teresa calling loneliness the worst human disease, and I imagined each man filled with love. Focusing on love prevented my worrying about Dad. I ran into the hall when I saw orderlies wheeling him to his room on a stretcher, writhing in pain. That old instinct to protect him welled up and I could do nothing.

After Dad came home, we buried Benjy's ashes in the back yard. Dad cried and cried — for himself, for Benjy, for us all. It was the first time I'd seen him cry since he'd found out he had cancer, although Mom said they had some good cries together.

Each day we had to flush a solution through the tube in the artery to Dad's liver. If we didn't clamp the tube properly, blood would spurt out all over. After working in the hospital this didn't frighten me. For Mom and Dad it was very unnerving at first. Taking responsibility for irrigating that tube was an important step in increasing their confidence that they could take care of Dad's needs at home.

The talk at home changed from "could he be cured" to "how long he might live." Dad hoped to make it to hunting season and Christmas. Together he and I were learning what Mom seemed born knowing—surrender. Instead of learning it from my friends with their seemingly free lifestyles, I was learning it from this modest middle-class couple who lived in the suburbs. Dad accepted he was dying nearly a year before he died so he was able to live fully his remaining time. Even after he accepted what was happening it took him a while to get used to not being in control.

I returned to New Mexico to continue writing; Suzy and her boys moved to Texas to live with Mom and Dad. Because Dad had chosen chemotherapy, I prepared myself to hear that he'd chosen to die in a hospital. Also, Mother, Suzy and Judy had said they didn't think they could handle his dying at home. Finally I could even accept that dying in a hospital, although contrary to my values, was OK.

In October, Mother phoned and remarked as an afterthought, "Oh, your father wants to die at home." At first I was afraid I'd misunderstood—then I was overjoyed. We were going to be home together and care for Dad ourselves! I couldn't wait to get to Texas. The hardest part—accepting that Dad was dying and making the decision where it would take place — was over.

Hunting season began. Dad was weak, in pain and determined to go. Each weekend we bundled him up, prepared food he hardly ate, and his friends took him hunting. He sat in the open door of the cabin, a potbellied stove burning behind him; his rifle, now almost too heavy for him to lift, sat on a table in front of him. He didn't shoot a deer . . . and it didn't matter. He was living — enjoying the silence of the country, the companionship of his friends — forgetting for a time he was dying. I'm grateful to those loving men.

When Dad walked out the door, we put him in God's hands and didn't worry about him . . . well, just a little. His weekends away, gave Mom and me time to take care of ourselves so we'd have the energy to care for him. I didn't have to wait up to make sure he remembered the 11 o'clock pain pills. Mom didn't have to wake up to help give the ones at 3 a.m., or worry about what to serve him for the next meal.

She dreaded figuring out what to feed him. There was little he could eat without gagging or throwing up, a physical problem Mom took personally as a reflection on her ability to nourish. She's a gourmet cook and sharing love with food was no longer possible. It was a painful part of her process of letting go. For those weekends, she wasn't reminded at each meal that he was dying.

When Dad wasn't hunting, he sat in his reclining chair in the family room next to the patio doors. After a morning hug, he read the print off the newspapers as usual, played with the kids, worked on his taxpayer revolt, and directed the finishing of the cabin at the river that he and Mom had started to build with their own hands. Mom continued to keep their financial affairs in order. I remember Dad sitting in his chair, smiling and saying, "I feel so healthy I forget I have cancer." He was healthy in his heart.

Neighbors brought over banana pudding, casseroles and roses and prayed for our family. Dad's sister and her husband visited from New Jersey. Auntie Thelma, Mom's sister and our fairy godmother, called long distance twice a week. Friends phoned every day. It was difficult for the ones who visited to see Dad so weak. And it was as hard for them to express their feelings as it was for Dad to express his. Judy would come over after teaching to eat and play cards with Mom. She often felt frustrated at not knowing how to help Dad.

Ben, 4, and Joshua, 9, brought a lot of joy to us all. As kids do, they went about playing as usual. As we shared their play, we'd forget about dying. They knew Gramps was dying and couldn't do all the things he used to do with them and that he was going to die at home. Shining little Ben would come home from school and drop his drawing and lessons on Dad's lap for approval. Ben was learning to read and they'd work together on letters and sounds.

For Joshua, Gramp's dying was harder. He'd recently left his father in Massachusetts and now Gramps was going to leave too. Like his grandfather he had difficulty in expressing his feelings so communicating was difficult. But he agreed with Ben who said, "I like it better when Gramps is home." For his birthday Josh was allowed to pick a dog from the pound. With Dad dying we'd been concerned that a new dog would be just more complication, but when he and Josh enjoyed the dog so much, we wished we'd done it earlier!

At times, we all took it personally when Dad grouched because he was losing control of the few things he still felt he had command over. One night after Mom or Josh was in tears over one of Dad's grouches, I got angry. "Dad, everything that is flexible has to do with life and everything that is rigid has to do with death. If people always have to play or do things your way, you may end up with no one to play with." I'd cleaned out my anger and he understood. It was an accomplishment for me to let him *see* me angry because he thought being angry was "losing control" and he'd never approved of it.

Unlike Mary and John, Dad had pain that was difficult to control. The liver tumor expanded until it pressed against the nerves of the solar plexus. He was depressed because he constantly hurt physically. I guess he put up with the pain because he thought pain had to be part of dying. I told him, "You need your energy to live the time we have. There's no need to tough out the pain." With the doctor's approval we upped the Dilaudid from a usually potent 12 mg. every four hours to even stronger dosages that would have been lethal for some. Before raising the dosage, we first tried other pain relief techniques — breathing into the painful area, hot water bottles on his stomach and/or feet, hot cloths on his forehead. Sometimes we survived a painful period without raising the dosage. He wanted to keep the dosage down because he didn't like sleeping so much.

For nausea he took Compazine one hour before the Dilaudid, and Ritalin, a stimulant, twice a day to counteract the sedative action of Dilaudid. For general well-being, I gave him Bach Flowers and massaged his feet once or twice daily, and focused on filling him with love.

Although we appreciated having medical support available we needed very little, except for pain medicine and information about it. We joined the St. Benedict Hospice Program so if we needed help, it could come to us. The hospice nurse visited three times, not because we needed her, but because it was required by the program. It reassured Dad to question her about his symptoms. It made me laugh with love to see the family worrying about not hurting the nurse's and social worker's feelings because we needed their help so little. If I hadn't had previous experience with dying, however, the program would have been invaluable.

Our chief outside supporter was Angie, the cancer research nurse from the VA, who soon became "family." She became personally involved and worked with us as equals. She was the go-between ourselves and Dr. Page. We phoned her with questions; she got answers, arranged prescriptions and brought us medicines and supplies. This saved us running around when we had little extra energy. Help like hers might be a model for supporting dying without the need for hospitalization.

Angie had me inject a needle into her arm to help me overcome the terror of shots I'd avoided facing with Mary. Because we'd traveled overseas a lot, I felt I'd spent half my childhood hiding under tables from people with needles. And now Dad might need Methadone injections. One day Dad said, "Deborah, I need a shot." I said "OK." Following the instructions in this book, I gave it to him. It was that simple. When I wanted to help him, I forgot my fear.

Another day, at the time of the celebration over the return of the hostages from Iran, Dad was in pain and we'd done everything we knew how to do. I hated seeing him in pain and I felt helpless and beaten. I went off alone and told God, "I've done my best and he's still in pain. He's in your hands. There must be something he has to learn from the pain."

Coming Home

When I stopped being Dad's protectress and accepted his pain (my pain), I felt at peace. Then a new idea came: I'd find some THC, the active ingredient in marijuana. It combats nausea and also reduces the amount of pain medication needed. He chose not to smoke marijuana, but was willing to take socially and legally acceptable pills.

After we gave it to him, Dad became a beaming Buddha. He sat in his chair radiating sweetness, beauty and love. The THC appeared to open his awareness to his own nature . . . and also to undermine his will. And *will* was holding Dad in his body. By Sunday afternoon he was nearly dead. He sat in his chair and looked dead. He could not talk or move.

Suzy, Judy, mother and I gathered around him. With tears running down her face, Mom tried to wake him. She couldn't. *This is it. Dad's going to die now.* We cried and told him we loved him. Mom remembered 'last rites' because Dad was raised a Catholic — and still went to Mass twice a year. Suzy volunteered to find a priest and got on the phone. We were huddled around Dad when we heard her say, "Well, he's *somewhat* Catholic." We all burst out laughing. Tears of laughter mixed with tears of pain.

Neighbors appeared and told Dad they loved him. Someone put a cross beside him and a rosary in his hand. The priest came and went. Dr. Charlie appeared saying he'd just dropped in for a social visit. Actually he'd driven 15 miles because a neighbor had called and told him Dad was dying. "Yes," he agreed, Dad was dying. We decided to carry him to his bed.

Six of us had him lifted in the air when Dad opened his eyes and said, "What's going on?"

52

Three Experiences With Dying At Home

Dad lived, and actively, another two weeks. He continued to love swinging outside with us in the winter sun, and playing with Joshua's new dog, Pizza. One of our last projects together was to paint Indian glyphs on a deerskin he'd tanned and stretched on a frame. The symbols he chose (three triangles, a man walking on water with an eagle coming out of his head, the sun and two fish) showed a man dying in peace.

Gradually he needed more attention. He used a cane to walk from the family room to the bathroom, ate almost nothing and often seemed to drift away. He was so skinny that we put a foam pad on his chair and bed at night for comfort and to prevent bedsores. We dropped the schedule for pain medication and played it by ear. We'd discuss the amount he wanted and whether he wanted pills or shots, then arranged a schedule so Mom and I could sleep as much as possible.

Angie asked Dad if he were willing to be interviewed for a newspaper story on dying. Talking used a lot of energy but Dad said, "Fine, if it will help someone." The reporter asked how he'd decided to die at home. He said, "I knew Debby's friends who died and their way sounded more like the way I wanted to go. I'd read her manuscript and heard about the hospice idea. I saw friends, fellow cancer patients, dying in the hospital . . . it seemed such an ignominious death."

The reporter asked Mom how she felt when Dad said he wanted to die at home. "If he was happier at home, we'd work it out . . . I couldn't have done this alone."

"What about joy and dying?" Dad answered, "Well, at least you don't have any more problems!" He and Mom both said, "We don't know about joy but we do feel peace."

"After you were diagnosed, how long was it before you could accept you were going to die?" "Well, I was shocked. I felt angry and afraid and 'why me,' all those things you read about. Right after I heard I had cancer, I ran into a doctor who gave me hope. He told me it wasn't the end; his mother was a healthy 86 and had had cancer for years. I held onto "It's not the end!"

"I'd like to tell people not to be afraid of dying. Dying gave me a chance to get rid of sadness and feel peace. You can combine dying with your ordinary life. And doctors and nurses can help us get over the gap before we realize we can live while we're dying."

A few days after the interview Dad said he didn't feel like walking to his chair. He stayed in bed except to go to the bathroom. Friends brought over foam wedges to prop up his legs and take pressure off his swollen ankles. Josh brought in his little TV.

That night we knew time was running out . . . and that it didn't exist. Mother and Dad rested together on their bed, leaning against each other. The beauty and peace in their faces spoke of the long journey shared together . . . and of the shared journey of all people. And love had made it worthwhile.

The next morning was sunny and springlike for February. I was happy padding around barefoot in jeans shaving and bathing Dad. We were alone. Mom had secretly gone to check out funeral homes; Suzy was working on the first issue of the newspaper she was starting; the kids were at school. Dad and I had a beautiful talk.

He already knew I didn't believe death was the end; that we just leave a body that is no longer useful to us. We'd talked before about reincarnation and my remembering our being together in other times. This time we talked of preparations. I told him about spiritual teachings that suggest that when you feel yourself lifting out of your body, keep repeating 'God' and follow the brightest light. Dad *heard* me and repeated, "OK, remember to say 'God' and follow the light."

Our talk ended when Dr. Page arrived with Angie for a social visit. Dad was pleased Dr. Page cared enough to drive 32 miles round trip on his lunch hour to visit. To him that meant he hadn't been just another number in the VA mill. Mom asked Dr. Page the old question, "How long?" He said, "two days, two weeks!" I knew that was inaccurate.

We spent that evening around his bed. Dad played with Ben — rolling up a magazine telescope to watch him play hide-and-seek with himself. Josh said goodbye on his way out to Cub Scouts. Dad and I watched the world news to see if Poland was being invaded as Mom worked on her Saturday Review "double crosstic." Dad gave us instructions on the light fixtures at the cabin and on giving away his hunting guns. Suzy came in; he told her he loved her and repeated how much he loved us all. He considered phoning to ask Judy to come but decided it would worry her. "I'll *probably* be here in the morning."

Angie came in about 9:00 p.m. out of a howling wind and rainstorm that the morning sun had never announced. After she took his vital signs, she asked if she could stay over and sleep on the couch. While we sat around him visiting, Dad was looking at himself in the mirror across the room. Suddenly he started and asked, "Do you see what I see?" I said I saw light all around him. He said he saw white light and rainbows, and when he saw the light, he knew he would die soon.

I asked again if he wanted me to call Judy and he said "yes." Judy came over and they joked together. "I love you,

Judy," he told her. She said a teary goodbye. We kissed him goodnight and he didn't speak again.

Mom and I were with Dad when he stopped breathing, a few hours past midnight on Wednesday, February 11. He was sixty-eight. Momma cried as she tucked the covers around him and said, "I love you, Daddy." I 'held the Light' as best I could. I cried as I'm crying now as I write.

I walked out into the dark and wind and down the front yard path beside the stretcher with Dad's body. "What is it to die but to stand naked in the wind and melt into the sun" (The Prophet). The ambulance awaited. "I love you Papa . . . stay with the brightest light."

I went back to the house and Mom and I crawled into her and Dad's bed. I heard Dad telling me, "If you hurt, let it out. Don't hold on until the pain cripples your will to live." I took time just now to cry again as I did that night. This time I lay on the floor beating it with my arms, kicking, crying and howling to release the pain from my body. I heard a trapped animal freeing itself . . . myself.

That night Mom held me as I cried. Now I am alone with the beating of my heart — a heart opened wider after releasing the pain.

In the morning, I *needed* to clean. I washed clothes with a fervor while Judy, Suzy and Mom went to the funeral home. Dad wanted a military funeral with a G.I.'s wooden box. This funeral home had no simple wooden coffins so they chose a grey metal one. They arrived home saying, "It's a good thing you weren't there." (Precisely why I hadn't gone.) We joked about my idea of using an ice pick to punch holes in the box so earth could return to earth more quickly.

The next day was a blur. I planned the eulogy I would give at the funeral service. I'd asked Dad's permission and he said, "OK, but keep it short." Suzy and I had the biggest fight we'd ever had. It grew out of unexpressed pain; neither of us felt appreciated by the other. All my clothes were at the cabin so I huffed off to buy something to wear. After Suzy's lecture on not always doing things my way, I thought maybe I should wear something conservative, not my usual style. Here I was making a production over what to wear. Unbelievable!

At one point I was standing in total despair in a shop door, when a saleslady asked if she could help me. "I need a dress for my father's funeral." She said, "Oh yes, black." And I said, "Oh, no, white, purple or peach!" I found a floaty peach dress that looked like "me," but chose a dark purple one so Mom and Dad's friends wouldn't be shocked. At home I told the story to Mom who suggested, "Why don't you go back and get the peach one if it makes you happy?" I was repeating the same old lesson: In the long run, doing what you want, instead of what you think you should, as long as you take responsibility for it, makes everyone happier.

The next morning I'm not sure if I steeled or centered myself to prepare for limousines, flower wreaths, all the funeral trappings. Last thing out the door Mom turned to me in mock seriousness and asked, "Have you got an ice pick?"

Joshua, who'd practiced reading the Twenty-Third Psalm the night before, backed out at the last minute. The part of me that was afraid to speak in public wanted out too. The rest of me wanted everyone to know Dad was alive and free.

With Dad's flag-draped coffin in front of me, I spoke shakily,

"My father is not dead. In this box in front of me lies only a shell. He's free and whole . . . Will you make today a day of joy and celebration as well as sadness?" . . . Dad said, "I'm not happy about dying and I'm not afraid . . ." He believes we'll be together again . . .

His cancer was a kind teacher. It gave him time to learn and to get his life in order . . . time to prepare for death. It taught him to give up control and surrender . . .

Dad's death is a victory. He chose how he'd die. He chose to accept death, to accept life. Because he lives in our hearts, it's impossible to lose him."

Mom, Ben and I went back a few weeks later to put daisies on his grave. We all knew he wasn't there. I held Mom's hand and read:

Do not stand at my grave and weep;
I am not there. I do not sleep.
I am a thousand winds that blow.
I am the diamond glints on snow.
I am the sunlight on ripened grain.
I am the gentle autumn's rain.
When you awaken in the morning's hush,
I am the swift uplifting rush
Of quiet birds in circled flight.
I am the soft stars that shine at night.
Do not stand at my grave and cry:
I am not there. I did not die.

— Anonymous

Ben and I sang "Zippity Duda."

NOTES

Called or not called, God is always here.

—Carl Jung

CHAPTER 2

MAKING THE DECISION
TO DIE AT HOME

*Everything can be taken from a man but one thing:
the last of the human freedoms — to choose one's
attitude in any given set of circumstances, to
choose one's own way.*

> — Victor Frankl
> Author of *Man's Search for Meaning*
> Survivor of Auschwitz and Dachau

When we can no longer control the circumstances of our
lives, we can still choose our attitude about them. We can
choose our attitude about dying. We can choose to see it as a
tragedy, teacher, adventure, or simply as an experience to be
lived. Our *attitude* will determine the nature of our experience. An optimist and a pessimist see the same world, only

61

through different lenses (attitudes). And as Norman Cousins said, "Pessimism is a waste of time. No one really knows enough to be a pessimist."

When we choose to surrender to life, we are free; and when we are free, we are in control. This paradox lies at the heart of our human existence.

To surrender and to be free we have to accept life as it **is** instead of holding on to how **we think it should be.** We can't change something we don't first accept. Surrender and acceptance are not to be confused with resignation and succumbing. Resignation and succumbing are *passive*— something just overpowered or overcame us and we had no choice but to give up. Resignation is self-pity and believing the illusion that we're powerless. Acceptance and surrender, on the other hand, are positive acts. "I choose to let go, to give up control and accept life as it is. And there will be things I can change and things I can't."

If we deny dying and death, we're prisoner to them. When we accept them, we're free and regain the power lost in resisting them. We let go of our resistance by *letting go.* It's easy to do and can be hard to get ready to do. The choice to let go must be made in the heart. A choice made only in the head, unsupported by the body, feelings and soul, is unlikely to be carried out.

If we remember that choice of attitude, the ultimate freedom, is always available, we make a spacious place in which to experience dying. We can be free whether we are dying ourselves or sharing in the dying of someone we love. We can be free whether we die at home or in a hospital. Choosing our attitude is easier at home than in an atmosphere that unconsciously says dying should be isolated from life and is, therefore, not OK.

Making the Decision

As our Western culture emphasized control over nature, death became the uncontrollable enemy. We gave doctors the responsibility for combatting this enemy. Death became increasingly a medical "problem" instead of a natural event. We gave away the responsibility for death (and life) to experts outside of ourselves — big institutions and big business. Until very recently life-sustaining technology said a good death is a hospital death and an unobstructed natural death is euthanasia. And people seem to feel that because we invented machines, we have to use them. So life ends up not to be for living but to justify machinery. We have become medical consumers.

Ivan Illich, in his scholarly and intriguing history of our attitudes and practices about death, *Medical Nemesis*, calls death "the ultimate form of consumer resistance." Illich goes on to say, "Today the man best protected against setting the stage for his own dying, is the sick person in critical condition. Society, acting through the medical system, decides when and after what indignities and mutilations he shall die." In the face of death we have felt powerless. This doesn't have to be. We're not dying to humour doctors by doing it *their* way or to make the medical community rich!

We have begun to take back what is rightfully ours — our life and our death.

You may remember Karen Ann Quinlan, a young woman from New Jersey, who brought to national attention the conflict between our technological capabilities and our human needs. In 1975, Karen became permanently unconscious after mixing drugs and alcohol. A year later the courts upheld her *right to privacy* and gave her parents legal permission to refuse *extraordinary* treatment for her . . .

even if that resulted in her death. Her respirator was removed and Karen was moved to a nursing home.

Her loving father, Joseph Quinlan, who visited her almost daily, said, "I understand that conceivably all treatment of Karen is extraordinary, that means the antibiotics and food and respirator. However, we personally have moral problems with our conscience with regard to the food and antibiotics."

Karen's parents decided to continue feeding her with tubes. One can only speculate on how being in the spotlight of national publicity and not having to pay for her care themselves affected their decision. Karen lived for 10 years in a vegetative state with her expenses paid for by all us taxpayers. After she died in 1985, her mother, Julia Quinlan said:

"My daughter Karen's condition, like that of so many today, raised profoundly disturbing questions that do not lend themselves to easy answers or ideal situations. My hope and prayer is that medicine, technology and law will work together so that we will not become slaves to technology, but rather, let technology with all its wonder enhance the worth, the dignity and the beauty of human life."

In some ways Julia's prayer, the prayer of many hearts tired of unnecessary human suffering, has been answered. Many U.S. courts continue to uphold our right of privacy, our right to refuse medical treatment we don't want — even feeding tubes — and our **right** to die with dignity.

Perhaps the money we spent on Karen was money very well spent. She made us think together about the quality of life vs. the quantity. Perhaps her life was a seed for the American Medical Association (AMA) 1986 policy statement that says it **is** ethically permissible for doctors to withhold **all** life-prolonging treatment, including artificial nutrition and hydration, from patients in irreversible coma and from dying patients. (Complete Statement in Appendix C)

Perhaps Karen encouraged us to act on the knowing of our hearts and say clearly, "Technology, you are our partner, not our master."

Once we gave the medical industry responsibility for our deaths, it became an act of personal courage to die at home. Now more and more courageous people are saying, "I don't want to go away to die. I want to die at home."

State and federal governments are financially supporting more home health care. Hospices that help care for our dying have developed all over the country. Insurance companies have added more home health care benefits to their services. Living Wills that express how we wish to be treated when we're dying are becoming commonplace. Death and Dying Courses are taught in universities and medical schools across the country. Once again young doctors are recognizing the value of a family practice, personal care and housecalls.

We're returning to dying at home — the old natural way which most of the world never questioned.

We have a right to die with **dignity**. Dignity in the dictionary means "worthiness." To me it means doing things in our own way. Dying at home we maintain the ability to choose our own way, whether it be a little decision like what time we eat, or a big one like whether or not to use life-sustaining techniques.

We have a right to die with **respect** — to see and to be seen. At home a person remains an individual, rather than "the patient in Room 204B."

Dying at home, we can influence the quality and quantity of our lives.

WHY DIE AT HOME?
THE ADVANTAGES

(You may want to share this list with the dying person.)

1. Most dying people are happier at home than in a hospital.

2. The dying person can influence the quality and quantity of his or her own life.

3. Respect and dignity are maintained.

4. The dying person feels wanted.

5. You feel useful and needed.

6. The continued presence of love supports you both.

7. You both have more freedom and control. The dying person can tell you what he or she wants. (No one is awakened at 5:45 a.m. for temperature taking or the 20th blood sample.)

8. You both can live more normally and fully.

9. The dying person can teach you something about living.

10. Home is more supportive of the shift from *curing* to *making comfortable.*

11. In a familiar and secure outer environment, both of you have more time for the inner preparations for death.

12. There is time and a place to express feelings of grief, anger, and love, so accepting this death and death in general will be easier.

13. When physical death occurs, there's time to experience what's happened without the body being whisked away to make room for the next patient.

14. There's no travel wear and tear between home and hospital. (No worry about loved ones driving at night in bad weather.)

15. You both can see or create your own version of beauty.

16. Food at home can be fresher and more appetizing.

17. Living at home costs less.

18. Be it a slum or a palace, it's home!

I met a lovely 92-year-old Spanish lady in the hospital who sat in a wheelchair hooked to tubes, babbling, mostly incoherently, about her bedspread at home, the curtains and the good milk. It seemed to me she was still expressing what she wanted most—to be home. Home is a magic word.

WHEN IS IT NOT APPROPRIATE TO DIE AT HOME?

1. When the dying person doesn't want to.

2. When the family would be too upset to care for him or her.

3. When the hospital can provide services that improve the *quality* of a person's life.

4. When the dying person wants to be hooked into intravenous feedings (IVs), etc., and you can't afford a regular nurse.

5. When there is no one at home to care for the person and you can't afford to pay for someone.

6. It may not be appropriate if there are small children in the family who also need care; not because it wouldn't be good for them to be present, but because you might not be able to manage it all. (If you can't get sufficient extra help at home, a residential hospice program may be a solution — see page 83).

7. If the dying person plans to donate organs for transplant, the death needs to take place in a hospital because organs are transplanted soon after death.

MAKING THE DECISION

Sometimes it's very clear-cut. The person who is dying says, "I want to die at home" or just, "I want to go home." If this happens, you, the family, can discuss among yourselves whether or not this choice will work for everyone concerned. Your preferences, as well as the dying person's, need to be considered. The decision to come home must be a joint one. **Only a family that wants someone to come home can give the care needed.**

More often the situation is not so clear. The sick person still may hope to get better and may well do so. Or, someone may not know or want to know how sick she or he is, and feel anxious, afraid and confused. And family and friends may feel the same. It's hard to feel clear about dying when we're getting a morass of conflicting reports from different parts of ourselves; body, mind, feelings and soul each report their own story or reality.

In the face of death, the rational mind is afraid because it can't understand or control what's happening. It **thinks** death is the end and fights it. The body's job is to stay alive. It **senses** that death means extinction and fights it. The feelings (emotions) **feel** confused because their work is to react to the other parts. The part that endures, the soul or consciousness, seems to make an arbitrary decision to leave, which instigates death, and then can't understand why body, mind and feelings resist and make such a fuss.

No wonder we feel confused by dying and death and often wonder what the heck is going on.

Only the heart is not confused. It **knows** the larger plan. It intuitively knows the whole. It **loves** each part and understands the sacredness of each. It **sees** the truth: life without the lens of fear. When we accept all the parts of ourself—surrender—the heart opens wide, the conflicting reports end, and we can live fully with dying. Mind, body, feelings and soul are aligned so we can make decisions based on all our needs.

If this feels like a tall order for you now, keep in mind it can take a long time to accept ourselves fully. We can practice by surrendering for brief moments at a time.

Give loving support and information to help everyone involved make the best decision possible at this time. Include in the information what you **want** to do, finances, your own state of health, child care and the availability of help. To avoid total exhaustion, **I recommend there be at least two people at home to take turns supporting the dying person.** In the following section on Financial Considerations and in Chapter 3, you'll find more information to help with the decision.

Probably you'll want to discuss the choices with a doctor. Remember, a doctor in this circumstance is a provider of information, not a decision-maker. Usually, she or he is accustomed to recommending the hospital for very sick people. If a hospital is recommended, ask how it can serve the dying person besides prolonging life. (In Chapter 4, there's information on finding a doctor if you don't already have one.)

A decision need not be permanent. If a person is at home and you still have doubts or it's not working out, a hospital, hospice or nursing home is always available. Returning someone can be emotionally difficult for all concerned, and sometimes it's necessary. Respect your feelings. **You are just as valuable as the dying person.**

Examine your motives carefully before bringing someone home. If guilt is the motive ("If I were a good person, I'd bring her home" or "I *should* bring him home"), you probably won't have the energy to keep going until the person dies. Love sustains us; guilt drains us.

Resentment begins with feeling or thinking someone *should* do or be something they aren't. "He *should* be cooperative" or "She *should* feel grateful." Keep in mind that people bring the same characteristics to dying that they do to living. A person with a difficult or demanding personality generally dies true to character. Although the process of dying may transform a personality, it would be foolish to expect it. **Do you want to care for the person just as she or he is now?** If you do, you will generally be able to meet the challenges. **There will be challenges**, and each is an opportunity for growth.

Pain management is one of the great fears of the dying and their families. **In most cases pain can be alleviated just as well at home as in the hospital.** In my experience dying people living at home have less pain than those in a hospital. Love is a very effective stress and pain reducer. If the dying person cannot take pills or liquids, a nurse can give injections or you can learn to give them yourself. With a nurse's help even IVs can come home. **Pain control isn't something to fear; just something to do.**

Another fear of a dying person is, "What will happen to my family?" When he or she sees you at home coping and handling well this terminal illness, the fear will be alleviated. At home there's time for making the appropriate arrangements.

Dying people also fear being a burden. Reassure them they're not and that their dying is part of the whole family's life. For example, when I suggested coming home while Dad was dying, Mom said, "But you've got to get on with your life, Deborah." My response was, "What happens in my family is part of my life." You might say to someone who wants to be at home but who fears being a burden, "Allowing ourselves to receive love and caring is just as important as giving them. Please let us return some of the love you've given to us by allowing us to care for you at home." Or to a real stubborn person, "Are you going to give the pleasure and privilege of caring for you to your family or to strangers?"

Dying people, as well as a lot of the rest of us, fear loneliness and being deserted. In Malcolm Muggeridge's *Something Beautiful for God*, Mother Teresa says:

"I have come more and more to realize that it is being unwanted that is the worst disease that any human being can ever experience . . . For all kinds of diseases there are medicines and cures. But for being unwanted, except there are willing hands to serve and there's a loving heart to love, I don't think this terrible disease can ever be cured."

Bringing dying people home reassures them they're wanted and won't be deserted. And we may have to reassure them many times. Being at home also alleviates loneliness.

Dying people fear losing control over their lives. In the hospital, the staff takes over and largely dictates what the patient can and must do, when you can see them, etc. You and the dying person don't have time to adjust **gradually** to loss of control. At home, on the other hand, you can take a few steps at a time toward giving up control which makes dying easier.

The feeling of being totally wrenched by an unnatural catastrophe, common in sudden deaths and many hospital deaths, is less likely to occur at home. You know you're doing all you can do. If the thought comes up afterward, "Maybe I could have done more," you're likely to let go of it much more quickly than if you'd been isolated from a loved one in a hospital. After caring for someone who dies at home most people report feeling peace as well as loss — a feeling of appropriateness and completion and a greater openness to the new life ahead. Mom said, "I feel good because Dad was so happy to be at home and die the way he wanted to."

Sometimes the dying person is medically termed 'unconscious' and has earlier expressed a desire to be home or has signed a "living will." A living will is a document we can sign any time in our adult lives instructing doctors to withhold or withdraw extraordinary life sustaining procedures during a terminal illness (see page 264).

Patients whose level of consciousness is uncertain may still let us know what they want. You can ask, for example, "Do you want to go home? Squeeze my hand for 'yes' — blink for 'no'." Use whatever signal you can invent using the abilities the person still has available.

Few people realize **we have the legal right to leave a hospital whenever we please,** with or without a doctor's approval. A family has the legal right to make a decision for a person who is "incompetent", not able to make or express his or her own decisions. Under these circumstances, the next of kin can take responsibility for checking the patient out of the hospital. You may have to sign a form stating that the patient is leaving the hospital "against medical advice." Attending physicians most frequently just drop a case if they don't agree, but they can resort to legal proceedings if they feel it's not in the best interest of the patient to leave. This is uncommon.

Hopefully you will have no difficulty in bringing a loved one home from the hospital. Most states have recently passed Living Will Laws which legally protect our right to refuse treatment. The American Hospital Association has drawn up a Patient's Bill of Right which also affirms this right. (See Appendix F). If you should disagree with a hospital staff about the *best interest* of a patient, see Appendix G for suggestions. Legally, it's assault and battery to treat a patient without his or her consent.

What is the *best interest* of a person who cannot express his or her own wishes? This is a difficult one. What is the quality of life of someone in a coma, sustained by tubes, with little chance of functioning alone again? What is in the best interest of a patient who expresses a desire to go home and the doctor disagrees?

Here, some profound thinking is necessary about the quality of life versus the quantity. In a hospital, a person may be kept alive longer but in what condition? What is the difference between a coma in which consciousness lifts out of the body to allow the body to restore itself and a coma in which consciousness leaves to prepare the body for death? When does physical survival cease to be a desirable goal? Each case is different. I believe answers come from an inner or higher source which we can reach through prayer or meditation.

Keeping in mind the considerations mentioned that are relevant for you, why not gather as a family to discuss the idea of bringing or keeping someone at home? Then perhaps each individual separately can pray, meditate, think and feel about the choices. At least sleep overnight before coming together again to share your preferences. If your decision is "home", affirm it together as a group, recognizing that you may still have doubts and that together you'll do your best. Not everyone has to do everything; one person may want to physically care for the person, another may prefer caring for the children. Remember you're a team.

This could be a good time to make an agreement that may save needless suffering later. It can happen that a medicine or something else we give the dying person speeds up the process of leaving the body. We cannot know the effects on each individual of all foods, medicines and treatments. **Affirm together that if a dying person dies as a result of something you administer with the best intention, there's no need for guilt or blame.** God or the mysterious and subtle workings of the universe simply used you to help that person out of their body at that time. **You are aligned with your purpose**: allowing someone to die at home with love around them. If this responsibility is too heavy for you to handle, a nurse may be hired.

In this gathering of family and friends, you may want to express your love and support for each other. Sharing loving energy will strengthen each of you. Whoever **needs** to share in this dying is who needs to be present for it.

Once you've made the decision for home, keep in mind that your focus shifts from *curing* to *making comfortable*. Now, do everything possible for comfort rather than to prolong life, as long as the dying person is in agreement. A dying person may want to prolong life for some reason . . . seeing a son or daughter graduate from school, a grandchild born, etc. People have a right to change their decisions.

FINANCIAL CONSIDERATIONS

Finances will probably be a factor in your decision to experience this dying at home or in a hospital. It's generally less expensive to die at home. John and Mary, for example, had few additional expenses; my father had none. Most people spend more on their final illness in a hospital than on all the medical care they receive in their whole life.

To keep or bring a dying person home, there must be at least two people to care for him or her. If you're working can you arrange leave from work? Can you afford to? Can you work part-time? Is there a hospice, a service to support dying people and their families at home, in your area? (See page 83) What are their fees? Do you have Medicare or private insurance that cover hospice or homecare such as doctor or nurse visits and medicine? If you don't have insurance coverage, can you afford a nurse or doctor if they're needed?

Compare these homecare costs with hospital costs not covered by insurance. Is the person eligible for federal or state disability payments, Social Security or Veteran's benefits?

Let's start with **hospice.** Most hospice homecare is covered by Medicare if services are given by a **certified** hospice. Services covered are:

1. Nurse and doctor visits.

2. Drugs for pain relief and symptom management.

3. Physical, occupational and speech therapists.

4. Home health aides and homemakers.

5. Medical social workers.

6. Medical supplies and appliances.

7. Short-term inpatient care, including respite care.

8. Counseling.

If the dying person is eligible for Medicare, call your local hospice and ask if they're certified.

Medicare hospice coverage does not pay for treatment other than for pain relief and symptom management of a terminal illness. You pay 5% of drug costs or $5 per prescription, whichever is less. Respite care is a short hospital or nursing home visit for the dying person to give the family a needed rest. You pay 5% of respite care, up to $492 (1986 amount).

Even if there's no hospice in your area, Medicare and Medicaid cover home care if there's a medically established need for "skilled service." The service must be given by a *certified* home healthcare agency under a doctor's direction. Both programs require an "assessment visit" by a registered nurse.

Now, let's look at private **insurance policies.** If you have one, check to see if it covers hospice care; an increasing number do. If not, what coverage is provided for home visits by a doctor or nurse? Insurance often covers 80% of the cost after a $100 deductible or 100% after $1,000. What are the limitations on homecare services? Nearly all policies specify a maximum number of visits covered. If the policy is written in Greek, call an insurance agent and ask him to explain the benefits to you.

Keep in mind that insurance companies are run by people. It's possible to negotiate with them. If your insurance doesn't cover homecare, consider asking your agent for help. You might say, "My policy with you doesn't cover home-care, but it does cover hospital care. If you will finance the care of my husband or _____ at home, it will save you a lot of money!" Oftentimes you can work out an arrangement.

Coming Home

If there's a hospice in your area and you don't have insurance, call them anyway. Often their fees are on a sliding scale dependent on your income. Many, but not all, will take care of a dying person who can't pay.

If there's no hospice and you don't have insurance, check the availability and cost of doctor and nurses' visits. Look under "nurses" in the Yellow Pages. Getting prices by phone may be difficult but you can often arrange a free nursing assessment visit in your home.

Nurses are categorized according to education and skills. For example, generally only a Registered Nurse (RN) can start IVs and give injections. A Licensed Vocational Nurse (LVN) provides general nursing skills. Homemaker Aides do bathing, personal care, housekeeping and running errands. Nursing costs vary, so shop for the qualifications you need at the best prices. The more training a nurse has the more you pay, so don't hire an RN to help bathe someone . . . unless you enjoy giving money away.

Visiting Nurse Associations (VNA) are non-profit nursing organizations. Their fee scale and services are similar to profit-making nursing agencies. Many of them receive funds from United Way and provide sliding fee services. Most nursing agencies divide their services into two categories, private duty visits and home health visits. The charge for a private duty RN from an agency is about $14 to $25 per hour (1987). The charge for an agency RN for a home health visit to perform a specific task runs from $50 to $80 per visit.

You can find a nurse through referrals or a newspaper ad. You may find a wonderful one and pay less. You will have to trust your own judgement because you won't have outside assurance about reliability and skill. You might call your county government to check if they have a Home Health Care Service or a Public Health Nurse who makes home visits without charge.

Talk with the nurse or nursing agency about your needs and resources. Unless you're working and need a full-time nurse, a nurse can train the family in ordinary nursing skills. You need to call only in the event of unusual challenges. In many cases only a few short visits are needed. Mary had about six, and Dad, three. The price of doctors' visits also varies so call and ask. Again, let them know your needs and resources. You may not need a visit by a doctor or nurse. We didn't with Dad although some visited because they wanted to.

To give you some idea what a home-dying can cost, here are the costs for Mary, John and my father. Mary had no insurance and practically no money. Her last month at home cost us $250. One day in the hospital cost $344 and was paid by the County Indigent Fund. A $55 phone bill was paid by Social Security. A $70 bill from a doctor who looked at Mary for three minutes and said, "Yes, she'll die soon" was returned with a note saying we had no money and I hoped his family wasn't hungry. We didn't have to pay $150 for six nursing visits because the agency had a federal grant. John's three weeks at home cost about $850. My father was covered by the military. His last month cost us nothing beyond the usual expense of running a home. All his medications were free from the VA hospital.

For further information on financial help, check the following sections in Chapter 3: City, County and State Services; Social Security; Veterans Administration.

Serving humanity is recognizing our common divinity.

— Phoebe Hummel

CHAPTER 3

SOURCES OF HELP

In one morning on the telephone you can find out a lot that will help you make your decision or, if you've already made it, get you started finding help if you need it. Here are the sources I found. You'll find others. New alternatives and possibilities spring up every day.

If someone says, "No, we can't help", ask if they know who can. Keep a list of the useful numbers by your phone. When Mary was dying, we had a bowl on the kitchen table where we put all those little notes we wrote about possible help. Share with the dying person what you find out unless it's clearly inappropriate.

You may not need much help, but you may feel more comfortable knowing where to get it if you need it in a hurry.

FAMILY AND FRIENDS

Family and friends may be your biggest help. Let them know that this person they're close to is sick and probably dying, that you're planning a home death, and ask if they're willing and able to help. You do them a favor by offering the opportunity to give of themselves and to face their own fears about dying.

People basically love to help and to feel needed. Your request might give someone who at the moment is experiencing life as meaningless an opportunity to find meaning. There's no need to think you're imposing by asking; everyone is free to say "no". Present a clear opportunity to which "yes" or "no" are equally valid responses. For example, "John is dying at home and we need help running errands, cooking meals, caring for him, etc. Is this a time in your life when you can help?" Let them know you're aware that there are times when it's not possible, and that's fine. **It may happen that some of your inner circle of friends may not be ready to face their own feelings about death and move to the outer circle.** People you hardly knew before may move to the inner circle.

You may even find a doctor or nurse among family and friends, or be referred to one.

Another idea is to form a neighborhood co-op to care for the sick and dying, a Caring Network. It would take a fair amount of courage for the first person to reach out but it could totally change our feeling of separateness — living isolated lives in city apartments and suburban homes. Starting a caring co-op might take just one phone call to those neighbors you don't know or one meeting at your house to ask for help. It might be organized around your husband, wife or child, then spread to include everyone in the neighborhood. Ms. Blossom can come over for an hour and sit with John. Julie can come for an hour after school and tidy up. Mr. Smith can mow the lawn. Mrs. Martinez can't come over but can bake a casserole. The Dudas could have the kids over to play. Mr. and Mrs. Levy can come sit with John and watch TV while you get away to the movies. Imagine what would happen to a neighborhood or an apartment house with everyone cooperating, feeling needed, having a sense of purpose and learning to love each other. What a joyful prospect.

MEDICAL AND HOME CARE HELP

HOSPICES

A hospice is a public agency or private organization that helps families care for a dying loved one at home. If there's one in your community, they can give all the help you'll need.

Hospice is a relatively new word in American health care. The word itself dates back to the Middle Ages at the time of the holy pilgrimages. "Hospice" then meant a "way station", a place for tired sick pilgrims to receive care. "Hospice" is the root word for "Hospitality" and "hospital."

The hospice idea was revived recently by a courageous English woman, Dr. Cicely Saunders, who was unhappy about the way her dying patients were treated in hospitals. To her, hospice meant a way station between this world and the next. The hospice she began in London, St. Christopher's, generated enthusiasm all over the world for better care of the dying. Today there are over 50 hospices in England and over 1500 in North America.

The main concern of a hospice program according to Dr. Sylvia Lack, an American hospice organizer, is "the management of terminal disease in such a way that patients live until they die, that their families live with them as they're dying . . . and go on living afterwards." A team of care-givers, including a doctor, nurse, social worker, counselor or chaplain and volunteers, become personally involved, to the degree that you choose, with you and the dying person. The nurse is on call 24 hours a day, 7 days a week, visiting you at home if necessary.

Hospices generally accept only patients who have been certified by their doctors as having a life expectancy of six months or less. Their emphasis is on alleviating symptoms rather than curing disease. Sophisticated pain control techniques allow most patients to live their remaining time pain free and alert.

All hospices emphasize care at home. A few have their own facility with a home-like supportive atmosphere. Some hospitals have a hospice unit in which hospice-like care is given.

If you're not sure if there's a hospice in your area, check the phone book under "hospice", call your hospital or the National Hospice Organization — (703) 243-5900. New hospices begin frequently.

VISITING NURSES

To locate a nurse, look in the yellow pages under "Nurses" or "Nursing Services." Call the agencies in your area and compare costs and qualifications. Don't forget to check if your county has a Public Health Nurse who makes home visits.

A visiting nurse can teach you basic nursing skills that relate to providing comfort, moving a patient, changing sheets, bathing and exercising. They can show you how to give non-intravenous injections and advise on feeding problems, enemas and other patient needs. They can answer the patient's questions and recognize when a doctor is needed.

HOME HEALTH CARE AIDES

Another important kind of assistance comes from Home Health Care Aides. Their services may include personal care, homemaker services, transportation and escort, companionship and counseling. Their training, supervision and cost vary so check around. There's not yet a national certification program but many home health care aides are locally certified after completing a training program.

To find an aide, call a medical social worker at a hospital to recommend an agency. Look in the Yellow Pages under Homemaker-Home Health Aide Services, Visiting Nurse Associations, Family Service Agencies or Social Service Agencies.

HOSPITALS

A hospital is always available if you need one. You can use one for particular services, even though the intention is to die at home. If your patient does have to go into a hospital for some treatment that will improve the quality of life, I recommend not leaving him or her there alone. Nurses, no matter how excellent, don't have time to attend to all the emotional and physical needs of their patients. If you do have to leave someone, don't feel guilty. They'll manage and perhaps they have something to learn on their own.

Even if you don't use a hospital, you can call the hospital's Director of Nursing Services for information about other services in your community.

FINANCIAL HELP

CITY, COUNTY AND STATE SERVICES

Financial help is offered to individuals and families at city, county and state levels. The names of the departments providing funds vary from area to area. Some of the names used are: Health, Health Services, Social Services, Welfare, Human Resources and Human Services. Look in the white pages of the phone book, under the name of your state, county or city. Often there's a **central information number** that can direct you to the right department. If you have trouble locating a service, call the county courthouse.

States administer federal programs such as Medicaid and Aid to Dependent Children.

It can be a headache finding someone in state or local governments who knows more than his or her little piece of the pie. However, there's generally someone and with perseverance you'll find them.

For example, after much calling around I found a woman in our county Social Services office who knew what help was available. She told me about a county emergency relief fund which pays hospital and nursing home bills, and about food stamps, daycare services for children, homemaker service for light housework, a group which does heavy work like cutting wood, and a rent subsidy program. In our county there's even an adult protection service which helps people who are confused or incapacitated to connect with these services — including the running around and the paperwork. These services are generally free if your income is below a certain level, or on a sliding scale.

Hopefully it won't be long before each county, city and state has a coordinator for benefits and services for the sick and dying.

SOCIAL SECURITY

Besides Social Security Retirement Benefits, Social Security administers five programs that may be useful to you and the dying person: Medicare, Disability Insurance, Dependent Benefits, Survivors Benefits, and Supplemental Security Income. They also determine eligibility for Medicaid in some cases.

The problem we encountered with Social Security was that their help didn't arrive before Mary died. Hopefully you'll have more time, and they'll complete their processing in time to be fully useful. Ask about Presumptive Eligibility which is designed to speed up the process.

Retirement Benefits. If you're 62 and not working and have paid enough into Social Security, you're eligible for monthly payments.

Medicare. If you're 65 and have paid enough into Social Security, you're eligible for Medicare. Medicare is a health insurance program similar to private health insurance. There's generally a deductible, and the policy pays a certain percentage over that deductible. Medicare can pay for hospice care provided by a certified hospice or for occasional part time skilled nursing services, home health aide or medical social worker services, and for medical supplies and appliances prescribed by a doctor and furnished by a certified home health care agency. If you already have Medicare, find a hospice or home nursing service that's certified by them. For more information, call your local social security office and ask them to send you "Your Medicare Handbook."

Disability Insurance Benefits. *Regardless of age*, if you're totally disabled and a doctor says you can't work for 12 months, or your disability is likely to result in death, you can receive monthly payments **if** you've paid enough into the system. Social Security requests reports from your doctor and determines if you're disabled.

You have to work under Social Security for 5 out of 10 years before you were disabled to be eligible. There's a 5 month waiting period where no disability benefits are paid. Payments start on the sixth month from the beginning of the disability.

Dependent Benefits. A spouse who is 62 or older, or people who have a disabled child in their care, or children under 16 may be eligible for payments.

Survivor Benefits. When a wage earner who has paid into Social Security dies, his or her survivors are eligible for:

1. A lump sum burial payment up to $255 payable only to a surviving spouse or a child entitled to monthly benefits.

2. Monthly payments—to a widow or widower 60 years old or if disabled at 50 years, divorced widow or widower married 10 years, minor child to 16 years, dependent parents, widow or widower caring for a child under 16 or disabled child (eligible for life if applied for before age 22).

Supplemental Security Income. This program is based on need, not on your having paid anything to the government. If you're 65, blind, or totally disabled, the government will supplement your monthly income to *bring it up to* $360 if you're single or $520 for a couple (1987). This figure goes up every January. Your resources must not exceed $1700 if you're single or $2550 for a couple. They don't count the value of a house, the land it's on and a car. Most states supplement Supplemental Security Income and pay higher amounts.

MEDICAID

Medicaid is a state-administered health program for people with low income based on need. Medicaid, unlike Medicare, pays nearly all medical expenses. There's no deductible. In some states you apply for Medicaid at your local welfare office, in others at a Social Security Administration office.

If you have questions about Medicaid, call your state Welfare Department or Department of Human Resources. For questions about other federal programs, call your nearest Social Security Administration office. Much of your business can be completed by phone. If you need to see them in person, ask which documents to bring so you don't waste a trip. If you're applying by phone, make a note of the date, who you talked with and the subject of the conversation in case you have to call again. To avoid a long wait, don't go on Monday, usually their busiest day.

VETERANS ADMINISTRATION

In your area there is a Veterans Service Bureau or Agency.

Any person who served in the U.S. Armed Forces with at least 90 days of wartime service and an honorable or general discharge, who's over 65 or totally and permanently disabled, is eligible for a pension. A single vet can receive up to $490 per month, a married vet $642 plus $84 a month for each dependent child. All your income is counted against the $490—they pay you the difference.

Depending on their income, a widow or dependent children of a vet are eligible for a pension and educational benefits. If the death is "service-connected" (for example, if the vet dies of an old wound, illness or condition acquired while in the service) there are additional benefits.

Eligible vets who need help caring for themselves can receive an "aid-in-attendance allowance" up to $937 if married or $785 if single. "Housebound" vets unable to leave home but who do not need other help are eligible for up to $600 a month if single and $752 if married.

If a vet has to go to a private hospital in an emergency, the receiving physician must call a VA hospital within 72 hours. If he or she is eligible, the VA will transfer the vet to a free VA hospital or will pick up the tab if the vet is too ill to be transferred. When a vet dies in a VA hospital or while being transferred to one, VA will pay to transport the body to the home town or place of burial.

A vet, his widow and any number of unmarried children under 18 can receive a plot and headstone free of charge in a National Cemetery. If a vet who is receiving a pension or compensation for service connected disabilities is buried in a private cemetery, VA will pay up to $277 for burial and up to $138 for the plot and interment. If the death is "service-connected," there's a burial allowance up to $1,015. VA will also furnish headstones and a burial flag. Funeral directors have the applications for burial benefits and will complete them for you, or you may apply at the nearest VA office.

The VA doesn't chase you around the country to give you money. You have to apply. They have other benefits not mentioned here and their laws and payments change often, so check with the VA if you think there's any chance you or the dying person might qualify.

LEGAL HELP

LEGAL AID SERVICES

These are government-funded, nonprofit services that can help with any type of legal problem including land transfers, wills and estate planning. There are certain income qualifications for receiving these no-cost services.

To find a legal aid service look in the Yellow Pages under "attorneys" or Social Service Organizations." If you can't find one there, call the county courthouse, bar association or a lawyer referral service.

STATE BOARD OF HEALTH
MEDICAL EXAMINER
COUNTY CORONER

At some point you'll need to know about the laws in your area regarding death at home and burial. This will enable you to plan a simple, dignified funeral that meets your needs and desires, and the legal requirements.

Look in the White Pages under the name of your state, county or city for the Board of Health, Medical Examiner or Coroner, or call your hospital or county courthouse and ask who to call. Funeral homes are not the best sources for this information because they have a vested interest in your spending as much money as possible.

MEDICAL SUPPLIES

RENTAL SERVICES

You can rent almost any of the supplies you'll need. First, see if you can find them free of charge. If not, rent by the month; the rates are less. Look in the Yellow Pages under "Medical Supplies — Rental" or "Rental Services."

THE AMERICAN CANCER SOCIETY

Local chapters of the American Cancer Society often provide free transportation to and from treatment. They may lend a variety of supplies: wheelchairs, hospital beds, commodes. They may also have dressing supplies. A San Antonio chapter provides disposable pads used for incontinent patients and a Santa Fe chapter has a wig for someone who loses her hair from chemotherapy!

CATALOGUES, MEDICAL SUPPLY COMPANIES AND HOSPITAL PHARMACIES

If you're unable to find no-cost or rental supplies, check Sears and Roebuck's and Montgomery Ward's home-care catalogues. *Comfortably Yours*, an attractive catalogue of aides for easier living, is available from: 52 West Hunter Ave., Maywood, N.J. 07607.

Medical Supply companies or pharmacies near a hospital specialize in selling supplies needed by patients at home.

COUNSELING

COUNSELORS

Counselors are people specially trained to help us with our feelings. If this dying process brings up feelings which you have difficulty dealing with, consider getting outside help, such as a therapist, psychologist or social worker. It's a sign of courage, not cowardice, to seek help from a professional if problems seem beyond your capacity to handle at this particular time.

You may already know people in your community who specialize in helping with emotional challenges. It will be most helpful to find someone who is relatively clear about his or her own feelings about death. Call a hospice for a recommendation. Check with a County Mental Health Association, Community Mental Health Clinic or a college. If you live in a city, look for a Council of Social Agencies or a branch of the Family Services Association. For a child, you might check first with the school guidance counselor.

THE ELISABETH KÜBLER-ROSS CENTER

Elisabeth Kübler-Ross, M.D., has been recognized as the foremost authority in the field of death and dying for over 20 years. I like to think of her as the American Mother Teresa and of course she is totally unique.

The purpose of her center is to encourage people to view life as a series of challenging experiences from birth through death, rather than as a threatening and painful ordeal.

Regular five-day live-in retreats called "Life, Death and Transition" are given throughout the U.S. and abroad for dying patients, their families and other caregivers such as nurses, doctors and clergy. The emphasis of the workshop is to help you get in touch with and release negative aspects of yourself so you can be more loving with yourself and others.

Participants have told me the workshops end up being a joyous celebration of life. People leave with a fresh sense of well being and contentment through discovering new values and a deeper appreciation for the gift of life. The cost is $550. Scholarships are often available for people with fixed low incomes, needy terminally ill patients or those in crisis.

Dr. Kübler-Ross has written the following books which are useful in increasing our understanding of dying:

On Death and Dying
Questions and Answers on Death and Dying
Death, the Final Stage of Growth
To Live Until We Say Goodbye
Living with Death and Dying
Remember the Secret
On Children and Death

She lectures in the U.S., Europe and Australia. If you have a chance to hear her, do. She's an inspiration.

For her lecture schedules and workshop locations, send a self-addressed stamped envelope. As a member you receive an excellent newsletter and an opportunity to support our human family in transforming fear. Dues are $15 to $30. The center also gives workshops for teenagers and young children, and has a catalogue of useful books and tapes available. (For address see Appendix A.)

THE CENTER FOR ATTITUDINAL HEALING

This joyful, loving group works with children and adults with life-threatening diseases. They use the principal "Love is the only energy there is" from *A Course in Miracles*, a series of books which teach using love to transform fear. Participants with life-threatening illnesses act as counselors for others with a similar challenge. Programs and support groups help young children, siblings, sons and daughters, adults and elders, share their fears and anxieties and support each other with love.

The Center has a Phone Pal/Pen Pal Program to extend love and support to children and parents across the country. It also has books, pamphlets, cassettes and video tapes available. The children have created their own inspiring book, *There's a Rainbow Behind Every Dark Cloud*, which I recommend for any child facing a life-threatening disease. The founder, Dr. Gerald Jampolsky, is the author of *Love is Letting Go of Fear*, *Good-by to Guilt*, and *Teach Only Love*.

Out of compassion for parents already overburdened with medical expenses, they don't charge for any of their services. There are currently forty similar centers in the U.S. and Canada. Call to see if there's one near you. (For phone numbers see Appendix A.)

SPIRITUAL SUPPORT

CHURCHES AND SYNAGOGUES

Your priest, minister, or rabbi will want to visit and share their compassion and services with you and the dying person. Obviously the richness of your spiritual and religious life will support you as you face dying.

Calling a clergyperson or rabbi is clearly the choice of the dying person. It would be disrespectful for the family or clergy not to accept a dying person as he or she *is* and to attempt a last-minute conversion.

A priest can be called at any time to give the "Anointing of the Sick," a celebration of God's healing sacrament. Previously called "last rights", it is now given at any time to the sick, elderly or dying.

There are no deathbed sacraments in Judaism, although there is a tradition of *vidui*, a statement of confession as death approaches. This may be the recital of the *Shema* as an affirmation of faith or the traditional Prayer for the Dying. From ancient times, Jewish tradition has prescribed a mourning ritual which is compatible with modern understandings about the grieving process.

EMERGENCY SUPPORT

THE FIRE DEPARTMENT AND EMERGENCY MEDICAL SERVICE (EMS)

In some places the Fire Department and EMS are in the same department, in others not.

Fire Departments are close to my heart because they still seem to work on the principal of brotherly love. Without their help we couldn't have gotten Mary out of that second story apartment! Many fire chiefs have told me to tell you, "If you need help, call us. We'll try or help you find someone who can." How's that for reassuring?

EMS helps stabilize people to take them to a hospital. They're available for any lifesaving activity. You may not need them for this.

Both EMS and Fire Department staffs are trained to solve unusual problems. For example, you're alone — no neighbors are home — and the person you're caring for falls out of bed. You need help to get them back in.

If your area uses 911 as the phone number for emergency help, call 911. It connects you to a central emergency information service who'll connect you to EMS or the Fire Department. If you talk with EMS, be sure to let them know you don't want the person taken to the hospital, if that's true. If your area doesn't use 911, call the Fire Department.

AMBULANCES

In case you have to move someone from one place to another who can't be moved by car, van or pickup, find out ahead of time about ambulance services and their costs. They generally require cash upon delivering the person. So be prepared.

He who binds to himself a joy
Does the winged life destroy;
But he who kisses the joy as it flies,
Lives in eternity's sunrise.

—William Blake
Notebook

CHAPTER 4

GETTING ON WITH IT: PREPARATIONS AND HOMECOMING

Know that you are not alone. Every heart in the world is part of every other heart. Even if there is no friend or family beside you, you are not alone. The energy that created and encompasses us is with us as we bring someone home to live until they die.

Strength beyond what you imagine is yours. Love protects and surrounds you as you meet each task of the day.

The everyday limits of time and space can be transformed into a sense of connectedness with all people. If you're feeling alone — as if it's all closing in or you just walked into a wall — close your eyes and imagine yourself part of a huge family that's experiencing the same things you are, even in the same moment. Think of the people before you who have experienced dying, family, friends, people you don't even know, and all of us who will experience it in the not so distant future.

Each heart in the world standing beside someone they love who is dying is connected with every other heart. Two hundred thousand members of our family die each day on our planet — one every 15 seconds in the U.S.

If you feel your heart is breaking, feel it breaking open. Hearts don't break closed. People close them. The courage or peace you may find in your Self is shared with us all.

Whenever you're troubled or don't know what to do next, ask from the quietest, deepest place you can find in yourself . . . and listen for the answer. Sooner or later you'll hear it. It will come with quiet reassurance. Trust what you hear. Your Self knows more than all those experts out there. Allow your sadness and fear, and know that you are more than these.

If you ask for help, it is given.

You cannot fail.

You are not alone.

WHAT DO WE NEED?

Once you've decided this person you love will live and die at home, choose the room or rooms that are most comfortable and convenient. Consider how much the person can move about and the location of bathrooms. Is the old room still the favorite? Could you hear someone call from that room? Or would a bell or buzzer system be helpful? If a room was shared, do the persons want to continue sharing it? Does the dying person like to be alone, or is a bed or couch in the living room, in the middle of the life-flow of the home, a desirable choice? Is there another place the family can be if the dying person wants to sleep or be alone? A cheerful, well-lighted bedroom not far from the main living space and kitchen is a possibility—or even a greenhouse or porch depending on the weather.

It's helpful to locate a bed so you have easy access on both sides. This makes moving and turning the person and changing sheets easier. Bedside tables are useful for bottles, tissues, medical supplies, flowers and other things you want handy.

Make a list of things you'll need and want and go about getting them. Look around for what you can find at home. A list might go like this (not all are necessary, not even the first):

1. A doctor (see the following section on finding a doctor).

2. Prescribed medicines, particularly those for pain control.

3. A nurse.

4. A sense of humour.

5. A hospital bed—only if both patient and family decide it would be easier. It's not always necessary and can be upsetting to give up your own bed even if a hospital bed might be more comfortable.

6. A commode (potty chair), bedpan or urinal. Commodes have a plastic can underneath that can be emptied. You can bring a bedpan or urinal home from the hospital or buy one. Urinals are only for men.

7. A wheelchair, walker, crutches — according to the patient's needs.

8. Extra sheets and bedding. If you have a choice, choose designs and colors the person might like. Waterproof pads for beds and chairs. (Electric blankets are not recommended.)

9. Extra nightgowns or pajamas that are easy to put on and take off. A nightshirt for a man might be easier than pajamas. If you sew, you could copy a hospital gown in pleasing fabrics and colors. Bed jackets or cardigan sweaters.

10. A glorious potted plant or bunches of wildflowers.

11. Massage lotion. Try an herb or health food store for natural products.

12. A TV, VCR, radio, and/or cassette player.

13. Drinking straws that bend.

14. An extension on your telephone cord. It might be ideal to have two telephones, one near the person (on which you can turn off the bell), and one in a private place where you can talk and let out your feelings.

15. Extra pillows.

16. Alcohol, cotton balls. Hydrogen peroxide or swabs for care of the teeth.

17. A plastic dishpan for bathing.

18. Paper towels and tissues. Also cotton towels.

19. Socks and nonskid slippers. Feet tend to get cold if the weather is at all cool.

20. A stand-up bed tray if the person can feed him or herself.

21. Two hot water bottles, one for the feet and one for easing pain.

FINDING A DOCTOR

This may or may not be a challenge. You need a doctor to give the patient and family assistance in making medical decisions, to prescribe medicines if necessary and to authorize nursing services, insurance benefits and hospice care. If the patient has to go into a hospital unexpectedly, a doctor can give directions that the patient's wishes in terms of treatment be respected. A doctor is useful for patient and family morale, although for day-to-day care a nurse may be more helpful.

You'll need a doctor who can understand the patient's desire to die at home and who is willing to support you. Try to find one who accepts death as a natural part of life. If you're able, discuss with the doctor how he or she feels about death and artificial means of prolonging life and how the dying person feels about these things. This could save finding out later that the doctor you chose feels death is a personal or professional failure and will prolong a life no matter how inhumane this may be. When things are critical, there's no time for philosophical discussions.

A doctor who's willing to work with you as an equal and be personally involved in this dying process will be the most useful. She or he needs to be available for home visits and phone consultations. Doctoring partially by telephone can save a lot of wear and tear on everyone.

You may already have a doctor who fills the bill or you may have to do some looking. Friends may know of one; call a hospice, free clinic or university medical school. A growing number of young doctors are interested in home births and deaths. Call the local or county medical association and ask for a doctor who makes housecalls. Look in the Yellow Pages under "Physicians — General or Family Practice." Initial inquiries may be made by phone.

If the patient is taking medication, pain relievers, etc., make arrangements with your doctor and have them available before you bring the patient home. If you will be responsible for giving injections immediately upon the patient's homecoming, get instructions, syringes and needles beforehand.

MOVING FROM HOSPITAL TO HOME

When the patient is ready and things are sorted out at home, you're ready for the next part of the adventure. If you're nervous, it's OK.

At any time the patient, or the family at the patient's request, can check him or her out of the hospital. As mentioned earlier, it's easier if the doctor agrees and very uncommon for one to try to stop someone going home by instituting legal proceedings.

Driving a person home in your car saves the cost of an ambulance. Use a wheelchair if necessary to move the patient to and from the car. If an ambulance is needed, be prepared to pay cash. The doctor may ask a nurse to call an ambulance or you can call.

THE HOMECOMING

This may well be one of the most satisfying moments of the whole experience for you and the dying person. Homecoming with John, Mary and Dad were times of joy and quiet satisfaction. Don't be discouraged if there are snags or difficulties. You are both learning and adjusting.

If there are children in the family, they may want to make their own kind of homecoming celebration. Wonderful, as long as it's not too tiring for the homecomer. Joshua, Ben and I made signs to welcome Dad when he came home from his chemotherapy weeks; once we dressed as clowns.

You've already completed some of the hardest work, making the decision and getting organized at home. You and the dying person are doing what feels right and are taking responsibility for your lives. The house probably feels peaceful and purposeful. The homecomer is often content or joyful and relieved to be in familiar, beloved surroundings. Even if it isn't their own home it feels like a place for living. The dying person regains more ability to direct his or her own life.

My own experience with homecomings has been one of rightness (not righteousness) in cooperating with life by taking responsibility for dying. My feeling of helplessness vanished, replaced by a new sense of purposefulness. **I'm doing what I want to do, being here for this person I love, and it feels good.** A feeling like this can carry you a long way through whatever lies ahead.

Sit down and put your feet up. Enjoy the satisfaction of your accomplishment and the beauty of home.

A human being is part of the whole, called by us the 'Universe,' a part limited in time and space. He experiences himself, his thoughts and feelings, as something separated from the rest — a kind of optical delusion of his consciousness. This delusion is a kind of prison for us, restricting us to our personal desires and to affection for a few persons nearest us. Our task must be to free ourselves from this prison by widening our circles of compassion to embrace all living creatures and the whole of nature in its beauty.

— Albert Einstein

CHAPTER 5

MEDICAL CONSIDERATIONS

WHEN TO CALL A DOCTOR OR NURSE

You may find it surprising how little you need a doctor or nurse if you accept that the person you're caring for is dying. Much of what we need from the medical profession is moral support.

A doctor is properly called for counsel and assistance with some specific procedure, **not to make decisions for you**. Ask for help and guidance to make the dying process as comfortable as possible. Don't let their advice dominate the experience. Listen to doctors knowing they have information you need and also that their life investment is in hospitals and medicine.

Call a doctor or nurse if you feel you're in over your head. Call if you feel you don't have sufficient knowledge to take responsibility for a decision. Call if you don't know what to do and panic, and the panic doesn't subside. Call about pain, developing bedsores, catheter problems, constipation. Call if the patient wants you to call. If you can't reach a doctor, call a nurse. In terms of practical care, a nurse is often more helpful than a doctor. A nurse can call the doctor and get orders for pain medication, etc.

There needs to be an **explicit agreement** about what the dying person wants the doctor to do. For example, a complication arises such as difficulty in breathing, perhaps due to pneumonia. Does the person want to be rushed to the hospital, which may prolong the dying process? In times past pneumonia was called "The Old Man's Friend" because it can help a person to die. Is there a reason to cure it so the person can die later of cancer? There may be.

The dying person can share his wishes verbally with the doctor and ask that they be noted in his medical record. Preferably a living will has been signed (page 261). If so, give the doctor a copy. The agreement or living will can be changed whenever the dying person chooses. Doctors feel freer to follow a patient's wishes if they know that the family understands that in a dying process, the dying person may die at any time and there is no blame.

WORKING WITH A DOCTOR

Working with a doctor can teach us a lot about trusting and taking responsibility for ourselves and about how we relate to authority figures. Doctors are just ordinary people with a medical specialty. They have a difficult role in our society, indicated by their unusually high incidence of alcoholism, suicide, drug addiction and marital breakups.

We have set them up as gods, as knowers of mysteries we cannot hope to comprehend and we feel cheated and angry when they don't heal us. Perhaps this inability indicates the *source* of healing is somewhere else. It seems a little silly to make gods of specialists in livers or nostrils and sillier still to turn our lives over to them. After years of working with people who expect them to be gods, many doctors start to believe it themselves. Then, when a patient dies, they take it as a personal failure — and we also see it as their personal failure.

Until recently, most of us have wanted doctors to be in control of our health. So they became habituated to being in charge and were astounded when someone wanted to participate in his or her own health. A patient and family who want to, are still often labeled "difficult". I suggest it is better to be called "difficult" than to abdicate our responsibility which may later cause us needless suffering. It is possible to find a doctor who's pleased and relieved that you want to participate and who will support you all the way.

Patients and families have generally reacted to doctors the same way people do to other authority figures — with feelings of hostility and/or intimidation. Neither attitude makes for an open, helpful relationship. In the long run it's not useful to have unrealistic expectations of doctors. They cause us disappointment and prevent doctors from being all of who they can be. It's not useful or accurate to assume, *the doctor knows and I don't*. The most beneficial relationship between doctor, patient and family might be **a partnership of equals.**

113

a. The family and patient see doctors as helpers, feel compassion for them and appreciate their expertise in an area (usually a limited one in terms of the total health picture.)

b. Doctors share their compassion and expertise with the family without suggesting they know it all and the family doesn't.

c. The patient and family take responsibility for themselves and don't expect doctors to make life decisions about any life except their own.

A doctor's life would be a lot easier if he or she didn't feel responsible for the life of each patient. When we feel responsible and things don't go as we'd like, we tend to feel guilty. A doctor can be **responsive to** and **not responsible for** a patient. Once we, as patients and families, get over the fright of not having someone else in charge, we'll feel a greater sense of responsibility for our own lives and increased confidence, power and dignity. A doctor's life might also be more meaningful if he or she is willing to be personally involved with patients and their families.

If during this dying process, you have a problem getting your doctor to answer your questions and hear your concerns, **be very direct.** Often harassed, busy and tired, doctors can seem like escape artists. You could say, "It appears you are too busy to talk now. I'd like to make an appointment to talk about John's treatment."

Here are three questions to keep in mind when you talk with a doctor:

1. Presently, in simple terms, what's going on?

2. What do you think is best to do from here?

3. How much of this treatment is to keep this person alive and how much is helping him or her to be comfortable?

After each question, repeat back to the doctor what was said to make sure you understand and everyone knows you understand. Review the conversation. For example, "Did I understand correctly that you feel . . . such and such?" You have a right to know what each treatment is for. And **there is no shame in asking questions until you understand.** Make notes if you have to.

I write down medicines prescribed, then call a pharmacist and/or read about them in a standard drug book called the *Physician's Desk Reference* (PDR). The PDR is easily obtainable by non-physicians — your doctor may give you last year's. You might check your local library for *The Essential Guide to Prescription Drugs*, by James W. Long, M.D.

The AMA 1986 policy statement that permits doctors to withhold *all* life-prolonging treatment from dying patients and the Living Will Laws passed in most states go a long way toward alleviating the problem of doctors, with good intentions, resisting or obstructing a patient's right to die.

Not withstanding, you may sense that your doctor feels death is a personal failure, professional defeat or a moral and legal dilemma instead of a natural event. If he or she is resisting or obstructing your loved one's right to die, you might discuss your feeling with him or her. Then, if death continues to be resisted, it may be time to get another doctor-helper.

If getting a new doctor is difficult and the dying person's wishes continue to be ignored, see Appendix G. For doctors and families of people being kept alive artificially, I recommend *Physicians and the Hopelessly Ill Patient, Legal, Medical and Ethical Guidelines.* The book is available from the Society for The Right to Die. (See Appendix A for the address.) It might be a kind gift for your doctor.

Be aware that it's OK to change doctor or nurse-helpers if the dying person doesn't like the ones you have. Having people around us whom we feel good about is our right. This doesn't mean pamper a *prima donna* who wants a new staff each day!

PHYSICAL PAIN AND PAIN RELIEVERS

The most consistently voiced fear about dying and death is physical pain, particularly in the case of cancer. You may be relieved to know that cancer is not necessarily painful. Some doctors estimate that 25 to 50% of advanced cancer patients experience no pain as a result of the cancer. For patients who are in pain, its management is important to enable them to live fully until they die.

Each of us reacts differently to pain because it's experienced by the whole individual, physically, emotionally, mentally and spiritually. A unique pain relief program must be developed for each individual. With skilled help, we can control pain just as effectively at home as in a hospital. Pain can, 90% to 99% of the time, be relieved with the right combination of medicine and dosing schedules.

Medical Considerations

Even as we move to relieve pain, we need to be aware of its purpose. Pain is neither good nor bad; it's simply a messenger that tells us something in our lives or bodies is not working and needs attention. It's generally pain that moves us to leave behind old patterns and ways of being that no longer work. The more a dying person clings to the body, the more pain she or he experiences.

Perhaps the role physical pain plays in the dying process is to loosen our attachment to our bodies and the illusion that we are our bodies. "Hey, my body is getting uninhabitable. I need to consider getting out of here." Notice there is an "I" apart from the body. Without a body there is no pain. **Death itself is painless.** Getting ready for it can be painful.

Dying people may be afraid to admit they're in pain, feeling ashamed to be "weak" or afraid of addiction or returning to the hospital. Encourage them to speak up and not 'tough it out', so they can use their energy to live well until they die. Having pain does not indicate weakness, just *humanness*. **Suffering is not noble.** Let the person know pain can be controlled at home so they needn't fear returning to a hospital. Reassure them that the therapeutic aim in their case is pain relief and addiction is not a concern.

Sudden unexpected pain, called **acute**, causes anxiety. Your attitude can do much to help the person experiencing it. Your fear and resistance to their pain increases their fear and resistance and their fear and resistance increases their pain. You can help by not saying for example, "Oh, pain, terrible. We've got to get rid of it right away!" Allow the person to learn what he or she can from it as you quietly move towards relieving it, if that's the person's choice. *Do what the dying person wants.* **No human being should be degraded by having to beg for pain relief.**

You might try using the word "sensation" instead of "pain." Taking the label off pain often changes our experience of it. Aspirin and different strengths of Tylenol can be used for *non-severe acute pain*. **If there is severe pain for which you are unprepared, call your doctor or nurse.**

Pain that endures over time is called **chronic. Chronic pain experienced by a dying person can generally be relieved.** Because we want to live until we die, it's important to know that **alertness and chronic pain relief can be balanced.** To be conscious at death is a choice similar to being conscious for the labor of birth. Some women like to be unconscious and wake up with a baby beside them; other prefer to be awake, cooperating with and participating in the experience. Perhaps dying is the labor pain of the soul. Some may not care if they're unconscious and others prefer to be present for their dying. It's a personal choice. There's no right or wrong way. Either way works.

Whatever the pain challenge, the patient and doctor decide **together** which drug or combination of drugs might be most suitable. A pain reliever that works for one person, may not work for another. A dosage therapeutic for one may be toxic for another. Consider drug allergies. (John Muir, for example, was allergic to opium and its derivatives, which include many commonly used narcotics.) A person may have to try a number of alternatives until pain relief and alertness are balanced. In the words of Ivan Illich, we don't want to turn "patients into pets," as many nursing homes do.

The secret of chronic pain relief is regularity. The pain reliever should be given at regular intervals **before** the pain begins and the dosage adjusted to handle the entire period. *Machos* and stoics do themselves and their families a disservice by waiting until they're in agony to take pain medication. Pain is much more difficult to control if it's very severe before medication is given.

A skilled person needs to set up the time schedule which can of course be changed at anytime to meet the patient's needs. Ask the patient to keep you advised of how she or he feels.

Recent studies and practice in many hospices indicate that *liquid morphine* is an effective pain reliever for dying patients. It's chief advantages are that it's easy to take and enters the bloodstream quickly. **The side effects of oral morphine and most narcotic pain relievers are nausea, constipation and sleepiness.** Nausea can be treated with anti-nausea agents such as Compazine, taken about a half hour before the pain reliever. Constipation can be remedied a number of ways (see page 133).

During the first few days of taking a narcotic, a person may feel drowsy. As the body adjusts and the person catches up on sleep lost while in pain, she or he usually becomes alert again and may live fully the remaining time. If drowsiness continues, the dosage can be adjusted. The morphine solution is usually given every four hours around the clock. Although, long acting morphine tablets, 12 hours, may be given before bedtime to eliminate waking the dying person and yourself in the middle of the night.

The morphine solution, called by hospices "MS" or "OMS", contains morphine, alcohol and cherry syrup. It's used instead of the "Brompton Cocktail" that originated in England which includes heroin and cocaine. MS or OMS may be mixed with juice, pina colada, Kahlua, Amaretto or any water-based liquid. For normal dosage, see the Hospice Physician's Standing Order Form on page 000 in Appendix B.

MS is dispensed with a prescription which must be renewed each time. So plan ahead.

If the dying person can no longer swallow or is vomiting, injections or Numorphan suppositories may be substituted. Sometimes Prednisone is given once a day in the morning to enhance the patient's appetite and sense of well being.

There are many other effective pain relievers. Another useful combination is Dilaudid in tablets, changing to Methadone injections if the patient can't swallow tablets. Dilaudid is now available in an injectable form called Dilaudid HP.

Narcotic means "sleep inducing." See the list of narcotic drugs commonly prescribed for chronic pain relief. Narcotics can be combined with Tylenol, Aspirin, nonsteroidal anti-inflammatories (for example, Motrin) or antidepressants to maximize pain control and minimize sleepiness. Some doctors consider Demoral a less effective drug for cancer pain.

PAY ATTENTION and stay flexible when using these drugs. For example, a doctor may say one shot should last five hours. The patient reports that it lasts only three. Consult with the doctor about changing the dosage. Don't be overly concerned if a much larger dosage than the one listed is necessary for effective pain relief. My Dad *started* with 12 mg. Dilaudid.

A new development in pain control is the use of pumps to administer the desired drug. A pump worn at the waist delivers a constant flow of morphine, for example, through a plastic tube to a small hypodermic needle usually implanted under the skin of the chest. The pump is particularly useful for people whose stomach or intestines have been severely damaged or for whom other forms of pain control haven't worked. You might want to ask a hospice doctor, medical oncologist or a pain clinic connected to a hospital or doctor's group if they're available.

NARCOTIC DRUGS COMMONLY PRESCRIBED FOR CHRONIC PAIN IN TERMINAL ILLNESSES

Name	Usual Oral Dose in milligrams (mg)	Usual Intramuscular Dose (injection) in mg
Demerol	150	50
Codeine	100	60
Talwin	90	30
Morphine	15	5
Oxycodone (Percodan, Percocet, Tylox)	10	7.5
Methadone	10	5
Dilaudid	4	1
Levo-Dromoran	2	1

(These doses are roughly equivalent.)

Commonly Used Medical Abbreviations

Abbreviation	Meaning
a.	before
a.c.	before food or meals
ad lib.	to the amount desired
b.i.d., b.d.	two times a day
b.i.n., b.n.	two times a night
b.m.r.	basal metabolism rate
b.p.	blood pressure
B.P.	British Pharmacopoeia
c.,c̄.	with
e.g.	for example

ext.	extract
fl.	fluid
gtt(s).	a drop, drops
h., hr.	hour
h.s.	at bedtime
I.M.	intramuscular
I.V.	intravenous
noct.	at night
NPO	nothing by mouth
p.o.	give orally
p.r.n.	as needed
q.d.	every day
q.i.d.	four times a day
q.o.d.	every other day
Sx	symptoms
t.i.d.	three times a day
Tx	treatments
U.S.P.	U.S. Pharmacopoeia

There are a number of alternatives to medically used drugs: Scotch, Bourbon or other strong spirits, biofeedback, heat, massage, acupuncture, hypnosis, color therapy. LSD, Marijuana, Mescaline and laughing gas — or laughing. The appropriate choice is determined by the dying person, influenced by the content and style of life before the illness.

Marijuana, Mescaline and LSD have been used experimentally with the dying process. The fear and hysteria built up around these drugs have obscured their useful medical qualities. The active ingredient of marijuana, THC, has proved effective in preventing nausea in chemotherapy patients. It acts as a mood elevator and tranquilizer, tends to retard weight loss by stimulating the appetite and potentiates pain medications so that less is needed. Mescaline and LSD, consciousness expanding drugs, seem to enlarge the framework in which a person experiences pain, changing the

Medical Considerations

experience of it and sometimes eliminating pain entirely. Laura Huxley in *This Timeless Moment* describes the death of Aldous Huxley, an innovative adventurer in the human mind. Huxley used LSD in his last days in order to experience his death as fully as possible.

Stanislov Grof and a group at the Maryland Psychiatric Research Center, doing research with cancer and LSD, made an interesting pain discovery. Grof and John Halifax in their book, *Human Encounter with Death*, reported that pain is relieved by a "transpersonal experience" (A mystical experience in which one goes beyond the usual limits of personality and connects with some large whole, perhaps God). See page 280 for one technique for guiding someone into a transcendent space *without drugs.*

Breathing and visualization techniques can be very useful in working with pain. If there's delay in getting a pain reliever, you might try them. In some cases, they may preclude your needing drugs at all. Breathing can be as useful for dying as it is for birthing. When we feel pain, we tense up and tend to stop breathing fully. Our cells don't get the oxygen they need to clean out toxins and keep the nerve signals straight, and the pain gets worse.

One of the first things to do for pain is to **keep breathing.** Unless someone has had previous experience with breathing consciously, he or she may focus on the pain and fear and forget to breathe. As the helper, encourage the person to breathe deeply, to **breathe into the area that hurts,** and then down into the toes. Ask the person to relax, to "soften" around the area that hurts, and open him or herself to the sensation of pain. As the person surrenders, gives up resistance, more oxygen enters the area and the pain may lessen. The body senses that its message is received and relaxes. Keep repeating, "soften, relax, open."

123

Paying attention to pain helps relieve it if we don't judge it as bad! It just is.

I find it helpful to combine breathing techniques with hot water bottles and foot massages. While the person is breathing into the area that hurts, partially fill two hot water bottles with hot, **not boiling**, water. Cover the bottles with a towel so you don't burn the person's skin and place them under the feet and on the area that hurts. If you don't have hot water bottles, put the person's feet into a bucket of medium-hot tap water. Put a hot washcloth on the forehead. Together these seem to keep energy moving through the body so pain is lessened or eliminated. Some people prefer ice packs and cold water. Either is OK. (Again, if the pain is severe and you're unprepared, call a doctor). If it feels right to you, add a foot massage to further relax the person and to stimulate increased circulation.

Breathing and foot massage are useful techniques for calming *anyone* in a stressful situation. You might want to take time for them yourself.

I sometimes hear talk in new age circles that taking drugs for pain is somehow not spiritual. That's baloney. Again, physical pain is a message that something's not working right in the body. The dying get the message loud and clear only this time there's nothing they can do about it. The body can't be fixed. Taking drugs is useful to free us to experience dying on other levels and not to fixate on one level—the body. If we're in pain, the body has our undivided attention. And if dying teaches us anything, it teaches us that we're more than just a body.

If, as many new age people believe, our essential identity is God, why torture God's body—or anyone else's—by not taking pain medication? That's cruelty. If we truly believe that everything is equally sacred, morphine is just as sacred as the herb from which it's derived.

SHOTS OR INJECTIONS

There are two types (routes) of shots or injections used for giving pain relievers: **intravenous**, in which the solution is injected directly into a vein, and **intramuscular**, in which it's injected into muscle tissue. Intravenous shots should be given **only** by a qualified doctor, nurse or medic. If necessary, you can give intramuscular ones. Ask a doctor or nurse to show you how and practice ahead of time on an orange. The following instructions and diagram will help you as well.

Don't panic. Giving an intramuscular shot is not difficult or dangerous, although it may be frightening to think about. You will likely forget your fear if someone you love is suffering in front of you and you could do something about it. Remember, love transforms fear.

Have the prescribed drug(s) and the correct size syringes and needles available. If you've had experience in giving shots, you can protect a person's privacy by giving it in the arm or upper thigh. If you haven't, it's best to use the buttock.

PREPARING AND GIVING AN
INTRAMUSCULAR INJECTION

1. Position the person comfortably to receive the injection and ask him or her to relax. If administering to the

How to Give an Intramuscular Injection

126

buttock, ask the person to turn the toes inward to relax the muscle. (The discomfort of intramuscular shots is usually due to tension in the muscle tissue.)

2. Swab the bottle top with alcohol. If you use an ampule, hold the top with paper towel and break it off, holding the base firmly and snapping the top toward you.

   Remove the sterile syringe and needle from the package and check that the needle is secure. If the syringe and needle are separate, screw them together without touching the metal needle.

3. Insert the needle into the bottle or ampule. (*For a bottle only*, first inject air into it — the same amount as the dose of medication. If you want 1 cc. out of the bottle, inject 1 cc. of air into it first.)

4. Pull the plunger until the correct dosage is shown on the syringe scale and remove the needle from the bottle or ampule.

5. With needle end pointed up, tap the syringe with your finger and push in the plunger slightly to remove excess air. (Don't worry about injecting small air bubbles with an intramuscular injection. It may be uncomfortable, but isn't dangerous.) It's OK if a little of the solution spurts out of the needle.

6. Choose an injection site in the **upper outer quadrant** of either buttock (see diagram). This is important to avoid the sciatic nerve or a large blood vessel.

7. Thoroughly clean the injection site using a cotton ball saturated with alcohol or prepared swab.

8. With the thumb and first fingers, press down, spreading the skin around the site.

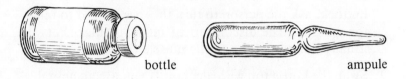

bottle   ampule

9. Hold the syringe up and, like a dart, quickly and deliberately thrust the needle into the buttock at a 90 degree angle. (You'll find this doesn't rule out gentleness.)

10. With the needle in place, pull back the plunger slightly to see if any blood appears in the syringe. If it does, you've hit a vein and must remove the needle and choose a new site.

11. Inject the medicine slowly.

12. Quickly remove the needle, and then apply gentle pressure on the site with the cotton ball or prepared alcohol swab.

13. Massage the area gently and firmly to help the medicine be absorbed.

14. Destroy the used needle by bending and breaking it. **Do not touch the needle after using it to inject someone who has a communicable disease.** Some pharmacies sell small, inexpensive needle disposers which are useful if you give injections often.

IVS AND DEHYDRATION

The question of intravenous feeding (through IVs) may come up for you. IVs are used to nourish people who can't eat or drink enough to stay alive. The decision whether or not to use IVs in terminal care raises again the issue of the quality of life versus the quantity. Feeding the body cells by means of IVs often prolongs the life of the body. The cost is discomfort, less ability to move and the need to have a nurse. Dad said, "When I've got those tubes in I feel like a patient. When I don't, I feel like me."

The result of not taking enough fluids into the body is dehydration. The chemical imbalance created by lack of fluids often causes a person to have a sense of well-being or euphoria. It's a relatively comfortable death. The main discomfort, dryness of the mouth and thirst, is helped by sucking on ice chips and clean moist washcloths. It generally takes only a few days for a debilitated person to die from lack of fluids.

If someone has not yet accepted that she or he is dying and wants to be fed intravenously, a doctor or nurse can show you how IVs work and problems to watch for. There can be local pain and inflammation at the needle site. The needle can slip out of the vein causing the liquid to fill the surrounding tissue. A qualified nurse needs to be there or come by often to check the IV. Bottles are changed three to six times a day.

Don't worry if a bottle runs out. Air is not going to get in and kill the person. If the fluid is not running, a clot forms around the needle and the needle then has to be changed. Ask the nurse ahead of time what to do if the tubing falls out, comes apart or has air bubbles.

One of our worst fears about shots and IVs is that air will get in and kill the person. Actually, a surprisingly large amount of air has to go **directly into a vein or artery** before there's a problem.

129

Sensitive Areas that Need Extra Massage to Prevent Bedsores

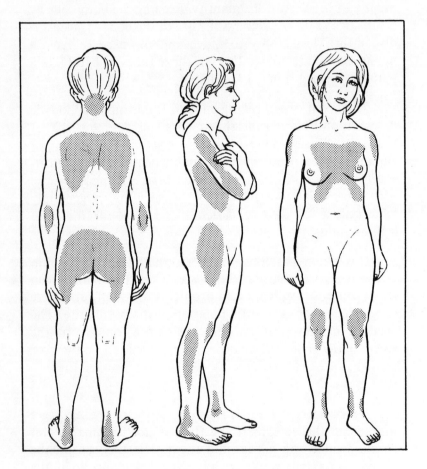

SKIN CARE AND BEDSORES

Skin care is important medically as well as to help a person maintain dignity and comfort. If the skin is not properly cared for, bedsores can result. Bedsores (dicubitus ulcers) are caused when skin tissue breaks down. The first sign of skin breakdown is red sore areas. They occur where prolonged pressure limits circulation of oxygen to the skin. Uncared for, they can become painful, oozing, raw areas where infection may set in. **The best thing to do about bedsores is to prevent their happening in the first place.** The less a person can move, the greater the chance of getting bedsores.

You can prevent them by **turning** a person in bed at least every couple of hours, **massaging** to keep blood circulating in the area, **drying** the skin well after bathing, and **exposing** the skin to air. Use a "sheepskin" (see page 196) under the person or an eggcrate mattress, a foam pad with indentations like an egg box. Hospices often use eggcrate mattresses. You can buy one for about $20 at a medical supply company. You may not need one to prevent bedsores if the person is massaged and turned frequently, but they are comfortable.

To protect the coccyx (tail bone), place a 4-inch foam cushion on a wheelchair or other hard seat. If the person is so thin that his or her bones stick out, place soft cotton materials, like flannel, over the bones for protection. Place a soft cloth or pillow between the knees when someone is laying on his or her side and has been confined to bed for a long time. Body surfaces that touch can cause pressure, friction and skin breakdown. You may also buy toughening cremes that contain tincture of Benzoin to protect the skin (Lanacane, Solarcain, etc.).

The basic idea is: if the skin is wet, dry it; if it's too dry, moisten it. Use a light skin oil like baby oil. Sometimes you're working with both wet and dry skin. Any areas exposed to urine need to be washed and dried well. Use a drying cream such as Desitin, or powder such as Johnson's Baby Powder or Mexana.

To prevent bedsores, many hospices use Stomahesive Wafers and/or Duoderm dressings. These bandaid-like dressings act like a second skin to prevent breakdown. Place a Stomahesive Wafer, for example, on skin that remains reddened over the coccyx, ankles, knees or hips. If the skin has already broken down—there are cracks, it looks mottled, black or like an abrasion—use a Duoderm dressing. Available at medical supply companies or some drug stores, Stomahesive Wafers cost about $12 for five 4'x4' wafers and Duoderm, about $22 for five 4'x4' dressings.

If areas of the skin do redden and break down, be sure to show the doctor or nurse and ask for suggestions.

ELIMINATION AND INCONTINENCE

Often a person who is very ill or very old will have problems with elimination. As diet changes and a person gets less exercise, organs are weakened and the bowels and bladder start loosening or become blocked. 'Incontinence' means loss of bladder or bowel control. Losing control over elimination, one of the most basic life functions, can be very demoralizing. A person experiencing this loss needs our compassion and caring to adjust. See page 207 for ways to assist the person physically and emotionally.

CATHETERS

A catheter is a flexible tube inserted into the urethra (the canal that takes urine out of the body), and is usually connected to a plastic sack at the other end. It's used when bladder control is lost and can help prevent skin deterioration due to wetness. For men, there is a kind of catheter that is not inserted into the urethra but fits on the outside of the penis like a sheath. It's called a condom catheter. You'll need instructions from a nurse in the use and care of catheters and things to watch for, such as infection.

An alternative for dealing with lost bladder control is disposable cotton pads or diapers (see page 207).

Tell the dying person about the alternatives and ask their preference. Some people find catheters uncomfortable.

CONSTIPATION

A blockage in the bowels can cause discomfort and pain and eventually may be life threatening. **Paying attention to and treating constipation is an important part of home care**, particularly if your patient is taking pain relief drugs that cause constipation. A general rule of thumb, use a laxative or enema if there has been no bowel movement for three days. **If there is undiagnosed abdominal pain, check with your doctor.**

Natural ways to deal with constipation are: activity, a diet adequate in fiber; drinking warm water, coffee or some herbal teas; and using a toilet or potty chair instead of a bedpan. A diet containing bran, lots of fresh vegetables, fruits and their juices (prune and apple particularly) is helpful. White bread, white rice, meat and cheese tend to constipate. Acidophilus, a natural intestinal flora, helps relieve constipation and diarrhea by reestablishing the balance of intestinal bacteria — very important for people whose own intestinal bacteria have been killed by antibiotics or chemotherapy. Yogurt contains acidophilus. It's available at health food stores in tablets or liquid.

Temporary constipation may be relieved by a natural laxative such as Nature's Way or a bulk-forming laxative like Metamucil. For chronic constipation, you may use a combination of stool softener and bowel stimulant such as Colace or Senokot-S (no prescription required). If more stimulation is needed you can add Ducolax tablets or suppositories to the above. Some hospices use Colace, a stool softener, and two tablespoons of Milk of Magnesia before bedtime.

An enema is a simple procedure many of us have already used at some time for constipation. You can buy a disposable premixed one, such as Fleets Enema, or mix one yourself. Here's a recipe: Dissolve two or three tablespoons of honey or one tablespoon of castile soap with enough water to fill an enema bag, or fill the bag with coffee or comfrey tea (drinking strength). Place a disposable pad (see page 207) under the person. Put Vaseline or cream around the tip to be inserted into the rectum. Roll the person onto his or her **left** side and gently insert the tip three or four inches into the rectum. Hold the bag eighteen to twenty-four inches above the person's hip and allow the water to flow *slowly* into the colon. Lowering the bag slows down the flow. Ask the person to breathe deeply and relax and to hold the solution as long as possible. When the person can't hold it any longer and needs to let go use a bedpan if going to a bathroom or potty chair isn't possible. Be sure to wash and powder the area afterward, then wash your own hands.

If the person fails to respond to a laxative or enema, a nurse or doctor will have to do a *digital de-impaction*, which means digging the stool out by hand with gloves on. An impaction is painful and unpleasant. It usually doesn't happen if you pay attention to constipation.

DIARRHEA

Diarrhea is the body's way of getting rid of something it doesn't want in a hurry. Unless it continues and/or the patient is getting weak from dehydration, it's often best to let it run its course. Cooked food, including white rice, tend to slow down diarrhea as do bananas and Jello. Acidophilus will help rebalance the intestinal tract bacteria.

If these don't work, simple diarrhea is easily treated with Kaopectate and Pepto-Bismol. If it proves more difficult to treat, you'll need a prescription for Lomotil, paregoric, codeine, etc.

Sometimes a *little* diarrhea is a sign that stool is blocking the intestine. Liquid passes around the stool and it appears to be diarrhea. If a person's fluid intake and movement are limited, and/or they're taking narcotic drugs and the bowel has not moved normally, give an enema. Unless there is severe abdominal pain, it can't hurt and may clear the blockage.

INSOMNIA (Sleeplessness)

The cares and concerns of a dying person may cause sleeplessness. If your patient has difficulty sleeping see if you can help without sleeping pills and barbiturates. Addiction is not a real concern with the dying, but why interfere more with delicate body balances? Some possibilities are to take, before bedtime, calcium tablets (2 grams), camomile tea, valerian with B-vitamin complex, a warm glass of milk, or tryptophan. Tryptophan is an amino acid in meat, milk and cheese. Turkey is high in tryptophan. (Remember how tired you felt after Thanksgiving dinner?) Try a warm bath, hot foot bath, a back rub or foot massage, or a guided meditation (see page 280).

Stroke the hair and scalp and encourage the person to let all thoughts float away and let the head feel spacious and empty, clouds drifting in and out. When I can't sleep I use the Bach Flower Remedy, Sweet Chestnut (see Appendix B).

Avoid coffee, black tea and all dark colored colas before bedtime. They contain eye opening caffein.

It's also OK not to go to sleep even when someone else thinks it's time. Encourage the person to read, write, watch TV, listen to soothing music or think for a while. If not sleeping continues to trouble the *patient*, ask a doctor about sleeping medications. Hospices often use 15 mg. Dalmane.

FEVER

If the patient starts to run a fever, you can treat it with aspirin unless there's an allergic reaction to it. Tylenol is preferable if the stomach is upset or the patient has a prob-

136

lem with ulcers or bleeding. A tepid or lukewarm sponge bath can be very effective in reducing a child's fever. For a high fever, you can wrap a child or adult in cold wet sheets and cover them with blankets. If the fever continues or increases, you may want to call a doctor.

DEPRESSION

A dying person may experience depression. For the useful role it plays in the dying process, see page 143. Depression tends not to be as long lasting or severe at home, where the person has more control over his or her life. If depression persists, the person may need help with counseling or mood-elevating drugs. I've yet to see severe depression at home.

Depression causes actual chemical changes in the body. Chronic pain wears us down until we feel depressed and hopeless. These feelings may lift when the pain is relieved, although some people become habituated to depression and it persists. To break the cycle, try to help the person refocus their energy. Because depression is often a result of not expressing what we feel, encourage the person to express sadness or whatever they're feeling and to live fully the time they have. Funny movies or stories may help. I also use Bach Flowers for depression (Appendix B). Some people may want to temporarily combine a pain reliever with an anti-depressant. Elavil and Sinequan are commonly prescribed anti-depressants.

Sometimes depression is a side effect of pain medications. Have your doctor change the pain medication or combine it with one of the anti-depressants mentioned above.

IRRATIONALITY

Irrationality is a temporary or permanent loss of connection with the generally accepted reality. You may not encounter it. I have a number of times, as a result of over-medication. If you do, attempt to find the *cause* or *unexpressed need* behind it. If possible, change the condition or meet the need.

Irrationality may be a result of pain, over-medication, exhaustion, blockage in the colon or emotional frustration. In these cases you can often reverse the cause. Sometimes it helps to change the person's physical position, for example, from lying in bed to sitting up in a wheelchair. Suggest a walk if it's possible.

Irrationality may not be reversible in the case of senility or a brain tumor. (Not all brain tumors cause irrationality. It depends on the part of the brain affected.)

If a patient who can't walk tries to get out of bed, hold him or her gently and firmly, talk with them, massage them or whatever occurs to you to do. For their own protection, they may need to be physically restrained. You can use a restraining chair, a wheelchair with a tray that locks into place. If the person's in bed, fold a sheet until it's one foot wide, place it across the chest and arms and tuck it snugly under the mattress on both sides. Your doctor or nurse can also advise you about different types of restraints.

For severe agitation or hysteria, which I've not yet seen in people dying at home, tranquilizing medication may be necessary. Haldol, Thorazine and Navane are commonly used. I regard them as a last resort when we've exhausted **every** other possibility. I would use them **only** to protect someone from harming themselves or others. Remember, we don't want to turn patients into pets.

If a person with a senile mind is sitting around not harming anyone and rambling to him or herself, the only change necessary may be in our attitude. Irrationality may serve a useful purpose in the dying process by allowing a person to disconnect from this reality and prepare for the next. If it's painful for you to witness, allow your sadness and remember that we all don't have to have the same reality, and we can respect another's. It can be interesting to enter the world of someone we've judged to be irrational and see what there is to learn.

* * * * *

Possibilities other than those I've discussed may arise and can also be taken care of at home. For example, if the dying person needs oxygen for comfort, you can rent an "oxygen concentrator." It's a little machine that gathers oxygen from the air, concentrates it and delivers it to the person through nose tubes or a face mask.

If the person is choking on secretions, you can rent a portable suction machine. There's even one kind patients can use on themselves. A nurse can show you how to use these.

Some other possibilities are included in the *Hospice Physician's Standing Order Form.* This form gives you an idea of what some care-givers do for their patients. You might want to share it with your doctor (see Appendix B).

If the person you're caring for has AIDS, see Appendix D for a homecare guide.

PRAYER FOR PEACE

(A version of the Prayer of St. Francis, used by Mother Teresa.)

Lord, make me a channel of your peace that
Where there is hatred, I may bring love
Where there is wrong, I may bring the spirit of
          forgiveness
Where there is discord, I may bring harmony
Where there is error, I may bring truth
Where there is doubt, I may bring faith
Where there is despair, I may bring hope
Where there are shadows, I may bring light
Where there is sadness, I may bring joy.

Lord, grant that I may seek rather to comfort
          than to be comforted;
To understand than to be understood
To love than to be loved
For it is by forgetting self that one finds
It is in forgiving that one is forgiven
It is by dying that one awakens to the eternal
life.
       Amen

God bless you
M Teresa mc

CHAPTER 6

BEING WITH SOMEONE WHO IS DYING

ELISABETH KÜBLER-ROSS' STAGES OF DYING

Elisabeth Kübler-Ross, a Swiss-born doctor and author, has served us all with great love. Her work with dying people and the attitude she brings to dying have given many people all over the world the courage to look at a part of our lives that we've not faced before. Working with hundreds of patients, she noted a process that most go through as they die. Most people don't consciously want to die and this process is the way in which they make peace with this change.

The stages—denial and isolation, anger, bargaining, depression, and acceptance—are a **process**, not a goal. It's the same process many of us go through in facing any loss.

Not all people go through all the stages; some skip stages and others move back and forth between them, sometimes from moment to moment.

The following description of the stages is just a clue to feelings you and the dying person may have. If our choice is to let people die in their own way, there's no need to push them through the stages to acceptance. A person can die with dignity even if he or she never accepts dying.

Denial and Isolation. Dr. Kübler-Ross calls this the *"No, not me"* stage. It appears in the beginning of a life-threatening illness and often reappears many times. *"It can't be true."* The patient may shop around for different doctors or treatments. She or he may not want to "talk about it" or may want to be alone or with people who don't know what's happening. Shock and numbness are common. Dr. Kübler-Ross suggests that we just be there lovingly when a person is denying and let them know, *"When you want to talk I'm available."*

A person may need denial to cope with impending death, to adjust to losses already experienced and to tolerate suffering or pain. Some die in denial—that's their way. As family and friends we may also experience denial. Check to see if the denial is yours or the dying person's.

Anger. The *"Why Me?* stage. Rage, envy, resentment. Anger at losing control. The anger is randomly projected, often on innocent people. *"You don't love me."* *"The doctors and nurses are incompetent."* *"Goddamn, God!"* Dr. Kübler-Ross suggests we not respond with nasty criticism or kill them with kindness. Better to rub it in. Affirm what's happening: *"Doesn't it make you mad?"* *"Don't you feel like screaming?"* The relief from venting anger may move the person toward greater acceptance of what is happening.

Sometimes the most loving thing we can do for a dying person (or people with a part of themselves dying) is to be a target for an outburst of anger. It's not hard to do if we **don't take it personally** and remember that expressing anger often helps a person move toward accepting dying. I'm not suggesting, however, that you be a "patsy" for an angry bully.

It's OK to feel scared if the person yells at you and it's OK to be angry with God. Imagining yourself in their place may help you understand. You'd be angry too!

Bargaining. The "Yes, me, but . . ." stage. *"It's OK for me to die if Eve and I can just take a trip to Hawaii first." "If I can just live 'til the kids graduate . . ." "If I live, I'll dedicate my life to God."* Bargaining is a temporary truce. The patient may seem peaceful. It's a good time to take care of wills and other business. Dr. Kübler-Ross notes that very few people keep their bargains if they do live longer.

Depression. The *"Yes, me"* stage. Sadness. Dr. Kübler-Ross talks about two kinds of depression: reactive, for loss of job, a breast, the ability to take care of oneself; and preparatory, preparing for the loss of life and family. The dying person needs time to be alone during this stage to make the emotional preparations. This can be a good time for quiet hand holding.

Depression is the womb in which a new choice or way of being grows. It's caused by holding on to someone or something we can't have or by holding in some feeling we haven't expressed — anger, sadness, guilt, even love. Robert Waterman of the Southwestern College of Life Sciences in Santa Fe, calls one form of depression "trapped love." "We feel depressed when we block ourselves from receiving or expressing the living love that we are."

143

Depression is useful for a dying person and family holding on to a body. Making a change or letting go eventually becomes more desirable than the greyness of depression. You may be able to help someone see which feeling needs expressing.

Acceptance. *"It's OK"* stage. Quiet, at peace, neither depressed nor angry. Dr. Kübler-Ross describes it as "time to contemplate the coming end with a certain degree of quiet expectation." The person is probably sleeping more; his or her concerns no longer relate to the outside world. It is "the final rest before a long journey." This period may be almost void of feeling. You can be there quietly, reassuringly. Again, resignation (giving up) is not the same as acceptance.

Our response to dying is like any other big decision we make in our lives. We can go from acceptance, having made a decision, back into bargaining or questioning that decision. It's very helpful to look for these stages in ourselves as well as in the dying person we love. It's important for the family to arrive at acceptance so their desire to prolong life doesn't contradict the patient's wish to die in peace. It's easier if we feel acceptance when we bring someone home, even if this feeling changes many times.

TELLING SOMEONE THEY MAY DIE

I worried about this when I began to be around people who were dying. Like most things we worry about, it didn't materialize in any way I had imagined.

The first time I told someone she was dying, it was indirectly and accidentally. A nurse at the hospital asked me to talk with a cancer patient who was dying and feeling depressed. I'll call her Rosa. I asked two nurses if Rosa *knew* she had cancer and was dying. Both said "yes." I talked with Rosa about her life and cancer and felt we had a beautiful visit. I left her feeling that communication had been opened and I'd be back to see her later. The next thing I learned, the head nurse and doctor were in a rage with "some idiot in the Pastoral Care and Counseling department" (me, as it turned out) and Rosa was furious! The doctor hadn't told her she had cancer or was dying. He felt she was too sick and would take the news badly! I got through all the anger directed at me without feeling terrible by remembering that I'd done what seemed appropriate at the time, and also that expressing anger would help Rosa accept dying. Unfortunately I was forbidden to see her again.

Generally the doctor will tell a person that she or he is dying. The doctor is the appropriate person to deliver the news of a possibly fatal diagnosis because he or she is *believable* on the subject of physical death.

Optimally, the doctor will have spent some time with the person and will be aware of how she or he is handling illness. The doctor may then sensitively give the person information about the disease and its possible or probable outcome *as the doctor sees it*. You can discuss with the doctor how this might be done best. It's **very important** that the doctor not take away all sense of hope. (See *Hope*, page 221).

The doctor might say, "At this point your medical situation looks difficult. I don't know anything we can do medically to cure you, but we can make you comfortable. It's always possible you'll have a remission or a new treatment will become available." **Leave room for miracles.** They happen.

In the past, many doctors, with good intentions, thought it kinder to alleviate a dying person's confusion by not speaking about dying. Now more doctors are straightforward in speaking with their terminally ill patients. If your doctor is not, however, you may want to talk with him or her about it. If we avoid telling someone the facts, we're assuming responsibility for his or her life. **We can be responsive to another person and respect his or her rights; we cannot be responsible for them.** If a person wants to deny they're dying, that's their right. It's not our right, however, to take it upon ourselves to make that decision for them. If we don't tell someone, we are denying them the opportunity to get their affairs in order and to do things they've wanted to do, which might help them prepare for dying. We deny them the opportunity to try alternative treatments. **It's more stressful to wonder if you're dying than to know.**

Once a *possibly* fatal diagnosis is given, there's no need to try to force someone to face it. Most people who want to know more ask questions. People who don't may want or need to pretend it's not happening. In one study, about 15 percent of the cancer patients surveyed did not want to know about a fatal diagnosis.

It may well happen that a person tells us he or she is dying and that we must prepare ourselves. Dr. Kübler-Ross says, "Everyone knows when they're going to die, although it may be subconsciously."

If it comes to you to tell someone they **may** be dying, you can do it only in your own way. You might ask, "How sick are you?" If the answer is, "Well, I'm very sick . . . or dying," you might say, "Yes, that's my impression too." Remember, you're not telling them it's the end. It can be a time of satisfying new growth. You might suggest that a very sick person ask God what's happening instead of a doctor.

If someone asks you what's happening and you answer honestly and without killing hope, communication remains open for sharing thoughts and feelings. A person may know she or he is dying and ask you only for confirmation. If you aren't honest this time, the person may not trust you or feel free to share with you in the future.

BEING WITH SOMEONE WHO IS DYING

How can we most usefully be with someone who is dying? Just by **being present with an open heart**, making space for what is happening.

An open heart is the most important thing we can share with anyone dying soon or dying later. An open heart is love without conditions and judgements. Not, "I love you if . . ." Just "I love you." No one is right or wrong. Fear, pain and suffering are not right or wrong. Dying is not good or bad. **Everything just is.** From an open heart we can sense all the needs of the person preparing for his or her great change. Listen, see and touch from "our" heart.

"Serving humanity," a phrase we hear a lot, is *recognizing our common divinity*. It doesn't necessarily mean being out there making the world over. Two people in a quiet bedroom can serve humanity. **We serve just by understand-**

ing that we're both individual expressions of the One. We're not *right* or "up" because we're still healthy, and they're not *wrong* or "down" because they're sick and closer to dying. Just two people surrendering to life, to all the things you may have thought life was about and discover it isn't. And the challenge is: Can we keep our heart open to the other's pain and sadness without closing it and shutting off our own pain? All pain is everyone's. Can we be open to what the dying can teach us about life?

We serve by recognizing that **dying is OK.** If we resist a person's dying, we can increase their resistance. If we pretend circumstances are different from what they are—deny what's happening—the dying have to play a painful charade with us. *Pretending*, not communicating, isolates people from one another and makes dying very lonely for everyone involved. Pretending can leave you both with the "I-wish-I-hads: I-wish-I'd-said . . . I-wish-I'd-done . . ." Instead, we can do and say what's in our hearts. We can be open to this natural life process called dying.

The ultimate gift of love is letting someone die in their own way. Our work is to make a **supportive space** in which this process can happen. Let the dying person be where she or he is and don't try to push them to where *we'd* like them to be. They're not here to die our way but their *own* way. Dr. Kübler-Ross has said, "Dying with dignity is not necessarily dying with peace and acceptance, but dying in character."

Discuss all decisions relating to the dying person with him or her—even making decisions about small things allows a person to maintain their sense of dignity and worth. Help people express their preferences. If someone is accustomed to saying "yes" to things she or he doesn't like or want to do, encourage them to say "no" to those things. You might want to practice this yourself. Rather than overprotect them, encourage a dying person to live each day fully. In the face of death, does it matter if someone dies a little sooner because he or she went fishing or to a concert or enjoyed a binge on lobster, chili or chocolate ice cream? We've nothing to lose that we won't lose anyway.

Don't assume you know how someone feels—*ask*. Don't force someone to eat or smile or be social. Those may be *your* needs, not theirs. Try to be sensitive to their need to be with people or to be alone to adjust to the transition. Ask "Is there anything else I can do for you?" This may uncover a need you couldn't have dreamed of. Once when I asked my dad, he answered, "Just don't stop loving me or helping me like you are."

Albert Schweitzer said, "There is a modesty of soul which we must recognize, just as we do that of the body. The soul, too, has its clothing of which we must not deprive it, and no one has the right to say to another, because we belong to each other, as we do, 'I have a right to know all of your thoughts.' "

Conditioned by our cultural fear of death, people expect a lot of difficult emotional and psychological problems around dying. In working with dying people and their families from many different backgrounds, I have seen few challenges the family couldn't handle. Those few related to guilt, which occurs less often at home than in a hospital setting.

Don't sit around fearing "problems" that may never appear. Here are some reassuring words from Dr. Sylvia A. Lack, from a paper she gave at the First National Training Conference for Physicians on The Psychosocial Care of the Dying Patient (what a mouthful!):

149

There is far too much talk in death and dying circles in this country about psychological and emotional problems, and far too little about making the patient comfortable. Any group concerned with service to the dying should be talking about smoothing sheets, rubbing bottoms, relieving constipation, and sitting up at night. Counseling a person who is lying in a wet bed is ineffective. . . . . If people are cared for with common sense and basic professional skills, with detailed attention to self-evident problems and physical needs, the patients and families themselves cope with many of their emotional crises. Without pain, well nursed, with bowels controlled, mouth clean, and a caring friend available, the psychological problems fall into manageable perspective.

This is not to say challenges won't arise, just that you will be able to handle them.

Polite conventions and courteous fictions that people have maintained all their lives may drop away when they're dying. Old prejudices, resentments and grievances may surface; long-hidden preferences (as for one child over another) may no longer be glossed over.

There may be conflict between family members or family members and care-givers. Conflict is not 'bad'. It's an opportunity to clarify values and an expression of caring, although a distorted one. Two people (or countries) are in conflict because they each care deeply about something, feel the other doesn't understand their feelings or respect their beliefs and believe they're 'right'. Resolving conflict involves appreciating the other's caring, respecting their beliefs and eliminating the judgements 'right' and 'wrong' so we can find a common ground.

The dying person may pass through periods of generalized hostility towards everyone. If you are the object of this kind of projection, know that **it doesn't matter.** You are who you are, not who someone else *wants* you to be· or imagines you to be. Someone may insult an image they have of you, but that is not you. You are not someone's reaction to you. Instead of reacting to the reaction, you can choose compassion and try to look deeper — to the person's essence. Mother Teresa calls it "touching Christ in his distressing disguise." We don't have to like someone's personality just because they're dying. We can always love who they really are.

We also serve by respecting our own needs. With the discomforts of dying, a sick person may become demanding. If you feel overwhelmed by their demands, tell them. We don't win prizes for being martyrs. If a person is acting irrational, don't be afraid to be firm. Again, look deeper to see what unexpressed need is being expressed and try to meet it. There's no need to be over-polite — for example, the dying person is afraid to ask for something or family members are afraid to do what comes naturally for fear of seeming pushy or hurting others' feelings.

Jealousy — feeling someone has something you don't — may come up. This is natural. Someone other than you may appear to be the special one. Look inside yourself . . . how much more special can you be? You were *born* with your specialness. There will always be people who can see it and people who can't.

A dying person can also be a joy to be with. Take a moment before you enter their room to "breathe in calmness." *Soften. Relax. Open.* Be as natural as possible. Here is time you may not have made before for the quiet joy of sharing as a family, couple or friends. The illusion of time — that there are things to do, places to go — can drop away . . . just moments for whatever is! Share your feelings and what's happening in your life. Ask the dying person's advice. His or her perspective from dying may be of great help to you.

When the person seems open, talk about what's happening, what they want done when they die, a will, what kind of burial. . . . Often it's evening or night when a person feels like talking. Listen and listen. If there are things you've wanted to say or talk about with them and haven't, use this opportunity. It will ease your grieving later.

People who are sleeping or appear to be unconscious can still hear you at some level. Say only what you would say if they were totally awake. People confined to bed pick up the 'vibrations' of everything around them, perhaps more so than a physically active person who has more distractions.

Something I do each time before entering the room of a dying person may be of use to you. I say a prayer, "God, use me for whatever this person needs if that serve the highest good of us both." Then I share my heart, sometimes with words or just with my eyes and hands.

It is a rare privilege to be with someone who is dying. I suggest you use this time to think about your own death, your own spiritual beliefs. As we accept someone else's dying, we move toward accepting our own. See what you can learn from this dying that's useful for your life. What is really meaningful in your life and what is it time to let go of? What do you want to be or do or say that you haven't?

Make the most of the inevitable by *living fully* each moment and letting go of any sense of separateness.

If you find yourself working on two levels, one which says "dying is OK" and one which says "his or her dying is not OK," be gentle with yourself. They will come together. There's an old circus adage, "You can't learn balance until you've learned to lose it."

When we truly let go, the quality of death changes. It becomes a "fresh breeze of God."

Trust yourself. Love yourself.

*   *   *   *   *

THE DYING PERSON'S BILL OF RIGHTS

This comes from the Southwestern Michigan Inservice Educational Council and appeared in Ann Landers' column. It indicates a growing concern among us about the rights of the dying. The bill shares the concerns of some dying people: more importantly it points toward the desire of the dying to choose what they want and don't want. For example, not all people want to die with someone present, but most want to make the choice.

I have the right to be treated as a living human being until I die.

I have the right to maintain a sense of hopefulness, however changing its focus may be.

153

I have the right to be cared for by those who can maintain a sense of hopefulness, however changing this might be.

I have the right to express my feelings and emotions about my approaching death, in my own way.

I have the right to participate in decisions concerning my case.

I have the right to expect continuing medical and nursing attention, even though "cure" goals must be changed to "comfort" goals.

I have the right not to die alone.

I have the right to be free of pain.

I have the right to have any questions answered honestly.

I have the right not to be deceived.

I have the right to have help from and for my family in accepting my death.

I have the right to die in peace and dignity.

I have the right to retain my individuality and not be judged for my decisions, which may be contrary to the beliefs of others.

I have the right to discuss and enlarge my religious and/or spiritual experiences, regardless of what they may mean to others.

I have the right to expect that the sanctity of the human body will be respected after death.

I have the right to be cared for by caring, sensitive, knowledgeable people who will attempt to understand my needs and will be able to gain some satisfaction in helping me face death.

* * * * *

HELPING THE DYING FIND MEANING

From the beginning of time until now, human beings have searched for meaning. Meaning gives us a reason to live, the courage to meet life's constant changes. We tolerate even pain if we can find meaning in it. If we've not done so earlier, as we die we ponder the meaning of our lives.

In hospitals dying people often lose their sense of life as meaningful. They lose hope and when they lose hope, they die.

One of the great blessings of dying at home is that we're still surrounded by people and things that give immediate meaning to our lives . . . as we search for ultimate meanings. Even at home a dying person may go through periods of finding life meaningless and his or her present suffering hard to bear.

We can't find meaning for others, but we can share ideas that may point them toward discovering new meaning for themselves. Before talking with someone about meaning, be sure they're comfortable and free from pain. Share what is true for you as a gentle gift from your heart, not as dogma that makes the dying person 'wrong' if he or she feels differently.

When someone is dying, many outside sources of meaning such as work and daily activities are no longer available. But instead of diminishing the meaning of life, surprisingly, dying people find life, just being alive, increasingly meaningful. With fewer outer distractions, they tend to look inward for the source of meaning. For many this is an unaccustomed place to look.

Looking inward they find that the very fact of being alive has meaning—that meaning is not necessarily related to what we are able or not able to do. Life is recognized as precious and meaningful in and of itself—even if the trimmings are limited. Life is meaningful because it "is." It doesn't have to perform, show off or justify itself.

To live fully, even in the face of death, is to live *now* in this moment. Only in the now of this moment can we experience the wholeness and holiness of life.

To help people find meaning in their lives is to help them live in the moment. Encourage them not to limit themselves to their pasts or their future, but to experience the unlimited *now*. For many this is difficult. We're accustomed to live off our memories of the past or our projections on the future.

Help the person you're caring for appreciate the preciousness of life . . . moment by moment. For in these moments, he or she will find meaning . . . and peace and joy.

If it's appropriate for you, help them to appreciate the gift of receiving.

Sometimes we forget the circle of love includes giving and receiving. For people who place great value on control or who don't often allow themselves to receive, accepting all the care a dying person needs is difficult. Needing and receiving make them feel helpless — 'worthless.'

Many of us are graceful givers. Not so many of us are graceful receivers. We prefer giving because we've been praised for it since we were toddlers and because when we're giving, we're *in control.* We haven't usually been praised for receiving. Often receiving was labeled 'selfish.' We're afraid of receiving because when we're receiving, we're *vulnerable.* And that's scary. Perhaps we also doubt we're worthy of receiving or fear feeling indebted.

Help the dying understand that receiving is just as valuable and sacred as giving. Using the words of your heart, help them understand the arrogance of always having to be the giver and denying others the joy of giving. Let them know that we help others to feel strong by allowing them to help us. You might perhaps remind a parent that they cared for all your needs for many years and you're grateful now to have a chance to return that caring.

Christians say, "The meek shall inherit the earth." Perhaps that's because they allow themselves to receive the gift of life.

Help the dying understand the importance of balancing *doing* and *being.*

Our culture rewards us for *doing* — for achieving success, controlling nature, remaining young and thinking rationally. It's not often that we get pats for just *being* — sitting quietly watching a stream, communing with God, listening to a child, being angry or old, crying or dying. We tend to forget the value of being — just being present for ourselves, for our feelings, or for the child, stream or dying person in front of us. We rush from one activity to another and then we're surprised when life feels meaningless — as if we've lost touch with something precious.

We've measured our lives by what we do. But life doesn't limit herself to doing. She includes being. She includes all that is. Being present for our dying is just as valuable as any project or task well done. Perhaps it's the most courageous thing we will ever do.

By helping the dying understand that being is as important as doing, we help them adjust to not doing all the things they're accustomed to do. If we primarily value doing, we can't accept death or find meaning in dying (living), and we can't help the dying do the same. Dying is a return to our original nature, *being.*

Help the dying to understand that the most important thing a human being can do, they can still do — love. No illness, no prediction of limited days, can change that. Is there a greater meaning for a human life than love — to love and to allow ourselves to be loved?

Help the dying to enjoy the harvest of their lives . . . to remember their storehouse of love and joy. Talk together about the things you've shared together as a family, as friends. Death cannot take away our memories. Memory exists far beyond the gates of death.

Help the dying understand that life is lived most graciously when control and surrender are balanced. Often we humans believe that we must be in control of our lives, and only if we are, are we truly living. We forget that surrender, accepting life as it is, is just as important.

Help the dying understand that they don't have to hold up life. They can let go and let life hold them up instead. To control is to do our will. To surrender is to let Life's will be done. Perhaps the underlying truth is that our will and Life's will are One.

If a dying person's religious beliefs give him or her a sense of meaning, support their understanding. Encourage them to explore their own teaching even more deeply—to move beyond dogma to the core of that particular teaching. The core of all religions is the same—love God, love yourself, love your fellow human beings and know that you are One.

Again, take time as you care for this dying person to consider what's meaningful for you. The day of your death will come. And the more moments you have lived in alignment with what's meaningful to you, the more joyful your life will be and the easier your dying and death.

GRIEVING

You can't prevent the birds of sadness from flying over your head, but you can prevent them from nesting in your hair.

—Chinese Proverb

Grieving is opening up to sadness or anger if we feel it, and releasing it. We need to grieve throughout this dying-living process to keep cleansing and clearing ourselves. If we don't we're liable to walk through the whole experience numb from the strain of holding our feelings in. When we become so full of sadness that we can't hold any more, we close our hearts. If we wait until "it's all over" to open the floodgates, the backed up emotion may seem overwhelming.

The gift of grieving is that it allows us to open to the great reservoir of sadness in each of us, much of it not even related to the dying process we're living now. Grieving is an opportunity to clean up old, old stuff — the "attic" or "basement" of our beings so we can move ahead with greater lightness, space and freedom.

Let the person you're supporting, man or woman, know that crying is a way to cleanse ourselves so we can live more fully. Cry as much as you need, to give yourself more space for living.

You might want to take a moment to read Chapter 14, Grieving (page 317).

PACING YOURSELF AND FAMILY MORALE

Let there be spaces in your togetherness, and let the winds of the heavens dance between you.

— Kahlil Gibran

The time factor is often the great unknown in a dying process. Unlike a home birth, in which the baby is born within a relatively short time, a dying process has no fixed time limit. Not knowing "how long we have" is hard for the dying person and the family. For this reason pacing yourself is very important.

160

Nobody can face death all the time, neither the sick person nor the family. Unless you take time for yourself, for letting out your feelings and taking care of your health, you may well run out of fuel before the process is over. An early all out effort can exhaust you and cause you to resent the dying person for taking so much of your time and energy. Contrary to all beliefs and appearances, you are not Superman or Wonder Woman, although a part of you may think you "should" be.

Before you get out of bed each day, you might want to ask yourself, "What nice thing can I do for myself today?" This might become a morning meditation in which you also focus on joy and love to give yourself more energy for the day. Meditation is not some mysterious Hindu or Buddhist practice. It means *living with awareness*. Being aware the toast is burning . . . being aware of God. Some people make it a sacred cow apart from everyday life. This is unnecessary. All of life can be a meditation.

Because you're probably spending more time at home than usual, do some things you've wanted to do at home and haven't. Pick flowers. Make a fresh juice cocktail. Take a walk. Write a letter. When Mary was with me I did a lot of sewing and caught up on paper work. Instead of thinking, "God, I'm getting behind," I could think, "Great! I'm getting stuff done I wouldn't if I weren't home so much." While my dad was dying I continued to work on this book.

Exercise, eat well and get as much sleep as possible. Try to eat balanced meals and not live on coffee and doughnuts. Taking stress formula Vitamin B and/or brewer's yeast may help soothe your nerves and give you energy. If possible keep your own bedroom. With Mary, I was comforted to have my own space—sleep in my own bedroom—and I could hear her if I kept my door open. If someone needs constant attention you'll need people with whom you can rotate sleeping. If you have no help, you may have to sleep in the room with the dying person . . . and you may want to anyway.

There are endless ways of dealing with our feelings as they come up. You already have your own ways; see page 219 for others. **Remember, whatever your feelings, they're OK no matter how they feel or look to you.**

Taking care of family morale includes doing enjoyable things for yourself as well as with the dying person. Don't be afraid to ask for help so you can go out or have time alone. Go to the movies, dancing, bowling, visit with friends and talk about it all. **You can be totally loving and not think about the dying person all the time.** Ask for help if you need someone simply to be with you. By asking, you give someone else a chance to share love. If they don't respond as you hope, respect their honesty. Perhaps they'll volunteer on another occasion.

The Quiet Mind (White Eagle Publishing Company) is a beautiful little book from England I've used for years to help me relax and sleep well. It's available through some metaphysical bookstores and The Elisabeth Kübler-Ross Center (see Appendix A for the address). I also highly recommend Malcolm Muggeridge's book about Mother Teresa, *Something Beautiful for God.*

SHARING AND FAMILY MORALE

Sharing with a dying person lets them know they still count. While you're emotionally letting them go, it's important for you to be conscious that they're not gone until they're gone.

What can you share? Share your feelings as it feels appropriate, but not to the point of burdening the dying person. It may be hard the first time — it gets easier.

Share time together. Share decisions. Share games. Are there TV programs or stories you can enjoy together? Read together. Remember good times together. Pray together.

What about asking the dying person to share the story of his or her life or making a tape recording as we did with my dad or a video? These memories may help the dying person understand the tapestry of his or her life, and be a source of joy and comfort to you.

You might want to ask yourself each morning, "What nice thing can we do as a family or group of friends today?"

See Appendix C for two games that may be fun to play with someone in bed whose mind is clear.

VISITORS

Put yourself in the dying person's shoes and realize — truly realize in your heart, not just in your intellect — that one day you could be, more than likely will be, in the same situation.

— Peter Weatherby
The Pilgrim Soul

The number of friends a dying person wants to see usually depends on his or her earlier lifestyle. People who enjoy having lots of people around will probably continue to do so. Someone more solitary will probably want to see only a few. Ask if the person wants visitors. Ask if it's OK for someone to bring along a child.

Visits with a dying person are usually short, unless the person indicates otherwise. Visits can take a lot of energy and some people feel drained afterward. If as a visitor, you're open to your own feelings, including sadness, your visit will likely give energy instead of take it. Ask the dying person if he or she is tired and perhaps the visit should end. If some of you want to visit longer, move to another room.

Let visitors know what mood the person seems to be in today. If they haven't seen their friend in a long time, let them know how she or he looks now. It softens the shock if visitors know, for example, that their old robust 180-pound friend is down to 100 pounds.

If the dying person has expressed a wish not to see someone, respect this wish. I advise not sending anyone into the room who's extremely upset or negative. You might first help such a visitor express his or her feelings with you. Then, if they have a real need to see the person, accompany them and stand by for the 'enough' signal from the patient. At the same time don't overprotect. The dying person and visitor may need to be alone to sort out a misunderstanding, and might both feel better afterward.

As a visitor, be sensitive to your friend, to what is appropriate to share with him or her now. Imagine what it feels like if someone says, "You look great!" or "Let's go fishing next spring." How would you feel if you received a 'get well card' and you knew you weren't going to get well? These are obvious clues to a dying person that someone can't handle their dying which make real communication impossible. The dying person usually agrees to play along and pretend the illness is temporary.

If business considerations need to be discussed, first check with the family to find out when it might be appropriate.

Instead of making general offers like "Call me if you need anything," make a specific offer. "I'll bring dinner tomorrow night" or "I'll take the kids to the zoo Saturday."

As people approach death, they need more and more time alone to prepare for the transition. Don't take it personally if the sick person doesn't want to see you or doesn't recognize you. This is not uncommon. There's no need to feel badly. Focusing inward and disconnecting from the outer world is a natural part of the dying process.

If you'd like to know more about ways to help, I recommend an excellent pamphlet called, *Is There Anything I can do to Help*. To order, see Appendix A.

ON CHILDREN

And a woman who held a babe against her bosom
   said, Speak to us of children, and he said:
Your children are not your children.
They are the sons and daughters of Life's longing for
   itself.
They come through you but not from you,
And though they are with you, yet they belong not to
   you.
You may give them your love but not your thoughts
For they have their own thoughts.
You may house their bodies but not their souls,
For their souls dwell in the house of tomorrow,
   which you cannot visit, not even in your dreams.

You may strive to be like them, but seek not to make
   them like you.
For life goes not backwards nor tarries with
   yesterday.
You are the bows from which your children as living
   arrows are sent forth.
The archer sees the mark upon the path of the
   infinite, and He bends you with His might that His
   arrows may go swift and far.
Let your bending in the archer's hand be for
   gladness;
For even as He loves the arrow that flies, so
   He loves also the bow that is stable.

—Kahlil Gibran
The Prophet

CHAPTER 7

CHILDREN

Ma, can we still laugh?

> — A child's question
> about dying.

CHILDREN AS MEMBERS OF THE FAMILY

Allowing a child to participate at home in the death of someone she or he loves can be an incredible gift. Children can learn early that death is a natural part of life. Without automatically acquiring our culture's fear, a child chooses his or her own attitude about death.

When a dying family member is isolated in a hospital, often with "no visitors under 13," the child has no way of

167

developing a healthy attitude. Even if our words say "death is OK," the child feels something is wrong because he or she can't see or share in what's happening.

Shielding children from death makes them fear it more and makes its acceptance more difficult when they're adults. Shielding children from our feelings when someone we love is dying teaches them to deny their feelings, which closes their hearts. Out of love, we have tried to protect them. Out of love, let us free them instead.

The loss of someone a child loves is more bearable if she or he has shared in the dying process. The shock is less if the child has time to adjust *gradually* to the loss. Being at home together allows this gradual adjustment, as well as time for what can be a very beautiful sharing.

A child's greatest fear is separation from or loss of a parent. At home together, parents can help the child understand that in our hearts we never lose anyone. We feel very sad someone won't be with us and we can feel joy for the love we'll always share.

The way to prepare children for someone they love dying, is to help them understand ahead of time about death. For many of us talking to our children about death ranks second in uncomfortableness only to the "birds and bees." And it's our responsibility to talk about death clearly and truthfully when it comes up. Helping children relate to the deaths of birds and animals offers an opportunity to help them develop a healthy acceptance of death. Don't discourage children from touching dead creatures. They can always wash their hands and it helps them to understand.

What a child imagines about dying may be worse than the truth. Euphemisms and white lies mislead and confuse a child about what's happening. If you say that someone who died has "just gone to sleep", your child may be afraid to go to bed. If you say, "God took him," your child may spend his life fearing or hating God.

Explain death in your own way. Use words or ideas a child can understand. Share facts (not too technical) as well as your feelings. Allow space for your child to develop his or her own understanding of death by admitting you don't know everything. Ask your child what he or she thinks. Be patient if children bring up the subject of death again and again as they try to understand it.

One way of explaining death is to say "Jimmie was too sick to get well and he stopped breathing." *Immediately* reassure the child that she or he will get well from flu or a cold, or any familiar sickness. Then go on to explain your spiritual beliefs. A friend's little boy, after the death of his brother asked, "Where is Damian?" His mother replied, "Always in your heart." She said his acceptance was happy and instantaneous.

Children are often afraid of the dark and of being alone. What they fear for themselves, they often fear for the dying person. It seems honest to reassure them, based on "near death" experiences, that there will be beautiful light, love and loving people to meet the dying person (see page 327).

When we talk with children about dying, it's important that we share our sadness as well as that the dying person is going to a beautiful place. This helps them understand the seeming contradiction between our words and our behavior. Elisabeth Kübler-Ross says we say, "Mommy is going to heaven," because it's true! But when nobody's celebrating, our children won't believe us unless we share our personal loss as well.

Unless we've helped our children understand in some way that there's life apart from the physical body, they won't believe Mommy is going to a beautiful place when they see her put in a hole in the earth. These days, in our materialistic world, "soul" is not a fashionable word. Perhaps it needs reinstating because it's useful to have a name for the consciousness apart from the body that never dies. Kübler-Ross explains "soul" to children using the metaphor of the cocoon and the butterfly. We leave the old shell to become something even more beautiful.

What children need most when someone they love is dying is reassurance. Reassure them that they're loved and will be cared for. Reassure them that they're safe and aren't likely to die for a long time. Reassure them that besides the absence of the dying person, their world will stay more or less the same. Reassure them that the death is not their fault. Children tend to take responsibility for everything that happens in their little worlds. Often they feel guilty when someone they love is dying. "It's my fault because I was bad."

Often when someone we love is dying, we become totally preoccupied with that person, particularly if it's a dying child. Remember to keep the circle of love open to the whole family. If you have more than one child, spend time alone with each. A crying child and a less demonstrative one both need attention. Tears are not the only measure of grief.

Include your children in what's happening. They can provide comfort and welcome relief from the intensity of dying. Including them can also prevent having to deal later with a demanding or uncommunicative child who feels unloved, rejected and/or guilty. You don't have to do anything special for them — they understand Mom doesn't have time to take them to the zoo. Just include them.

Sometimes we shower attention and gifts on a dying child forgetting our other children may feel jealous. It's common for children to feel jealous, to wish a dying brother or sister who's getting all the attention were dead and then to feel guilty. It might be helpful to say to a child you suspect feels this way something like, "I would understand if you're angry because I spend so much time with Annie . . . or if you sometimes wish she were already dead. You know, we just have a short time with her and you and I will probably have our whole lives together."

Remember not to make a dying child seem perfect in every way. It's too high a standard for our other children to live up to.

Include your children in the family's grief. Let them see you grieving instead of trying to hide it. This provides a healthy model for accepting and healing their pain now and in the future. Children shielded from your feelings may feel rejected. It may be distressing to see Dad cry, but "business as usual" is more distressing. Wildly excessive expression of grief may not be wholesome and may cause a child to fear their feelings.

Encourage children to express their feelings, fears and fantasies. Let them know it's OK to cry — "Big strong people cry sometimes" — and it's OK to be angry. They may be angry because you can't prevent the death. They often feel angry that they're being abandoned. Don't put unnecessary burdens on children by saying things like, "Be brave", "Now you'll be the man of the house," or "You have to take care of Daddy."

Children usually adjust easily to being around a dying adult or child if they're told what's happening and are included. They adjust more easily than adults if they haven't been overly conditioned to think death is terrible. Don't *shunt* the kids off to Gramma's or Auntie's. It's likely to increase their fears. Do *send* them if you need a break. Children can feel the difference.

Children feel good about sharing the responsibility of making the dying person comfortable. They feel important to be included in this family event. Let them participate in any way they want. Ask for their help with tasks they can handle. Hugging, holding and cuddling are some of our best medicines. Children are the experts.

Help your children keep up with other relationships and continue to have friends in to play. Watching children play quietly may delight the dying person; if not, ask them to play in another room. Ben and Josh were *a big help* to us in terms of joy, humour, entertainment and keeping life in perspective.

Help your children express their feelings by encouraging them to say whatever they want to the dying person. Encourage drawing and telling stories. Stories children tell that don't correspond with an adult's reality are not necessarily lies. They're children's ways of sharing their reality which can help us understand how to better support them.

If you have school age children, let their teachers and school counselor know someone in the family is dying. They're usually glad to give extra support. Don't be concerned if children are distracted from school work and their grades drop. They go through the process of grieving too. If they want to stay home from school and help, consider occasionally letting them do so. A very special school is happening in your own home.

Some children's books I love that focus on death and dying are: Ethel Marback's *The Cabbage Moth and the Shamrock* (Star and Elephant Books, Green Tiger Press), Fynn's *Mister God, This is Anna* (Ballantine Books) for older children and adults, and Leo Buscaglia's, *The Fall of Freddie the Leaf*.

TO PARENTS OF DYING CHILDREN

Mamma, Pappa, don't be afraid.

— A dying child

Your child will give you the support you need.

— A mother whose child died at home

I have not yet worked with children dying at home. I have worked with parents of dying children and parents grieving after the death. Because our children are *people* as well as children, much of the information in this book may help you support your dying child.

For most of us, accepting a child dying is much harder than accepting an adult dying. For a mother and father, it may be the hardest thing you'll ever face. And there's no preparation other than living and loving fully each moment and holding our children lightly, knowing they are just on loan.

There are no words that will take away your pain if your child is dying. Perhaps there are some ideas that may help prevent bitterness or resentment.

Often when a child is dying we feel bitter because a child has "everything to look forward to," "their whole life ahead of them." We experience time as linear and sequential and feel a child who dies young was **incomplete**, cut off **before their time**.

Perhaps it would help to remember that a child is complete and whole at each moment in the *process* of his or her life. Our vision might be more like the Native American vision. The original Native Americans understood time as an "expanded present."

> Most native people did not understand their lives as a sequence of goals (getting an education, getting married, raising children, being an elder) at the end of which lay a sense of final completion. For them, once one entered adulthood, often at the age of only 10 or 12, life was complete. One could only continue to grow in that state — in the way a sphere, already complete, can continue to expand, to become fuller. There was no thought of not having done enough in one's life, of being too young to die, or of still having your whole life ahead of you.
>
> With that continuous sense of a full life, no one was tyrannized by the prospect of death. **Any day,**

Children

> but especially one in which you were living to the
> hilt, was a good day to die.
>
> —The American Indian Mind
> *Omni Magazine*

I believe it's accurate to enlarge that understanding to
include all ages. Everyone is complete at every moment.

When a child is dying, we often ask ourselves "Why?",
a question for which we may not find a satisfactory answer.
I encourage you instead to ask, "What can I learn?" "What
have I learned from my child?" Even now, if you're willing,
close your eyes for a moment and think and feel about what
you've learned. Among your answers, I imagine, will be
love—unconditional love—and joy.

I ask you from 'our' heart, **"Is there a greater purpose
for a human life than to be a teacher of love and joy?** Are
going to school, growing up, getting a job, getting married
and growing old more important?"

Besides coming to gain experience to be fully who they
can be, perhaps each child comes to teach us love—that
quality that allows us to experience the sacredness of life.
Your life and my life are sacred. Perhaps children who come
for only a short time, come to remind us not to take anyone
or anything for granted . . . that every moment of life is a
precious gift. I believe there's no such thing as a 'child', only
wise old souls in children's bodies.

Even as you grieve for an incredible loss, as your heart
breaks open, celebrate love.

I believe there is so much love in each of us that we
create a child partially as a place to put that love. Often we
give all our love to our child and forget to love ourselves.
Then, if he or she is dying, we feel like love is dying as well.

175

Perhaps a child dies to give us an opportunity to remember that we are love. One mother, after her boy died, said, "He made me see the love inside myself."

The physical loss of your child is a great sadness that must be grieved for. It is not the loss of your love. Love is the very nature of your being. It doesn't die, even when your child, the object of your love changes form. It is redistributed. Do not burden your child with responsibility for your love or burden yourself with fear of its loss. That's more than either of you need to bear.

The pain we feel when a child is dying comes not only from believing love dies, but also from **holding on**. No one can tell you how or when to let go, to surrender your child to life. The moment of acceptance of the breathing in and out of the universe comes in its own time and way. Perhaps it's useful to remember the child was never really 'yours' to begin with. She or he always belonged to Life, to God.

Pain also comes from expecting ourselves to be perfect parents. We pooh-pah the idea of being perfect ones, yet we secretly expect ourselves to be. Often we feel angry and guilty when we can't prevent our child's death. You could not prevent your child's death any more than you could prevent a river from flowing to the sea.

Forgive yourself for being so hard on yourself. Forgive yourself for all the things you did or said you now regret. Forgive yourself for all the things you didn't do or say you think you *should* have. **Forgive your child for dying.**

You will survive this experience. **You will survive.** Life goes on even if you've forgotten quite why.

Even as survival dominates your consciousness, hold the seed of hope. You feel love even as you grieve and you can feel joy again *if* you'll let yourself. Some parents won't.

Children

They feel it would somehow be disloyal to their child – a sign they didn't really love them. Others have allowed joy again – perhaps a more fitting tribute to a child, to a teacher of love, than suffering.

I've asked many parents what they learned from their child's death. I still remember the radiant faces of two mothers, one of whom had two children die, as they answered, "Joy." They weren't joyful that their children died. They had learned from them that life is precious, love is all that really matters and each moment is best lived fully because we don't know how many we have. A life lived from these understandings is a joyful life.

Unfortunately, we live in a culture that often measures love by suffering. Suffering is proof of how much we love. We expect parents of dying children and those who died to wear invisible scarlet letters over their hearts. We expect them to be "scarred for life."

I regularly hear grieving parents and professional care-givers say to other grieving parents, "You'll never get over it", "You'll never stop grieving," "You'll never be the same." With good intentions, they condemn parents to a lifetime of pain. When someone hurts more than they've ever hurt, telling them it won't stop is like kicking them when they're down. It makes me mad. And it's not true, unless you believe them and make it come true. Many parents do stop grieving and return to living fully without the haunting shadow of pain.

What you never stop is not grieving, but loving your child and remembering them. True, you'll never be the same and that doesn't have to be negative. It may be a blessing.

At the same time we expect parents not to stop grieving, we also expect them to act as if nothing had happened.

Coming Home

Sometimes this short-circuits the grieving process and the result is self pity. There's nothing wrong with feeling sorry for ourselves. We all have. As they say, "It's easier for others to count our blessings." Self pity, though, doesn't feel good and there's an alternative—grieving.

Time does not heal. It just pushes things into the back of our consciousness. What heals is what we do with time. Grieving heals. The way home to joy is through the heart of our pain. We have to grieve until we come out the other side of it.

You don't have to go into the heart of your pain alone . . . unless you want to. Your husband, wife, wise friend or counselor can accompany you without interfering. If you want to be physically alone, or you are, walk into your heart with God, Christ, Buddha or whomever is meaningful to you.

The widow of the poet Dylan Thomas wrote a book with the saddest title I've ever heard, *Leftover Life to Kill.* Grieve now, dear mother and father, so you don't have leftover life to kill. An emotional wound needs the same priority attention as a physical wound. For ways to work with your feelings, see page 219.

A tragedy is a loss without meaning. Tragedy literally means in Greek, "the song of the goat." Your child dying is a great loss, it doesn't have to be a tragedy. A tragedy would be to go through the ecstasy and agony of creating and releasing a child and not to learn what he or she came to teach you—love and joy.

Celebrate your child even as you live through this experience. Use this opportunity to give love to yourself, to the child *inside you.* In case you've forgotten, you're as important as your dying child.

In your own way, honor the great gift of your child.

CHILDREN

At the age of 2-1/2 years, Ebony became very sick. For almost a year we lived at the hospital, going through endless tests, drugs and tears trying to understand why her central nervous system was breaking down. We never did get any real answers as to what went wrong or why.

Three months prior to her dying, I was at the height of my grieving. I was so angry with God! But God was big enough to handle my anger, and helped me understand the wonderful healing that comes from death. A week before Ebony's death I came to total acceptance of the purpose for her life and I was at peace.

During the last day of Ebony's earthly life, my husband and I took turns holding her in our arms. I remember feeling exactly the same way I did when I was giving birth to her . . . the same pain. The dying was like going through labor again. Tears . . . and tears . . . I felt I could not take much more pain. When she died, it was like the crowning — such relief, such peace, such utter joy!

My child's body lay dead in my arms and I was feeling total joy and peace. I knew this was the greatest healing for her. What more could I want for my child who had suffered so much the past year.

—Karen Rockwood

NOTES ON DYING CHILDREN

I'd like to share a few ideas I've encountered during my work with dying adults and parents whose children died.

According to parents and other care-givers who work with dying children, children generally die more easily than adults. They have less fear of death because they haven't been as conditioned as adults have to fear it. Perhaps they're less fearful because they're closer to their *source*.

Except in unusual circumstances, children are happier at home than in a hospital. Most fear going to the hospital. They're afraid of being separated from you, of being alone in unfamiliar places where unfamiliar things happen. Sometimes they don't tell us how they really feel because they're afraid we'll take them to the hospital. Once you've decided your child will die at home, let him or her know you'll stay home together if it's at all possible.

If a child must spend time in a hospital, I encourage you to be there as much as possible. Consider asking permission from the doctor to take turns sleeping in a chair or bed beside him or her. This isn't always possible and depending on the personality and age of the child may not be advisable. Remember your other children and your husband or wife also deserve your care.

Children, like adults, fear mutilation. Having your child practice giving shots or other necessary procedures on a stuffed animal may ease the fear.

Consider putting a dying child's bed in the living room so he or she can live and be cared for in the middle of the family. There you can rest and cuddle or sleep together.

Children

Kids generally want to be like other kids. Within the limits created by the illness, help them to do this. They don't want people to feel sorry for them. Let other children or adults know that.

Help them feel as happy and secure as possible by not overwhelming them with your grief. This doesn't mean not to share your sadness. Again, hugging and holding are great healers for you both.

Dr. Kübler-Ross reports that even three or four year olds can talk about their death. It may be in a symbolic way.

Encourage a child to draw pictures about what she or he is feeling. What the child draws in the upper left quadrant of the picture supposedly indicates his or her feelings about the future and dying. Encourage a child to talk about the drawing by asking, "What's that about?" If we deliberately 'guess wrong' a few times about the meaning of something in the picture, often the child can hardly wait to blurt out his or her truth. For more information about dying children's drawings, read Dr. Kübler-Ross's book, *Living with Dying*.

You might ask a dying child, "What do you think it would be like to die?" This could open a conversation that might alleviate some fear for both of you. It might be an opportunity to share your spiritual beliefs.

Encourage an older dying child to write a letter to you, the parents, or to brothers and sisters.

Have you told your child how much you've loved being his or her mother or father?

If I had a dying child, I might turn to The Center for Attitudinal Healing and The Elisabeth Kübler-Ross Center for support (see pages 94-96). Dr. Kübler-Ross has written *A*

Letter to a Child with Cancer (The Dougy Letter), a beautiful explanation of life and death. (See address in Appendix A to order.)

A DYING BOY'S LETTER TO DOCTORS AND NURSES

I am dying. . . . No one likes to talk about such things. In fact, no one likes to talk about much at all. . . . I am the one who is dying. I know you feel insecure, don't know what to say, don't know what to do. But please believe me, if you care you can't go wrong. Just admit that you care. This is all we search for. We may ask for whys and wherefores, but we really don't want answers. Don't run away. Wait. All I want to know is that there will be someone to hold my hand when I need it. I'm afraid. . . . I've never died before. . . .

— Ron Klingbeil,
A 13-year-old who died of leukemia

YOUR MARRIAGE

Sticks and stones are hard on bones,
  aimed with an angry art.
Words can sting like anything,
  but silence breaks the heart.

—Anonymous

Children

In the mornings I lay in bed, hiding under the sheets, hating my husband for having someplace to go, for getting away from home, for having work to lose himself in . . . . I felt we should have been growing closer during our suffering, getting strength from one another, instead, we were miles apart, sustaining a quiet politeness, drinking too much and pretending in others' company that we were doing alright . . . . Sometimes I feel like I need to wear a sandwich board which reads, "Don't push me. I may shatter."

— Nancy Whittington
A mother whose child died

You may already be aware that a dying child can put a severe strain on a marriage. After the death of a child, a marriage rarely stays the same. It usually gets better or worse. Divorce rates after a child's death are very high. To avoid being a divorce statistic, you'll have to work at it.

We like to imagine parents leaning together to support each other emotionally as they care for their dying child and after the death. Yet that's often not true. If both parents are overwhelmed with grief, neither is available to be leaned on.

Sometimes the relationship between a mother and a dying child is so intense that it excludes, to varying degrees, the father. A father has a different, and often unappreciated, set of circumstances than a mother when his child is dying.

Often a mother is able to stay home and devote her whole being to her child; the father feels compelled to continue working. At work he's expected to function normally, so he hides his pain. He comes home exhausted from the strain of functioning 'normally' and holding in his pain. Then the mother expects him to express his feelings and if he doesn't, she's angry because he doesn't care *enough*. Our culture hasn't taught him to express his feelings. He can't stuff them down one minute and pull them up the next. Whatever he does, he's "rongo in the congo."

Don't expect your partner to grieve in the same way you do. You're two different people and you each have your own way of dealing with grief. Expecting your partner to respond **your** way, is the way **you** set yourself up to feel angry and/or resentful. Anger and resentment are our responses to unfulfilled expectations.

Keep communication open as best you can. Keeping it open might be simply saying, "I love you and I can't talk now. Let's talk after supper." Schedule time to be alone as a couple. I know that's difficult, but wouldn't it be worth it to preserve or improve your marriage? Often one partner is able to talk more easily about what's happening. A less talkative partner can listen and may eventually talk too.

Don't harbor little grievances. Talk about them before they're a huge pile of ammunition. What's the unexpressed need underlying the grievance?

Blame is harmful to any relationship. It's devastating to a marriage when a child is dying or died. A grieving partner can't handle accusations, spoken or unspoken, such as "It's your fault he got worse because . . ." or "It's your fault she died because . . ." Spare each other. You're both doing the best you know how.

Your sexual relationship may disintegrate when your child is dying. If in time after the death, it doesn't return to normal, seek a counselor. Inability to relate sexually points to a deeper lack of communication.

Financial worries caused by a long illness strain a marriage. If you're in over your head financially, consider a debt counselor instead of taking your fear out on each other.

If your marriage is suffering because you're so locked into pain you can't nurture it, see a counselor or social worker skilled in grief counseling. Find a support group such as Compassionate Friends. See page 337. I highly recommend *Healing a Father's Grief.* This $1.35 booklet might give you the highest return on your money you've ever received. (To order, see Appendix A.)

Love yourself and your partner. Take care of each other. Forgive each other. Respect your individual ways of grieving. Keep communication open. **Your partner will be here when your child is not.**

One way to define marriage is as a commitment to move to the truth together. The truth is love. Your child is your teacher.

TO ALL PARENTS

"I'll lend you for a little time
   a child of Mine," He said,
"For you to love the while he lives,
   and mourn for when he's dead.
It may be six or seven years,
   or twenty two or three,
But will you, 'til I call him back,
   take care of him for me?
He'll bring his charms to gladden you
   and shall his stay be brief
You'll have his lovely memories
   as solace for your grief.

I cannot promise he will stay
   since all from earth return,
But there are lessons taught down there
   I want this child to learn.
I've looked the wide world over,
   in My search for teachers true
And from the throngs that crowd life's lanes,
   I have selected you.
Now, will you give him all your love,
   not think the labor vain,
Nor hate Me when I come to call
   to take him back again?

I fancied that I heard you say,
   'Dear Lord Thy Will be done;
For all the joy Thy child shall bring,
   the risk of grief we'll run.
We'll shelter him with tenderness;
   We'll love him while we may
And for the happiness we've known,

186

Children

Forever grateful stay;
But shall the angels call for him
   much sooner than we've planned
We'll brave the painful grief that comes
   and try to understand.' "

—Edgar A. Guest

You are love. You come from love. You are made by love. You cannot cease to be love.

The whole manifestation is the manifestation of love. God himself is love. So the love which comes from the source, returns to the Source—and the purpose of life is accomplished in this.

—Hazrat Inayat Khan
The Purpose of Life

CHAPTER 8

MAKING THE SENSES COMFORTABLE PRACTICAL HOME CARE

For in the dew of little things the heart finds its morning and is refreshed.

— Kahlil Gibran

Nothing is worth doing unless it's done with joy.

— A Deva

Caring for someone means making the senses of the body comfortable, as well as the feelings, mind and soul. A joyful loving attitude as we provide physical care helps a dying person maintain or regain comfort and dignity. If we feel someone is glad to help us, we feel free to ask for what we want and need. On the other hand, if we feel we're a burden or nuisance, we're often afraid to ask. You might let the person know, "I enjoyed giving you a backrub" or "Helping you is a pleasure, Dad."

I hope you're beginning to sense that this adventure you've begun can be a beautiful experience and even a creative art which you develop in your own way to please your patient and yourself. True creation comes from joy. Can you imagine duty creating a flower? Let yourself really enjoy creating comfort and beauty.

Dying well is a concern as old as we humans. What has changed is the meaning of "well". *Art Moriendi* (Dying Arts), which taught the art of dying, was one of the world's first do-it-yourself books. In the 15th century, Caxton produced a book, *Art and Craft to Knowe ye Well to Dye*, which included instructions for everything from the art of blowing your nose to weeping well.

Part of making people feel comfortable is knowing what you're doing. I suggest tacking a schedule or list on the kitchen wall for anything you need to keep track of. The list could include times for medication, diet or who's going to be with the person if several people share the caring. Stay flexible, a list is just an aid. Remember, one of the reasons for being at home is doing what the dying person wants or needs instead of what's convenient for a hospital staff.

TOUCH

Your daily life is your temple and your religion.

— Kahlil Gibran

Touch is a way to share the love and caring in our hearts. It's important to all of us in endless ways, especially when we're

190

dying. Touching is a way to express with the body that something beyond the body is important. A person is loved even if his or her body is no longer attractive or is even unpleasant to see.

In many slow deaths from cancer the body may become very unattractive physically. You may feel repulsed. It's a natural feeling. Keep your heart open and remember your touch is received by the person who owns the body. Neither John, Mary, nor my father had bodies of great beauty when they died, yet each was a person of great beauty. By touching a dying person freely and lovingly, we're saying, "I care about you. You're more to me than just a body." This helps people understand that their bodies are only a part of who they are and helps them prepare to let go.

MASSAGE

Massage is a beautiful way to touch and make a person comfortable. It also helps prevent bedsores. Even if you've never given a massage before, you can do it.

You may massage the head, hands, feet, back or whole body. Do what you have time for and feel comfortable with. I'm particularly fond of foot massages because sometimes I'm too tired to do a person's whole body. While massaging someone's feet I often get the image of anointing the feet of Christ. The hands and feet both have nerve endings from all the organs in the body. By massaging them you stimulate and relax the whole body. (If you want to help a specific part, see Appendix J.) To avoid loosening possible blood clots, skip massaging the legs of people who have had recent surgery, have been bedridden for a long time or are elderly.

Here are some simple massage instructions:

Coming Home

1. Before you start make sure the room is warm enough and uncover only the part of the body you're going to massage.

2. Think about your love for the person.

3. Feel your hands as an extension of your heart and rub them together to make sure they're warm.

4. Let go of rushing around. Focus completely on this person.

5. Quietly enter the rhythm of their breathing. Align your breathing with theirs.

6. Gently place your hands on the person, knowing the flesh may be very tender.

7. **Trust your hands.** They may be uncertain at first, but soon your instincts will open to what feels good to both of you. Light flowing strokes can be very soothing.

8. Don't be afraid to ask, "Tell me what feels good and what doesn't."

9. If your hands feel heavy or cramped, gently take them off the person for a moment and shake them.

10. Pay particular attention to bony areas like the tailbone or shoulder blades. If they are white or reddened, use your finger tips and rub in small circles around them, not on them. This will increase the blood supply and help prevent bedsores.

11. When you're through, keep your hands quietly on the person for a moment, then lift them off very slowly and gently. (I say a little prayer to myself that God bless the person.)

12. If you remove your hands abruptly, the person is likely to feel a little deserted and shocked, negating some of the good feelings of the massage.

13. Cover the person when you finish and help them feel cozy. They may drift off into tranquil sleep or feel so secure and loved they want to talk about things unsaid before.

14. Wash your hands in cool water to clear energy you may have picked up.

You're probably feeling better now yourself. What we give to others is always for us as well.

HAIR

For many of us it's a treat to have someone comb and brush our hair, for others it's awful. Tangled hair can be uncomfortable, and who wants to look like a scarecrow? If visitors are coming most people will want to look their best. It's also very satisfying to have clean hair and scalp that can breathe. If a person cannot care for his or her own hair, you can do it. Brushing and combing may be part of a morning bathing ritual or done any time.

There are several alternatives for cleaning hair. Hospitals generally use "no rinse" shampoo . . . you pour a little on the hair, massage it in and then towel dry the hair. You can bring "no rinse" shampoo home from the hospital or buy it at a hospital pharmacy. At a regular drug store, you can buy shampoo that sprays on like a white powder, dries and you brush it out. If someone can sit safely in a shower stall, you can wash hair and bathe at the same time.

You can also wash someone's hair in bed if you need to. Invent a system that works for you and the patient. Be well organized ahead of time because hair washing is very tiring for someone who is weak. You'll need a pan, towels, and plastic to keep the bedding dry.

If the person can't sit up, put pillows covered with a plastic trash bag and a towel under their neck. Check the water temperature. Then lean the head backward into a plastic pan to catch the water as you pour it through the hair. Gently towel dry the hair as much as possible. If the weather is cold, use a hairdryer to prevent chilling.

If you can't or don't want to wash someone's hair yourself, you might ask a beautician who's been trained to work with people in bed. You can locate one through a hospital or visiting nurse association.

Note: Don't forget to cut the person's fingernails so they don't scratch themselves. Some people enjoy a manicure, fingernail polish or light makeup. A man may need help with shaving.

CHANGING SHEETS

An important part of touch is having clean fresh sheets. A rubberized flannel undersheet helps the bed stay clean. Consider bringing outdoor freshness in by hanging sheets outside to dry in the sun.

Change the sheets whenever they're dirty, wet, sweaty or the person wants them changed. This may be several times a day or once every two or three days. You may save

Changing the sheets with a person in bed

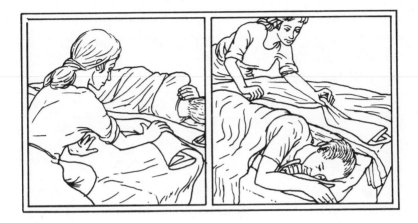

some changes by keeping towels around in case your patient spits up. It is tiring for both of you to change linen very often.

If the person can't get out of bed, you'll have to change the sheets with them in bed. A visiting nurse can demonstrate how, or use these instructions:

Before any procedure directly involving your patient, explain what you plan to do and ask if it's OK. Have the clean linen handy before you begin.

1. Take off the top sheet and cover the person with a bathrobe or towel.

2. Roll the person onto his or her side with their back toward the center of the bed. Put the siderail up (on a hospital bed). Be careful the person doesn't slip off the edge.

3. Facing the backside of the patient, loosen the bottom sheet and roll it up until it's along his or her backside.

4. Position the clean bottom sheet on your side of the bed and tuck it in. Fold up the rest close to the rolled dirty sheet.

5. Help the person roll over both sheets to the side of the bed you've already fixed.

6. Move to the other side of the bed, pull away the dirty sheet and tuck in the clean one.

7. Change the pillow cases.

8. Help the person back to the middle of the bed and put on the top sheet and covers.

"SHEEPSKINS" AND PILLOWS

"Sheepskins," pillows and eggcrate mattresses (see page 196) are important aids for comfort and preventing bedsores.

An artificial sheepskin is a washable synthetic pad about 3 ft. by 3 ft. You place it under a patient from shoulder to buttocks. They're available from a hospital supplier and some fabric stores, or bring them home from the hospital. (You've paid for them!) Have several on hand; one for the bed or a chair, another to exchange for a soiled one.

Have extra soft plump pillows available. For a change of position for a person lying on her back, place a pillow under the knees to prop them up. For a patient on his side, place a pillow between the knees so they don't get raw from rubbing together. If a pillow feels too bulky, use a soft flannel cloth. Tucking a pillow in behind the back feels cozy and prevents rolling. Pile pillows at the foot of the bed under the top sheet to make a tent so the person's feet don't get tangled in the bedclothes.

You can also buy foam rubber wedges shaped like triangles. They're useful to position swollen ankles and calves to knee height, which alleviates some discomfort. Sheepskin booties are useful to protect someone's heels who's in bed much of the time.

HUGGING, HOLDING AND CUDDLING

This is not the name of a law firm. They're a cure for loneliness and our illusion of separateness. As long as they come from unconditional love, I don't think we can over-hug or over-cuddle. Sharing love and warmth may include a person's sexuality. This is OK.

Don't be afraid to ask for a hug. Your asking gives people a splendid opportunity, and if they don't want to give or share one they can always say 'no.' I suggest you call a morning 'hug time' for your family. It's a great way to start the day. Jog to a friend's house for a hug. I once started a 'morning hug' for my construction crew. We were the happiest workers on the site.

Your hugging, holding and cuddling with a dying person obviously needs to be very gentle and appropriate to their needs.

Hug, hold and cuddle away!

197

MOVING THE PERSON

HOSPITAL BEDS

A hospital bed has some advantages for the comfort of the dying person as well as for the helpers. You can easily elevate the person's head or knees to change positions. The height of the bed is adjustable so that the person's feet may touch the floor when they sit up, which makes getting in and out of bed easier. The adjustable height also helps prevent back strain for the helpers because they don't need to bend down as far to assist the person. Transfers from bed to wheelchair are also easier because you can make the two surfaces the same height. It's easy to hook up a trapeze to a hospital bed. A trapeze helps a bedridden person to lift the upper body or to turn himself.

The disadvantages of a hospital bed are it's not the person's own bed and cuddling is more difficult. Giving up their own bed is hard for many people. We used hospital beds with John and Mary. When Dad was asked if he wanted one, he didn't even bother to reply. He wasn't about to give up the bed he had shared with Mom for the last 43 years.

If you reach a point when you feel a hospital bed would be less strain for you both, explain the advantages and ask delicately. Sometimes a little inconvenience is better than a change.

You can rent a hospital bed with electric or manual controls from a rental company. The manually operated ones are less expensive and perfectly adequate. On the other hand, some people love to push buttons and be able to change positions when they want to.

Making The Senses Comfortable

WHEELCHAIRS

A wheelchair gives a person who can't walk greater mobility and a change of scenery. Finding one is easy. The American Cancer Society, some veterans organizations, and other service groups loan wheelchairs, and rental companies rent them at reasonable monthly rates.

There are a variety of models including one with a tray that locks in place if your patient's getting up and wandering around is a concern. If you have a choice, choose a model that most suits the needs of the person.

To prevent accidents make sure the brakes are on before helping someone move in or out of a wheelchair. See the illustrations for how to move a person from bed to wheelchair and back, or up and down a curb.

MOVING A PERSON WHO NEEDS HELP

During a home dying, you'll have challenges helping the person in and out of bed, to a chair, to the bathroom or potty chair, etc. Be sensitive to how much help the person needs. Overhelping undermines a person's sense of worth and dignity. Encourage the person to help him or herself unless it's too difficult or too discouraging. Move them the way they want to be moved. Support them in places they can't support themselves.

A visiting nurse can most easily demonstrate methods of moving a person, including a transfer belt. I'll share some ways I use; you may invent your own.

It's important to learn to move someone with the least amount of strain on yourself. One person can probably give

199

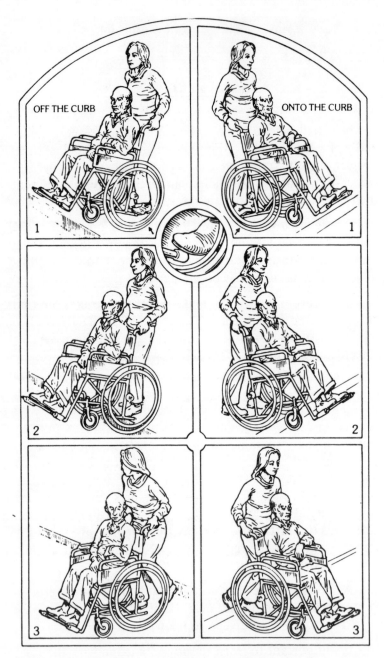

How to get a person in a wheelchair up and down over a curb.

all the support needed in the beginning. Later, you may need two. Some principles of healthy body mechanics when lifting and moving are: whenever possible, keep your back straight; use thigh and stomach muscles; bend your knees and keep your weight over them; take a wide stance with one leg in front of the other with your weight evenly distributed; hold the person close to your middle, your center of gravity. Don't life a weight you can slide.

To help someone out of bed. Imagine yourself in their place; sense what hurts and what's hardest for them about moving. Plan in advance with the person how you're going to lift or move them. What might get in your way? Any furniture or slippery rugs? Use non-skid slippers or bare feet.

If the person is moving to a chair or potty chair, place the chair at the side of the bed with its back facing the foot of the bed. When the person is ready to move, take a deep breath and relax yourself. Relax your knees. If the move is to a wheelchair, make sure the brake is on and arm or foot rests aren't in the way. Then:

1. Roll the person on her side, facing you. Drop the siderail if there is one.

2. Raise the head of a hospital bed.

3. Slide her legs partially over the side of the bed.

4. If she can't sit up alone, put one arm around the back of the shoulders, supporting the neck, and with the other arm gently pull her forward.

5. Stop a moment to let her get her balance sitting up. Make sure her feet are squarely in front of her.

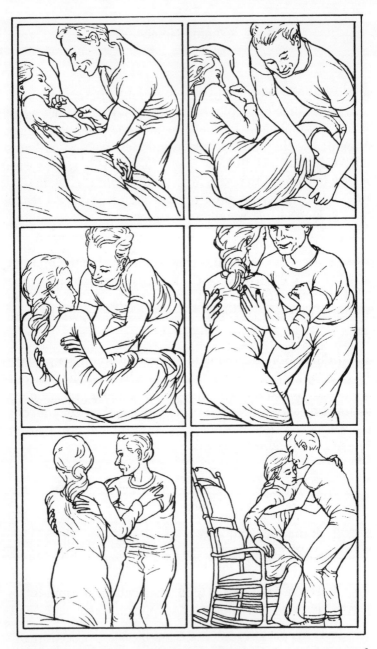

How to help a sick person from bed to chair. Awareness of balance and leverage is important.

6. If she can't help, face her, bend your knees and put both arms around her, under her arms like a big hug. I sometimes put a hand under one buttock.

7. Brace one of your knees against her knee to prevent falling if her knees buckle, and gently lift her up. (This is the waltz!)

8. Let her get her balance standing and, in this hugging "waltzing" position, move toward your destination.

9. If she doesn't need this much support, hold her under the armpits from the back.

To help a person in bed turn to their side. Raise the siderail (if any), place one hand on the far shoulder and the other on the far hip. With your feet apart, gently roll the person toward you. Most patients can help by grasping the siderail or bed edge on the side they're turning toward.

Moving someone up in bed. (toward the head of the bed). This can be done by one person if the patient is light or can help. Two are necessary for a heavy person who can't. There are a number of possibilities:

1. If the person can help, have him bend his knees. Remove the pillows. Standing beside him, slide your arms under his back and thighs. Then, shift your weight forward toward the head of the bed as he pushes upward.

2. If the person can't help, use the same procedure as above, or two people can lift him with their arms under the head, shoulders and hips.

203

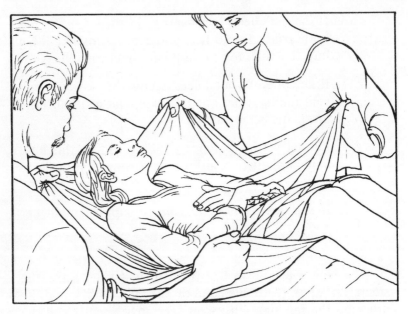

Moving a Person in Bed with a Draw Sheet

3. A tug or draw sheet is a doubled sheet placed under someone from neck to buttocks. It's used by two people to move someone up or down the bed. Place it between the bottom sheet and the sheepskin. Stand on opposite sides of the bed and roll the ends of the draw sheet toward the person in the center of the bed. Grip the rolled part firmly and lift-slide the person up or down. Be sure to support the person's neck.

After moving someone, help make him or her comfortable. Rearrange pillows and the pad between the knees and straighten the gown or nightshirt.

Remember the Princess and the Pea? People in bed are often super-sensitive to things you might not notice or feel. Some little irritation makes a person feel crazy if they can't move enough to do anything about it. As death approaches you may have to move a person frequently. Trust your own loving tenderness. Relax and keep healthy body mechanics in mind so you don't strain your back. If you do (I have), don't be shy about asking someone for a massage.

SMELL

What smells good when you're sick? Flowers, fresh air, sheets full of sunlight, incense, perfume? Ask your patient what smells she or he doesn't like. Perhaps the smell of food cooking is nauseating. Smell is more highly developed in some people than others, but most of us like to smell good and smell good things. Good is different for everyone! One character in the play *The Mad Woman of Chaillot* loves garbage because "it's the smell of God's plenty!" Smell has a lot to do with cleanliness.

CLEANLINESS
BATHING AND CHANGING

Regular bathing is important for the health and comfort of your patient. If someone can't bathe or shower, bathe them in bed. Is assisting the person to sit on a stool in the shower possible?

Generally morning is a good time for a bath, but ask. Make sure the room is warm enough so you don't have to deal with frostbite after the bath! Chilling can be a problem. I use a natural sponge or cotton washcloth and a plastic pan for water. Find out what water temperature the person likes. Soaps without lots of perfumes and additives cause fewer dry skin problems. Have soft towels handy to cover the body parts you've already washed. Be sure to gently and thoroughly wash the genital area as odors tend to collect there. There's no need to splash around so much water that towels are needed under the person, but place one next to the person to catch occasional drips.

After bathing, use a skin cream or lotion to prevent itchy skin. Alpha Keri is used by many hospitals and there are natural products available at health food stores. Using baby powder around the genitals may prevent rashes. After her bath I gave Mary a short foot massage with cedar oil to stimulate circulation in her body. (Cedar oil is used by some Native Americans for purification.) If circulation is poor and the person has cold feet, put on socks or knitted slippers or use a heating pad or hot water bottle. Remember to test the temperature and frequently check the areas touched by the heating pad or bottle.

Change gowns or pajamas at bath time and whenever necessary, yet not so often it tires the patient. Gowns that open in the back are easier to take off and put on. Ones that go over the head are a pain in your back when the patient can't easily sit up.

TEETH

Cleaning a person's mouth is important. It's awful to go through the day with "bottom of the bird cage mouth." If toothpaste becomes too messy, you might change to hydrogen peroxide. If a person can't brush their own teeth, do it for them with peroxide on a toothbrush or Q-tip. Spongy swabs containing a special cleanser can be brought home from the hospital or bought from a hospital supply store or pharmacy.

Someone who wears dentures may want to continue using them. This is fine as long as they don't pose a danger. Consult a nurse or doctor.

ELIMINATION

We need to bring all the compassion and caring we have to help people adjust to losing control of elimination. They usually feel ashamed and embarrassed. You might point out that the situation could just as easily be reversed; she or he could be helping you. Remind a mother or father of all the years they cleaned up their child. A cycle is completing itself, and we're reminded we're not just a body.

A catheter is one way to handle loss of bladder control. Another is placing a disposable cotton pad under the person, which also works for loss of bowel control. Chux and Curity Disposable Underpads are available at medical supply stores and drug stores. Keep nightgowns or shirts out of the way and change the pads when necessary. Women can use a thick sanitary pad for extra absorbency. Men who dribble at night can lie on a seamless shower cap filled with cottonballs.

After elimination, wash skin thoroughly and use powder or drying creme to prevent irritation or skin breakdown.

Not all dying people lose control of their bladders or bowels. If they do, they're generally on a bland diet with few animal products so the smell isn't bad. If it makes you nauseous, put Tiger Balm or perfume under your nose and breathe through your mouth. Remember, this may be you later.

To the end, Mary and John were able to get to a toilet or potty chair. My dad used a bedpan once and lost control of his bowels once when he was drugged too heavily to wake up in the night.

As long as someone wants to and is able to get to the bathroom or potty chair (bedside commode), I suggest helping them, even if you think a bedpan or urinal might be easier for everyone. But do suggest a bedpan or urinal if getting to the bathroom or potty chair is so exhausting it doesn't leave much energy for more enjoyable activities.

BEDPANS

There are two kinds of bedpans. The flatter kind (called a fracture pan) is easier to push under the buttocks.

To use one, roll the person to his side, position the bedpan under the buttocks, then roll him back onto the pan. Or, with a more mobile person, ask her to lie on her back, bend her knees and bring her feet up as close to the buttocks as possible. Put one hand under her lower back and lift up as you place the bedpan under the buttocks with the other hand. Ask her to help, if possible, by pushing up the hips.

You might leave the room and ask to be called when they want to get off the pan. Flush the contents down the toilet.

Bedpans and plastic urinals for men are available from large pharmacies and medical supply companies.

SIGHT

BEAUTY

Beauty heals. For a glimpse of the power of beauty, take a moment to remember how you've felt throughout your body when you've seen something you found incredibly beautiful.

Recent studies indicate that the pineal gland, whose function has not yet been scientifically determined, is stimulated by beauty.

In the past, the person you're caring for may not have made much time or space in his or her life for beauty. Perhaps you can help them open to an experience of themselves they may not have had before—so that in dying the adventure of life continues.

Imagine yourself in the place of the dying person. Try to experience his or her vision of beauty, then do what you can to fill the room or home with it. Each vision will be different. Beauty to someone may be the old stained hat he always wore on fishing trips. Hang it up where he can see it. It may be a painting or weaving or the way sunlight comes through an old lace curtain. If you have a choice, choose a room with windows so the dying can still experience the outer world, the sky, trees or the apartment next door. The sunlight that comes through the window will nourish body and soul.

Hang up beautiful old or new things, move furniture, add a lamp or a bird feeder. Gather wildflowers; go to a florist. Check first with the person you're caring for. Maybe beauty is leaving things just the way they are.

You might also suggest that the person spend time imagining things she or he finds beautiful.

COLOR

We're just beginning to remember the effect color has on us human beings. Play with color. Ask the person which ones she or he likes. Dying people often prefer the lightness of colors to the deepness — a rose or peach instead of deep wine. For me, for example, dying with a reddy-brown bedspread would be torture. Keep color in mind when you gather sheets, pajamas, nightgowns, bedjackets and bedspreads. If someone has a craving for a certain color, it means she or he needs it at some level of their being. To the extent you can, meet the desire for a color as you would a craving for a certain food.

Sunlight contains all colors, which is one of the reasons it nourishes us. If we're experiencing perfect harmony we don't need more of one color than another. Most of us though, need more harmony in our lives and could benefit from specific colors. This is particularly true for people with dis-ease.

There are many books about color and its relationship to different diseases and states of mind. Many don't agree on which color does what, so once again we have to trust ourselves and experiment. I recommend *Color Therapy*, by Reuben Amber. It includes the history of the use of color in healing and practical ways to work with color.

Here are some general ideas to test. Greens through clear azure blues tend to be calming; yellow energizes.

210

Peachy pinks help depression and people who tend to stay alone. (Some say peach is the color of love of humanity.) The range of orchids, lavenders and purples connect us to our spiritual nature. (Dad's favorite color when he was dying was purple.) Orchid relates to transcending matter. Some think cancer is related to deep grief, which is helped by greens, and lack of enthusiasm, which is helped by yellow, an emotional energizer. Orange vitalizes the body. If the dying person wants browns and grays, you might ask why. Those colors sometimes have to do with fear and pessimism, and your asking might bring up some unfinished business the person may want to talk about.

As you support this dying process, if you get a craving for a yellow dress or tie, treat yourself to it. There's usually enough money for what we really need and 'yellow' can be just as real a need a food or medicine.

TELEVISION

Lest I get carried away with beauty and color, we also look at TV with our eyes. Ask the dying person if he or she wants a TV in the room, and if so, when they want it turned on and off. If there's only one TV in the house, the person can still cooperate and sometimes watch someone else's favorite program. When someone's watching their favorite show, you might want to enjoy time alone.

Dad and I watched the world news together and with Mary I used to insist on seeing M.A.S.H. because it made me laugh.

*   *   *   *   *

Here's another visual idea from a friend: She prominently displayed a picture of her husband taken when he was healthy. When he was thin and gaunt and not so wonderful to look at, it was a reminder to everyone that he was still the same human being and still deserved love and consideration.

HEARING

SOUND

Sound has been used for soothing, purifying and healing since the beginning of humankind.

"In the beginning was the Word, and the Word was with God, and the Word was God". (John:1) Does "word" mean "sound"? Many people are just beginning to be aware of sound's role in the creation. At some level we've all been aware of using sound to heal: lullabies, Native American chants in the sweat lodge, Gregorian chants in the monastery, hymns in church. Sound and some kinds of music clear our minds so new energies can emerge.

At home the dying person is blessed with not hearing doctors' beepers and clanging meal trays. Enjoy the sound of silence. Enjoy the sounds of home: birds singing, a child laughing, the same old leaky faucet.

Experiment with giving the gift of sound to the person you're caring for. Would a bell help a weak person call you more easily? What about a cassette player and some of the new nature recordings like a stream, whales singing or ocean

waves meeting a beach? Would hanging wind chimes outside the window be soothing? Some say chimes are the
sound of the heart. They've been used for centuries in China
and Japan. You can buy inexpensive ones at most import
stores.

MUSIC

What kind of music does the person like: Ask. It may be
'soul', Beethoven's *Ninth Symphony* or Mozart's *Ave
Verum*. What about flute music? Some say it's the sound of
the soul. Pachebel's *Canon in D* allows an opening to great
peace without intruding. I like Georgia Kelly's harp music,
Seapeace, and Steve Halpern's *Eventide*. You may discover
other healing pieces.

If you and the dying person have made music together,
keep it up as long as you can.

Using the words appropriate for you, you might suggest that as the person listens to music he or she relax and
breathe in the music, tune into the harmonies. Music can be
the needed break from the problems and routine of dying.

If someone seems to be holding in anger, it might be
useful to play a piece of music you know she or he doesn't
like. It could help release the anger — and you'd have to be
willing to take the consequences!

READING TO SOMEONE

Being read to is enjoyable for many people. Ask the person
you're caring for. Reading can be a quiet, relaxing time for

you both. When our attention is focused, not wandering among our everyday problems, other parts of ourselves are set free. Being read to also helps keep the mind active and prevents boredom. Being read to is not for everyone. Mary loved it. When I asked Dad if I could read him one of my favorite books, Allen Boones's *Kinship with All Life*, he didn't even answer, which was an answer.

What about storytelling, prayer or meditation? Often there is time for just talking together about the things we really care about . . . wonder about.

Be sensitive to noises that may be irritating or painful to the dying person (like banging doors, scraping furniture, vacuuming, etc.). Quiet for healing and final preparation is vital. Ask the person if there's too much noise or chatter.

Remember the sound of words of love. Use them generously.

TASTE

Taste is a sense some will enjoy right until the end of this life, even when other bodily functions have closed down.

From my present vantage point, if I were dying, I'd want Cadbury's chocolate instead of mushed carrots. This may change when my time comes! During Mary's last week, she craved butterscotch sundaes (or her memories of them) and we ran out to get them. She could take only a few bites and generally spit them up, but she enjoyed the taste so it was worth the effort. Dad craved raspberry sherbert and grape popsicles. Perhaps the digested sugar helped keep their minds clear.

DIET

Before terminal care, diet is very important. There are all kinds of different theories about purifying diets and which diet is most appropriate for which disease. If you're interested, check a health food store for books. Do what the patient and you decide is best. You can always change your minds. If you give someone a certain food and later learn another could have been better, remember you did what seemed best at the time.

I suggest avoiding artificial and chemically processed foods. When you're sick, your body has enough to deal with without the chemical preservative, artificial coloring, etc., that the food industry uses. Fresh fruits, vegetables and grains are usually appealing and easy to digest. Avoid hard to digest fried foods.

Once you've decided and accepted that you're providing terminal care, consider giving the dying person whatever food he or she wants. Consider again the quality of life versus the quantity. It is possible that a reaction to a certain food might cause someone to leave a body earlier than expected.

If the sick person finds some foods unpleasant, it probably means he or she would have difficulty digesting it. If a person is indifferent to food, serve what's tolerable.

Chips of ice or iced drinks may reduce nausea and be refreshing. For a variety of flavors, freeze fruit juices in ice cube trays. If chewing is tiring, mash foods or put them through a blender.

If someone is on a liquid diet, make delicious healthy combinations of fruit juices with yogurt, raw eggs, or wheat germ and powdered vitamins. With a vegetable juicer, com-

215

bine carrots, celery and spinach. Straight carrot juice is wonderful — if the liver is functioning well. Create and experiment. Use a beautiful glass and straws that bend to make drinking easier.

Remember those grim hospital meals wrapped in cellophane or metal on plastic trays? Serve food as attractively as possible. What about colored napkins, a child's cut-out, a tiny racing car or a flower on a food tray? For Mary I traded for beautiful hand-painted plates with rabbits and cats on them. Beauty and music can sooth digestion.

Sick people often ask for a certain food and then can't eat it, perhaps because of nausea or blockage in the digestive tract. **If you're caring for someone who can't eat, their difficulty does not reflect negatively on your ability to nourish.** It just means that changes are taking place in their body.

For a mother or wife accustomed to sharing love with food, watching someone she loves not eat can be very hard. (For Mom, Dad's not eating was the hardest part of caring for him.) The dying person can help by saying he feels loved even if he can't eat. Family members can help by suggesting other ways to share love, like massage or reading aloud, and pointing out that her presence alone radiates love. **Dealing with your feelings when a loved one doesn't eat or eats very little is part of the process of letting go.**

Joy is prayer — Joy is strength — Joy is love — Joy is a net of love by which you can catch souls. God loves a cheerful giver. She gives most who gives with joy. The best way to show our gratitude to God and the people is to accept everything with joy. A joyful heart is the normal result of a heart burning with love. Never let anything so fill you with sorrow as to make you forget the joy of Christ Arisen. We all long for heaven where God is, but we have it in our power to be in heaven with Him at this very moment. But being happy with Him now means:

> loving as He loves,
> helping as He helps,
> giving as He gives,
> serving as He serves,
> rescuing as He rescues,
> being with Him twenty-four hours,
> touching Him in his distressing disguise.

— Mother Teresa

CHAPTER 9

LIVING FULLY WITH DYING

OUR FEELINGS

As we come more into the understanding that working with the dying is a way of working on ourselves, we find that working on ourself means dying . . . letting go of the separate self, of every foothold and gesture that maintains our identity as apart from others and our original nature, our profound oneness with all that is.

—Stephen Levine

To live fully with dying we have to accept all of ourselves, including all our feelings—the ones we like as well as the ones we don't. Each feeling is a teacher.

Take time to **feel** your feelings. This may sound silly but it's not. A lot of us ignore or run right over our feelings in the rush to **do** the next thing. Then we're surprised when life feels meaningless or as if it's going too fast.

Supporting a home dying is an opportunity to slow down, to reappraise our values and to balance **doing** and **being.** When they are balanced, life regains meaning, mystery and excitement. We then tap into a spring of limitless energy and have all the strength we need to support this dying person. Without the rest and nourishment of *being*, the constant activity of *doing* is exhausting. We make up for our backlog of fatigue by allowing ourselves to be. Then, to prevent feeling again a deep down tired-out, we can rest as we go along by **being fully present for whatever we're doing or feeling.**

Regaining this balance may shake up intellectual ideas and cause us to swing from one emotional peak to another This is fine . . . part of the process of surrender. We swing until we regain our balance — perhaps until we make a friend of death.

As you support this dying, accept the wisdom of your being; trust your feelings. After taking time to feel them, express them in a way that's appropriate for you. Once you've felt and expressed a feeling, send love to the part of you that feels it — your angry self, sad self, impatient one, lonely one, disgusted one, or the child in you. Then let go of it. If you have trouble letting go, try one or more of these: yell (possibly in a car), take a walk, jog outside or in place, take a deep breath, drink a glass of water. If you feel really scared or crazy, call a friend, counselor or whoever feels appropriate. Do whatever you can think of to release the feeling, then breathe in peace. Make time to reflect on what your feeling may have been trying to help you understand.

Remember, the dying person is not the only one under stress.

The following feelings aren't in a particular order. If you feel drawn to one, go ahead and read it now.

HOPE

Hope is a reliance on the future that protects us from a "now" that is too painful. It's the question mark that is sometimes more desirable than an answer. As we walk through the darkness, hope may help sustain us.

It plays an important and complex role in the dying process. Nearly all dying people have hope in varying degrees, although the focus changes. At first they hope to regain their health, then to live a little longer, then to die an easy death. Hope is useful to sustain them through suffering, endless tests and treatments, being in bed, and losing control.

Don't crush hope in the person you're caring for. He or she needs it until acceptance is reached. Hope gives time to come to terms with impending loss. It can be a sustainer and/or a form of denial. Whichever it is, we need to support hope and be truthful at the same time. For example, "Your tests don't look good and it's possible the treatment will reverse this" (if that's true). We can always encourage someone to hope to live well until he or she dies.

The idea that there may be a cure around the corner, a new breakthrough in treatments, may help someone through a huge amount of discomfort. Breakthroughs are always possible. In the last couple of days before Dad died, he remembered with gratitude the doctor who gave him hope on the day, two years earlier, when he was first told he had cancer.

In her book, *On Death and Dying*, Dr. Kübler-Ross makes two important observations about hope:

> The conflicts we have seen in regard to hope arose from two main sources. The first and most painful one was the conveyance of hopelessness either on the part of the staff (hospital) or family when the patient still needed hope. The second source of anguish came from the family's inability to accept a patient's final stage; they desperately clung to hope when the patient himself was ready to die and sensed the family's inability to accept this fact.

When dying people express loss of hope, they generally die in a very short time.

LOVE

Our whole business this life is to restore to health the eye of the heart whereby God may be seen.

— St. Augustine

Love is the worker of miracles that restores health to the eye of the heart.

Just now, if you wish, take a few minutes to slowly read the following meditation. It is even more enjoyable if there's someone else at home who can read it to you. Use the meditation any time you need some extra love.

> Remember some time in your life when you held and were held by someone you love, a child, a parent, a husband, a lover. Feel that again . . . remember how soft and open and full you felt . . . how safe and comfortable! Remember what your breathing was like and breathe that way now . . . feel the wholeness. Now give to yourself that love your were feeling with someone else. Give your love to yourself as you have given it to others . . . feel the fullness in your heart. There is a giver and a receiver in each of us that keeps the circle of love flowing. We can give and receive love inside of ourselves, as we give and receive love outside with others. Feel yourself surrounded and enveloped by love. (It's there all the time whether we feel it or not.) Feel it giving you the strength you need for all the details, decisions and maybe crises involved with this dying process you're supporting. If you feel 'heavy' from worry, feel the heaviness lightening or lifting off.

When we feel the love inside us, instead of looking outside for someone to love us, our own loving abundance makes everything easier.

As you support this dying with love, you will likely experience that love transcends and transforms time. One of the reasons we love to love is because it moves us beyond the ordinary limits of time. Remember that sense of timelessness? The beauty and intensity of a relationship are often increased when one can see its end in time (death). Love, though, doesn't end with time; it belongs to eternity and dying is *leaving time for eternity.*

The presence of love gives the dying person a supportive place and time in which to experience the incredible changes taking place within him or herself. When we bring someone home we generally feel full of love; later, sometimes, it's difficult to maintain this feeling through tiredness, pressure or complications. Sustaining love is easier if we are aware of who we are and where love comes from.

I'll share with you my reality or vision of who we are to give you a context for understanding what I say about love and fear. If there is truth for you in my reality, or any other, it will resonate in your own heart.

In the beginning was God (unity, energy) and God was without form. For God to have form there must be duality — a positive and negative charge. God created light and dark.* The passive dark had no need to express, but the active light did. The part of God that wanted to express created humankind. The light is unconditional love; the dark is the space to receive it. When the light fills the darkness, there will be no more form. We return to God formless.

---

* Other words for God are: The One, The Source, The Creator, The Word, Truth, Reality, Life, sound, spirit, the void, Father, Heaven, formlessness, eternity, infinity, Brahma, Tao, Dharma, Allah, The Great Spirit, The Kingdom, The Ultimate, the prime cause, the first mover, that which endures indefinitely. Some other words for light: The Light, Sun, The Son, Christ, Christ consciousness, universal intelligence, the life force, The Holy Grail, giver, and yang. For the dark: form, creation, earth, Earth Mother, the manifestation, the expression, Darkness, receiver, and yin.

Living Fully With Dying

The formless Absolute is my Father, and God in form is my Mother.

— Kabir

Once we were created, we got attached to the form and forgot the formless. We forgot that God could not express without us. Fear was created when the first human beings judged that duality and separation are the same thing. Fear, the illusion that we're separate from that which created and encompasses us, prevents us from remembering we are God and love in form. When we remember, we experience no separation between God in form and God formless. We are both.

Life and death, to me, are a process of remembering we are God and love. Sharing in the dying of someone we love can accelerate our remembering. **We've cheerfully acknowledged the devil in ourselves, maybe it's time to just as readily acknowledge the god in ourselves.**

But if love underlies all of existence, why do I see cruelty, hate, greed, violence, guilt and insensitivity all around me? Why do love and fear seem to go together? How come I'm afraid to love? How come I'm afraid to receive love? Why am I afraid when I do love someone — afraid I'll be hurt, afraid he'll leave me for another woman, be in an accident . . . or die? Why do I see unhappiness in my relationships and in those around me?

Because, after we were created we judged we were separate from love, felt afraid and loved conditionally. "I'll love you if . . . if you remember my birthday . . . if you cut your hair the right length . . . if you have the right color skin . . .

225

if you have the job I think you should have . . . if you'll never leave me . . . if . . ."

Unconditional love eliminates fear. Love is the absence of fear. Just, "I love you." "I love you whoever you are . . . whatever you do . . . even if you leave me . . . even if you die. I love you without conditions and without expectations of anything."

Fear holds love a prisoner in the solar plexus where it's a possessive feeling. When we dissolve fear by loving unconditionally, love moves up and opens the heart. When our hearts are open, we experience everything as love; there is nothing other. We've remembered who we are. We know love is the quality of our being and we experience God.

When we love unconditionally, we take responsibility for our love. It's no longer dependent on someone else— their presence, what they're doing or what they might think about our loving them. When we take responsibility for our love, love connects us to joy, not to sadness and pain. And when someone we love is dying, we don't feel like we're losing our love.

We love by loving, not by talking about it or preaching. When we love the person we're caring for unconditionally ("I love you . . . even if you're denying that you are dying . . . even if you're afraid . . . or angry . . . or cranky"), we simultaneously love ourselves without conditions. While loving others can open our hearts, to keep them open we have to love ourselves.

A common misunderstanding about love is that the heart is a container with a certain amount of love in it and we can give only that amount. This is the idea of scarcity— There's not enough love to go around. The heart isn't a container; it's more like a funnel that draws from limitless love. We can give more than we think we have and never run out. There's abundance, not scarcity. There's plenty of love for everyone.

Cruelty, greed, hate, violence and guilt are fear's distortions of love, and so are healed by love. People like Mother Teresa show us it is possible. My experience with dying people and women prisoners has taught me that **unconditional love is the only thing that truly heals.** When we love this way, we recognize who someone really is, beyond the limited set of beliefs and concepts they represent themselves to be. This heals.

One of the endless examples of the healing quality of love involved a young man with liver complications whom I visited only once. After 56 days in the hospital, no one could understand why he wouldn't let go and die. From his mother I gathered he hated himself because he'd been an alcoholic, had lost his job, and his wife and children had left him. I shared my beliefs with him — that I felt the purpose of a life-threatening disease is to help us remember who we are, Love; that he was not the personality he manifested as a result of a malfunctioning liver. I told him that at the deep level where all of us are one, I loved him. He died two hours later. The purpose of words is to love, to heal and to serve. **If you love somebody, tell them.**

Once we remember we are love, we're responsible for living that truth in our daily lives by loving unconditionally. Don't feel badly or judge yourself if you don't do it all the time. We each love in the ways we're able to at each moment. . . . We live with the paradox, "Everything is perfect" and "There's always room for improvement."

*We are love not because we love, but we love
because We Are Love.*

— After Schuon

*Love is the Nature of God. He can do nothing
other. Thus, to be God, love at each moment.*

— Angelus Silesius

The great gift the dying give us is the opportunity to remember we are love — the same gift we can give to them.

COMPASSION

Unlike charity, which has taken on the connotation of doing something for someone to absolve a sense of guilt, compassion comes from putting ourselves in the other's place and knowing, 'There by the grace of God go I.' Unlike pity, which belittles both giver and receiver, compassion makes us both stronger.

When you're with someone who's dying, it helps you both if you imagine yourself in the dying person's place. **The more we enter the world of the dying, the better we serve them and the more we learn.** We're better able to understand a need for help for dry lips, a need to talk or to be alone, even a need that may seem ridiculous to us. We learn more about our own inevitable death, and although this may bring up our fears, in the long run it will ease our fear of dying.

Love and compassion will get you through unpleasant tasks like cleaning up if the person is throwing up or has lost control of their bowels. "I could be out of control like this and know that someone has to clean up after me." In the process of putting ourselves in the other's place, we're cleaning up our own life (and death) because we're not so likely to see ourselves as separate.

Remember compassion for yourself. You deserve loving kindness as much as the dying person does. We often remember compassion for others while forgetting we're due it as well. People often feel unworthy or think that's being selfish. It's not. We're more compassionate with others when we're compassionate with ourselves.

FAITH

What is faith? Unquestioning surrender to God's will.

— Swami Ramdas

Faith is the belief of the heart in that knowledge which comes from the Unseen.

— Mohammad B. Khafif

For me, faith is trust in Life (unity, God) — moment to moment. It's trust that whatever happens is part of an orderly harmony of all that is. It's the knowing of the heart that transcends the thinking of the mind. The province of the mind is time; the province of the heart is eternity. To have faith we need the larger vision. Religious faith or beliefs may or may not play a part.

Faith allows us to feel peace and joy, even when we cannot understand what's happening in our lives. What appears to be separation, confusion or chaos is transformed in the light of unity and perfection. We all have faith to some degree or we'd stay awake at night worrying if the sun will rise again. So it seems that faith alleviates fear and gives us more freedom to live fully.

Because faith is a knowing of the heart and we can't 'know' in someone else's heart, it's useless to try to convince others to believe exactly as we do. Although we can share our experience, only their own experience can really convince them. Respect the faith of the dying even if it's unlike your own. Dying people quite often have visions or revelations that give them new or renewed faith that sustains them though the process of leaving the body (See page 292).

A person who has little faith is no worse or better than one who has lots. All of us have different ways of learning. Doubt and cynicism are valid ways to learn discrimination. Discrimination may in the long run be the ability to look so deeply into things that we eventually see unity in everything.

Generally people who have chosen a rational/ intellectual lens through which to see the world or who think being in control is the most important factor in life, find surrender (giving up control) very frightening. At one time or another, and that may be at death, everyone learns surrender. Once we surrender and see that the sky hasn't fallen in, we may choose surrender again. Then surrender becomes an act of faith, not just hollering "Uncle" because the pain was too great. Doubters and cynics gain faith from their own experience, not by accepting what someone else says they ought to believe. I call that integrity.

We have faith by choosing faith — and rechoosing it and rechoosing it. Each day, each moment, we have an opportunity to choose faith in unity or to choose to see separation. If the doubter in us comes up and says, "There may be no tomorrow," we can thank it for expressing its reality and if we want to, rechoose faith.

Faith that dying is part of the breathing in and out of the universe, and not an end, facilitates the dying process. Dying is more easily accepted by a person who feels a sunset is not the end of the sun and shedding a body is not the end of life. She or he will likely pass more quickly through the stages of dying — not skipping fear or anger but spending less time with them. Likewise, your work with a dying person is easier if you trust the rightness of the process. If you both have faith, dying can be a beautiful adventure into the little-known.

JOY

Joy is the essence of our being
The light that shines through us
The stars of our own recognition.
It's the sun in our heart that reminds us
Life is as divine on earth as it is in heaven.

It's a candle that lights the darkness.
It's given us to remind us
Who we were before we were born.
The gift is always present.
It only waits for us to acknowledge its presence.

I remember joy in seeing a shaft of light in a stairwell, being tucked in bed, loving someone and discovering they loved me, finding a solution to a tough problem, greeting my father home from the war, playing with seaweed, walking barefoot on dirt roads . . . and caring for my friends and father when they were dying.

Others may remember joy in playing in water bursting from a fire hydrant on a hot day, winning a race, painting a picture, celebrating the harvest, watching a shiny-eyed child running up the driveway, childbirth itself. Remember joyful times in your life and remember how you felt — perhaps a quiet radiance or as if a light suddenly lit up within you so bright that you could barely contain it. Joy is the spontaneous recognition of our wholeness or holiness.

Joy may be an unexpected quality of the dying process you're now living. It can be there if you allow it, not making judgements that you shouldn't feel it.

Nurture your joy. Be a joyful servant. A very good "goodbye" can be to live joy-fully.

Joy is the next step for humanity. Many people think we've been so unloving with each other and with the earth that the next step is more suffering. This is unnecessary if we see what happens in our lives and in the world, as opportunities to learn instead of as punishment. Joy is the next step if we stop running away from pain. "Joy is your sorrow unmasked" (Kahlil Gibran). Resistance causes suffering. We don't have to resist the circumstances of our lives. And even if we do, eventually we'll get so fed up with the resulting suffering that we'll holler Uncle and just let go — surrender — which opens our hearts to joy. We may kick and struggle all the way home to joy — and we'll get there because it's the natural state of our being. We can't escape joy.

If the person you're caring for is angry and looking for a target, you're likely to be one if you're radiating joy. "How can you be so happy when I'm here suffering?" We don't have to give up our joy for someone else. That's the old Guilt-Con Trick. You can explain that you're not happy they're suffering but are happy to be with them and caring for them. Nourishing your joy is part of taking care of yourself so you can live fully through a dying process.

The joy I experienced caring for John, Mary, Dad, and other dying people was unexpected. It was the joy that comes from being open to someone else and seeing yourself in them. A moment of spaciousness. A new awareness. An expansion of time. Nothing to do, nowhere to go, nobody to impress. Hearts opening. Two seemingly separate beings becoming one again.

GUILT

I told you I was sick.

—Epitaph on a tombstone

Guilt is a way we punish ourselves for learning . . . for not being perfect yet. It's a tool for manipulating ourselves and others.

Our culture's emphasis on both the past and the future promotes thinking like, "If I'd just done something differently in the past, things would be better now." There we go screeching into guilt — the Monday morning quarterback is at it again!

The underlying pattern of guilt is, "To be a good person, I should . . ." We are intrinsically good, valuable and worthy, and continue to be so, even if we never complete one "should." The established *shoulds* may not be appropriate for our growth. If you complete a *should* that is not your own choice, you are giving up your power and choosing to be a martyr or victim. A martyr is someone who thinks suffering is noble; a victim, someone who doesn't act on what their body, mind, feelings and soul tell them.

Most of us divide our lives into two piles — what we *should* do and what we *want* to do. If we do what we *should*, we feel resentful and martyred or victimized. If we do what we *want*, we feel guilty. Perhaps a little voice says over our shoulder, "Irresponsible hedonist!" And so it goes. We bounce back and forth between the piles feeling split in two . . . and joyless.

To live joyfully and die contentedly, or even just to grow, we have to stop splitting ourselves in two. The people I've observed die the most contentedly, the most peacefully, are the ones who lived the most fully — who did more of what they *wanted*, without feeling guilty, and less of what they *should*. These wise teachers helped me understand, **the only real preparation for death is to live life fully.**

An alternative to dividing ourselves in two and feeling partially alive is:

Do what you want to do, if it doesn't physically hurt others or their property, as long as you're willing to take responsibility for it. With freedom always comes responsibility. If you don't want to do something, and want to feel whole, don't do it or change your attitude.

For example, you're caring for your dying husband or wife at home. You want to get away, get out of the house, go to the movies. GO. Your feelings are the voice of your soul (consciousness) telling you what you need. They're not the tempting of some imaginary devil. When we cooperate with our feelings, the universe seems to provide the support we need. In this case, that might be someone to stay home with your husband or wife or someone to drive you to the movies.

To continue the example, you get home from the movies, the supper dishes are still in the sink and you don't feel like washing them. DON'T. In the great scope of the universe, who really cares anyway. Certainly not the dishes. Or, perhaps you consider the bigger picture and think, "I need some outer order in my life now. I don't like the kitchen a mess or waking up to dirty dishes in the morning. I want to wash them now." You're then free to wash the dishes without resentment because it was your choice, not the choice of some invisible tyrant. Perhaps washing the dishes even becomes a source of quiet relaxation or a water game.

Again, a simple change in attitude changes our lives because our attitude determines the nature of our experience. The ultimate human freedom is freedom of choice of attitude.

"But, but, but," I hear, "if everyone ran around doing what they wanted life would be chaos. People want freedom, but they also want harmony and a certain amount of order in their lives." In my experience, doing what we want, **as long as we take responsibility for it**, doesn't create chaos.

Life may feel a little chaotic initially as the people around us adjust to our getting stronger — to our ceasing to be victim to the terrible tyrant of *should* and reclaiming responsibility for our lives.

In the long run doing what we want, creates not chaos, but increased harmony, strength, integrity and respect for life. It encourages not irresponsibility but a deeper or wider understanding of the meaning of responsibility. Responsibility, to me, includes acknowledging the sacredness of all of life. We're responsible not only for our outer life, but also for our inner life, including our feelings, and following their wise guidance.

Because guilt makes us feel separate from each other and God, self-forgiveness is one of the most important things we can learn. We need to be as loving and compassionate with ourselves as we are with others — plus some, because people tend to be harder on themselves than on others. ("I forgive myself for anything I did that now seems unloving or unwise.") Each of us is who we can be in each moment of our lives and we can be open to change. Once we forgive ourselves, no one can flog us with guilt.

A dying situation often brings up feelings of guilt, although caring for someone at home helps prevent most of them. At home, there's time and a place to express whatever you now feel or have felt in the past . . . thereby avoiding later regrets and remorse from not having said or done what you might have. If you have to take someone back to the hospital or nursing home, know you are worthy even if a home dying is more than you can handle. Instead of feeling guilty, change "I should keep Grandma home" to "I'm a valuable person too and I need help."

Besides not feeling guilty yourself, be careful not to make your patient feel guilty for dying. Saying, "I could go to the store if I didn't have to wait to give you your medicine," or "Don't leave me with all this," makes a person feel guilty and/or ashamed. Be aware of one pattern guilt takes: If we feel guilty about how we've treated someone, we sometimes make them look bad to justify our treatment of them!

Being honest with the dying person helps prevent guilt. Honesty isn't ridding ourselves of guilt or getting ourselves off the hook at the expense of someone else.

Guilt is also prevented by asking the patient what she or he wants whenever possible.

As I mentioned before, there's always the possibility that you'll do or give something to the person that will result in their death before you expect it. If you've earlier agreed to do your best, and acknowledged you can't know everything, you may prevent useless guilt. Remember my giving the "liver flush" to Mary? Spare yourself.

Be compassionate with yourself. Forgive yourself . . . over and over again. Instead of feeling guilty, congratulate yourself for outgrowing some old thought or feeling that is no longer appropriate for you . . . for increasing your wisdom.

Guilt, along with blame and punishment, are ideas we need to let go of if we want to live joyfully . . . or even survive.

HUMOR

There are no tortuous roads to climb, for an instant of humor transports a soul into another world, a bright hopeful world where anything is possible.

— A Deva

A friend found W.C. Fields on his deathbed reading the Bible and asked him why he was reading it. Fields answered, "I'm looking for loopholes."

Humor can cause a smile, a tiny chuckle or a big love-full belly laugh. Enjoy it. It's a source of deep nourishment for your voyage. Humor gives perspective to a world where it is *seriously* needed. If we can laugh together, we may be able to cry together and more. We can become one again. Whenever possible, try to see the humor in the situation you're facing now. As long as humor comes from your heart, it can't be harmful. Only cynicism and sarcasm have a destructive side.

Remember Charlie Chaplin? Remember how he increased our compassion for one another and reminded us of our common humanity? We laughed because he lightly showed us our conflicts and our pomposity. Laughing can be a great equalizer; it opens the heart.

Humor usually helps unless we use it to escape our feelings. A joke is a new vision, not just a way to mask pain or uncomfortableness.

Dying may be emotionally confusing for everyone involved. Humor helps us detach for a moment so we can

see it more objectively. Humor helps the dying person deal
with the frustration of needing help and not being able to do
things she or he took for granted before. It helps make their
situation seem less overwhelming and helps maintain a feeling of naturalness in the home. It releases blocked energies
so we can see the larger picture. The details of life don't bog
us down nearly so much if we laugh at ourselves, alone and
together. We're really in a very leaky life-boat and we might
as well enjoy it!

The belly laugh we had when Mary told us we were
"rushing" her loosened the tension of many heavy days. The
laugh we had when my sister told the priest that Dad was
"somewhat Catholic" opened our hearts and released our
fear. It would have been difficult to support them until they
died without the lightening-up quality, the levity, of humor.

At a very deep level, humor heals.

Remember those funny old family stories together . . .
like the time Uncle Willie got caught . . . or Grandma found
out . . .

Do you know why angels can fly? They take themselves
lightly.

ANGER

*A bull in a small pen is likely to kick the fence
down.*
A bull in a large meadow has room to move.

—Stephen Levine

Anger is an escape valve for the hurts and frustrations we pick up in the process of being human. We feel frustrated and hurt when we're attached to someone or something (life, for example) and things aren't going the way we think they should. ("I'm angry because I hurt because Dad shouldn't die.") Anger is a step on the way to surrender, a healthy sign as long as we don't hold on to it.

The amount of anger (or rage or violence) we feel is a measure of just how much hurt and frustration we're holding in. We can defuse anger by recognizing and expressing the hurt and frustration underneath it. We can transform it into compassion if we're willing to acknowledge we feel it. Many of us learned as children to hide our anger for fear of being punished for it. Now sometimes it's hard for us to recognize and/or acknowledge we feel it.

We transform anger into compassion by accepting that feeling angry is OK, by feeling and expressing the underlying hurt or frustration, and by accepting life as it is instead of holding on to how it should be. For example, the anger I first felt when Dad was dying was transformed to compassion only after I'd thrown some plates and rocks and cried, and changed "he shouldn't die" to "he is dying."

It's perfectly natural to feel anger when you're supporting the dying process of someone you love. Your sense of loss, abandonment, insecurity, feeling that this dying is taking too long or that the person should feel grateful, etc., can bring up anger. You may feel anger when someone says they want to live and you feel they're not really trying. What they may really be saying is not "I want to live," but "I'm afraid to die."

Sometimes with all this talk of acceptance and surrender, we feel angry if someone doesn't accept they're dying.

Living Fully With Dying

Remember that people can die with dignity and be angry down to the wire. Perhaps that's a test for us. Do we really want them to die with dignity, their own way?

Let your anger out. The universe can absorb it. Our bodies can't. By not expressing anger we hang on to control, and the price is high. We can't see very clearly from inside hurt or anger. Unexpressed anger can turn into nagging, irritability, depression, high blood pressure and other serious illnesses or a big blow up later.

Freeing anger — accepting and expressing it — helps you and the dying person prepare for your loss and can help you both move toward acceptance. A dying person may not feel free to let go and die if people around are holding on to anger.

People often assume that expressing anger and hurting others are one and the same. It may be more hurtful not to express it. Protecting someone from anger says we don't trust them, that we know what's good for them. We're taking responsibility for their feelings and response, and assuming they're too dumb or unperceptive to recognize we're angry. In the long run, these things are a lot more hurtful than saying, "I'm angry with you. I love you and I'm angry."

If it's not appropriate for you to let out your anger in front of others, or you're afraid of the backlog of anger inside you, go off alone and bellow, throw balls, beat pillows, etc. If you have a wise friend or counselor, express the anger with them. Elisabeth Kübler-Ross suggests taking a foot and a half of rubber hose and beating on something you can't hurt until you can't beat anymore. I use the side of the bathtub. I prefer cleaning off black rubber marks to cutting myself off from joy later.

It's all right for people, even children, to see us angry. Children need to know anger exists, what it's about, that it's OK to feel it, and how to deal with it. You can explain to children that you aren't angry at them or the person who's dying, but angry because you're frustrated and hurt. Let them know you can love someone and be angry at the same time. Encourage them to let out their anger in a way that doesn't physically hurt themselves or others. Maybe you could go off somewhere together and throw rocks. We lessen the amount of violence in the world by encouraging our children and everyone else to express their feelings.

I've heard people say about someone dying, "I'm angry because I love him so much." My response is, "Be angry. I know you love him. I know you hurt." Hurt was probably the immediate cause of the anger, fear and loving conditionally the deeper causes (loving the person if she or he is here with me like I want).

We're moving toward loving unconditionally. "I love him including his need to die."

FEAR

All know that the drops merge into the ocean
But few know that the ocean merges into the drops.

—Kabir

Dying and death may bring up more fear than any other circumstance of our lives. Supporting someone dying at

242

home is an opportunity to face and accept this fear so we can transform it — and open wider our hearts.

Fear makes us feel alone, like separate drops that are not part of the ocean. It's caused by believing we are separate. Once we mistakenly believed we were alone and separate, we made judgements that confirmed our belief. Judgements are limiting beliefs that we have projected into the future which prevent us from living without fear *now*. Our judgements prevent us from experiencing the underlying unity of everything that is.

For example, if your experience was: When I was seven my aunt died and I felt hurt and confused. Nobody would answer my questions and Mommy and Daddy acted strange. The judgement probably was, *"Dying is terrible"* or *"I'm afraid of death."* Even more likely, you didn't have a chance to experience that first mysterious death for yourself.

Parents' or friends' judgements — *"Death is frightening"* or *"Dying is the worst thing that can happen"* — were communicated verbally or non-verbally, leaving no possibility for you to experience dying and death for yourself. This is the way fear is passed from generation to generation. Your response to death from then on was probably controlled by a judgement you made at an early age.

And all the judgements we've made in the past rule our lives until we consciously change them.

Descriptions, on the other hand, are not projected onto the future; they leave us free to experience the future as it comes. We can change a judgement — "I'm afraid of dying" — to a description. "Once my aunt died and I was afraid. I don't know how I'll feel the next time." Or, "I know a lot of people are afraid of dying. I don't know how I feel because I haven't experienced it." Changing a judgement to a description leaves our energies free for the freshness of each new moment.

Fear creates what it fears. We attract everything that lies in our energy field. We attract what we fear in order to give us an opportunity to look at, understand and release it. I was afraid of hospitals, blood, shots, sickness and death, so I was drawn to work with dying people in hospitals to transform those fears. Fear isn't "bad". It's just another teacher pointing the way home to more love.

If you feel afraid of dying or of anything else, don't over-ride the feeling by insisting, "I shouldn't feel it." Our feelings and instincts help us select the experiences that are right for us; if we ignore them we can end up with situations or people we don't like. Fear means we're not yet ready to accept an experience. Forcing an experience on yourself is not loving all of yourself unconditionally. As long as you try to force yourself to accept something you're not ready to accept, you'll feel separate and will find it difficult to accept other people and their feelings unconditionally.

When you feel afraid, feel the fear and don't assume that's all of who you are. It may help to say, "Oh, there's that part of me that believes I'm separate . . . that *part* that's afraid of dying . . . of taking risks . . . of snakes" instead of "I'm afraid of dying . . . etc." Send love to the part of you that feels separate and fearful and look for the judgement that confirmed it. Words like good, bad, right, wrong, always, never, can't and should often indicate a judgement. When you understand the judgement, you can release it by forgiving yourself for making it, and change it to a description. The next time you run into the same old fear, experiment with focusing on love instead of the fear. Over a period of time you'll find there are fewer things you're afraid of and you'll attract into your life fewer things you don't want.

We don't need fear. Fear is the absence of love. It can, however, show us where our love is needed. "But," someone says, "fear warns me of danger!" Isn't it awareness or instinct for survival, not fear, that warns us of possible danger? "But I have to teach my children to fear knives and cars for their own safety." Teaching with fear is one way. Another is to use love and patience to help children understand that knives are neither good nor bad. They're useful to cut sandwiches and if used carelessly, they can cut us. We can help children understand potential dangers like knives and cars, and trust their survival instincts, or we can surround them with a miasma of our own fear. Using love and patience we can help children understand dying without making it a fearful experience.

As you support a dying process, you may experience some of the fears of the dying person and some unique to being the one who remains behind in the everyday physical world. Your fear about what life will be like without this person you love, particularly in a husband and wife relationship, is usually matched by his or her concern for you. How will you manage the children or the business? Talking together about fears and planning possible solutions and alternatives eases the adjustment to life without the other person. Talking together may also help a dying person accept death who feels afraid or guilty about deserting the family.

Your fear of loneliness matches their fear of loneliness. "Here I am alone dealing with the daily problems of life"/ "Here I am alone, dying." Share those feelings. "I hurt because you're leaving me."/"I hurt because I'm leaving you." Isolation, considered a major problem in the dying process, is greatly alleviated when your hearts are open to understanding each other's fears and pain. Facing your fear or resentment now— "I'm not strong enough to stay here alone" or "I hate you for leaving me with this"— prevents remorse later.

Worry comes from fear about what's happening now or what may happen in the future. Worry goes on inside our heads. If you feel worry coming up, take a few deep breaths, relax, breathe love into your heart, see if you're doing the best you know, and let go of the rest. This will give space for a new idea or solution to come to you. Or it just may be that whatever you're worrying about needs to happen to give someone an opportunity to learn from it.

Remember, at each moment in our lives we choose, consciously or unconsciously, love or fear. And what we choose determines what we experience.

EMOTIONAL PAIN AND SUFFERING

The amount of emotional pain and suffering around a dying is directly related to the fear around it. Fear makes us resist what's happening or may happen in our lives and the resistance causes emotional pain. When we stop resisting, stop seeing the world as we think it should be, emotional pain lifts. Suffering is a habit of pain, sadness or hurt. All of these are prevented and healed by accepting life as it is.

Pain is a useful message that something in our lives is not working. It's no longer needed when we pay attention to it, locate the resistance that caused it and let go of it. When I was fighting against my dad's dying, I was in terrible pain. Holding on to him was obviously making me miserable. When I let go and accepted he was dying, I no longer hurt and was free to enjoy the time we had together.

Each journey to acceptance is unique; a lot of fear and arrogance made mine long and painful. Arrogance closes us to parts of life. Humility, being open to everything, makes the journey a lot easier.

While we're on our way, we need to be open to and accept our pain. Resisting pain just causes more pain; the pain is prolonged and becomes suffering.

If we grieve right away when we hurt, our pain is not stockpiled and doesn't become suffering.

If you're thinking, "Well, I don't want to hurt but I do," accept what you feel. You can't change the hurt until you acknowledge you feel it. Feel it. Express it in your own way. Love the *part* of you that hurts. Release the *should* that caused it. (Some typical *shoulds* are: "He shouldn't die," "She should love me," "They should do things my way," "Life should be happier," and "Pain, starvation, pollution and war shouldn't exist.")

If we accept our pain, we can accept someone else's pain. If we run away from our own, we'll run away from another's. Although we may be able to protect someone for awhile, in the long run it's impossible to protect anyone from emotional pain. We need it and create it until we accept life as it is.

We often deny people the opportunity to learn surrender when we try to 'jolly' them out of their pain. Have you ever felt like hollering at someone who was denying your pain? "There's no reason to feel bad." "You shouldn't feel so sad." "I know exactly how you feel." "By next week . . .

month . . . year you won't even remember." When someone says these things, people often respond with anger, which may distract them from feeling their pain and learning from it. Give the people you love a chance to feel their pain so they can learn from it and let go of it.

Pain is the breaking of the shell that encloses your understanding.

— Kahlil Gibran

Taking on someone else's pain is as useless as denying it. Then two people, not just one, are suffering and the world is darker. Every time a heart is glad, it increases the light in the universe.

Taking on someone else's pain is one way to avoid feeling our own. (Something I did for most of my life.) Only when we clean out our own reservoir of pain can we support someone in pain without losing energy (burning out). What, then, can you do for someone who's hurting emotionally? Have compassion and share love. "I know you hurt and I love you." Once the person has felt the pain, if they're ready to release it, perhaps you can help them see what they're resisting and suggest alternatives.

God doesn't pin a medal on us because we suffer. There may be a part of ourselves that has an investment in our suffering. "If I suffer, I'm a good person." "I get a lot of attention when I suffer." "If I suffer, I don't have to take responsibility for my life." There may be a friend or relative who has an investment in our suffering. "If you were a good husband, you'd be suffering because your wife is dying." **We express love by loving, not by suffering.**

248

Suffering and pain are no longer an indispensable part of the human experience. They're optional. No one forces us to resist the circumstances of our lives. Pain can help us to learn and grow and it's possible to learn instead by awareness. We can look for patterns that might cause us pain before we hurt or when we feel a little edgy. Waiting until we're in agony before we pay attention is a hard way to learn!

It's possible to make a decision now, at this moment, in your heart to accept the circumstances of your life and you'd never have to feel emotional pain again (unless you started resisting again). This may not be probable, but for me, just knowing it's possible is comforting. As a friend of mine says about the idea of being free from pain, "That's scarier than infinity!"

*   *   *   *   *

Before John and Mary died at home, I thought dying was mostly about fear and suffering. There was much less of both than I'd projected. I found that sharing their dyings and Dad's, and facing my own fear and pain, opened my heart wider. I understand now that fear and pain have, all along, been teachers about love and joy.

I know in my heart the day will come when we no longer need our old teachers. You and I, each in our own way and our own time, will graduate from the school of fear and pain and live joyfully on earth. I believe this dying you're sharing brings your graduation day closer.

I celebrate your journey and I thank you.

All distinctions are false: The moment you say, "This is good and that is bad," you have divided life and killed it.

— Lao-Tse

CHAPTER 10

LEGAL CONSIDERATIONS

The legal considerations around a pending death reflect the degree of complication in a person's life. They relate principally to how a person wants to distribute the property she or he has collected. The laws governing property distribution are complicated and vary from state to state. I can most usefully familiarize you with some of the terms and procedures you may meet.

Help the dying person get their business affairs in order. If you're not asked, ask if he or she needs help. It's often useful to have a power of attorney, a legal document that gives you authority to do things in someone else's name. This authority, which includes the right to sign the person's name, can be general or for a specific project only.

All fifty states now recognize what is called a *durable* power of attorney. An *ordinary* power of attorney often becomes invalid if you become incompetent. A durable power of attorney remains effective, or in some states becomes effective, if you become incompetent.

Giving someone the power and responsibility of carrying out our wishes if we're no longer able is an important decision. You need someone you trust not only to do business transactions for you, but also to make medical decisions if you can't. Consider who might be appropriate and discuss your wishes with them.

Because state laws vary and because empowering others to make decisions for us is so important, ask a lawyer to advise and assist you in drawing up a durable power of attorney. It can be a useful addition to a living will (page 261) to insure that you're allowed to die with dignity — your way.

A joint bank account is also useful so you'll have cash available if you live in a state where bank accounts or other assets are 'frozen' (can't be used) after a death. Locate, if they exist, the dying person's will, insurance policies, safety deposit box and keys, deeds to all properties and/or a burial plot, all securities, numbers of all bank accounts, automobile titles, pension plans, profit sharing plans, trusts, copies of income tax returns, any power of attorney, Individual Retirement Account (IRAs), mortgage papers and/or charge accounts.

WILLS

A will is a legal document expressing how we want to distribute our material possessions and provide for our heirs upon our death. In legal-ese, a person who dies with a will dies *testate*, or without a will, *intestate*.

Legal Considerations

Some of the advantages of making a will are choosing the person we want to administer distribution of our property (called the executor or personal representative), choosing who gets what (in case we doubt our survivors will follow our stated wishes), naming who will have custody of minor children, providing for an incapacitated adult, lessening the possibility of future legal disputes over property ownership. A will can also be a love letter to our heirs.

A person with small children and no spouse will probably die more peacefully having made clear arrangements for their care. Instead of a blood relative, many people name as guardian the person most likely to love and guide the child to adulthood in a way consistent with the parent's views.

If the *estate* (what we leave behind) is small, a will is not always necessary, although generally advisable. Property jointly owned, joint or "pay on death" bank accounts, insurance proceeds, Series E Bonds, and death benefits like Social Security, VA and union benefits *bypass* a will, but are counted for tax purposes.

If a person has a large estate, estate planning can save money in federal and state taxes. It's a complicated business which requires a good lawyer who specializes in estate planning. Finding a suitable lawyer may be difficult. Ask someone knowledgeable, such as a trust officer of a bank, an accountant or your local bar association, to recommend one or more lawyers they consider qualified in this area.

A simple will takes a lawyer from one to four hours to prepare by the time she or he talks with you, drafts the will and has it typed. Fees range from $50 to $100 or more per hour, so a simple will may cost between $75 and $300. Before hiring a lawyer, ask how much he or she charges. If after the initial consultation you decide to retain the lawyer, reach a clear agreement on fees. If your income is low, check with a publicly supported legal clinic or your local bar association may have a plan for no-cost or reduced fee services.

A VALID WILL

One of the main reasons to have a lawyer help write a will is to insure that it's valid (will stand up to a legal challenge). What constitutes a valid will differs from state to state. For many of us it seems simple. It's a piece of paper Grandpa writes saying to whom he wants to leave what. But the laws that determine the validity of a will place more importance on *form* than on content. A will must include property distribution, name an executor, and be signed and witnessed by two (sometimes three) people who sign in the presence of the author (testator) and each other.

A will may be partially or completely invalidated for many reasons:

1. The author was *incompetent* to make a will. (What legally constitutes incompetent varies by state.)

2. The author was under *undue influence* by other people. (Someone influenced the author to write the will in their favor.)

3. The will is not executed with the *formalities* required. (Each state requires formalities such as a certain number of witnesses, author must sign each page of the will, witnesses attest they know it's a will they're signing.)

Most wills are invalidated because of the formalities.

We have enormous latitude in the *provisions* of our wills, but not in the *form*. The formalities make good business for lawyers.

HOLOGRAPHIC WILLS

A holographic will is one that is signed, dated and written *entirely by hand by the author*. It must include disposal of property and name an executor. No witness is required. It's recognized as valid in the following states: Alaska, Arizona, Arkansas, California, Idaho, Kentucky, Louisiana, Mississippi, Montana, Nevada, North Carolina, North Dakota, Oklahoma, Pennsylvania, South Dakota, Tennessee, Texas, Utah, Virginia, West Virginia, Wyoming, Maryland (if written by someone in the armed services) and New York (if written by a soldier, sailor or mariner.)

If you live in one of these states and don't own property in another you can write your own will, although a lawyer would not recommend that you do that. A person who has property in more than one state needs a lawyer. In some of the states listed, it may be possible to type or dictate a holographic will. Check with the court in your area that has probate jurisdiction.

NO WILL

A lot of people die intestate, without a will. When people die without a will, their property is distributed according to the *law of intestate succession* or the *law of descent and distribution* of the state in which they live. Property jointly owned, life insurance proceeds and death benefits bypass the law of intestate succession.

Under laws of intestate succession, property generally goes first to the surviving husband or wife, then to their children and then to other blood relatives. In community property states, property goes first to the children then to the husband or wife. If you care who gets your possessions, it's a good idea to find out the law in your state so you don't create problems for your survivors. A legal clinic or lawyer can help you.

In some states, for example, if you have a wife and one minor child, the law distributes half of the estate to your wife and half to the child. If the child is a minor, the court will name a guardian, who is normally the surviving parent. But the guardian may have to put up a bond (post money) and *must* get permission from the court to spend any of the child's money, and must file an accounting with the court each year. This means time, money and nuisance for the guardian which can be avoided by writing a will, perhaps with trust provisions. *Trust* is an agreement between you and a financial institution or person to handle money or property for you.

For the enjoyment of it and/or to avoid dealing with lawyers and courts, some people simply give away their property before they die. Legally we must file a federal gift tax return on all gifts given to one person worth over $10,000 per year (or $20,000 per year if the spouse agrees). Each year we can give tax-free gifts of this size to as many people as we choose. If one gives larger gifts and dies before filing the tax return, the executor is responsible for filing it.

THE EXECUTOR OR PERSONAL REPRESENTATIVE

The executor or personal representative is the person named by the writer of the will to take charge of his or her financial affairs and distribute property after death. If there's no will, an administrator-executor is named by the court. The work of the executor may take up to a year or two if the estate is large or complicated. She or he is paid by the will writer's estate for the work done. The payment varies by state; it's 'a reasonable fee' or a percentage (1% to 5%) of the estate.

The following discussion of the legal responsibilities of the executor is excerpted from *Law for the Layman* by attorney George G. Coughlin:

1. **He (she) may take the assets of the estate into his (her) possession.** (This means the executor takes control of the assets of the estate and obtains full information about all the deceased's belongings. She opens a bank account in the name of the estate and transfers the deceased's accounts to her name as executor. She collects the proceeds from insurance policies if they're payable to the estate (otherwise the money goes directly to the beneficiaries) and looks after stocks and bonds. Executors need to keep detailed records of all financial proceedings.)

2. **He (she) may sell and liquidate personal property and convert the assets of the estate into case.** (If cash is needed to pay debts, the executor can sell personal property and real estate.)

3. **He (she) may pay debts and funeral and administration expenses.** (This involves placing a notice in

257

newspapers that any creditors of the deceased present their claims. If state and federal taxes are due, the executor is responsible for paying them.)

4. **He (she) may distribute the estate to the beneficiaries.** (After all debts, expenses and taxes have been paid.)

PROBATE

Probate is the name used by the courts for the administration of an estate which includes opening and closing it. It documents legal ownership of inherited property. According to Phillip Stern, author of *Lawyers on Trial*, "Probate is up to 100 times more expensive here than in England, and that's because England 'delawyered' the process. In this country we end up paying two and a half to three times as much in fees to probate attorneys as we do in funeral expenses."

Probate is necessary if a person dies with a will, or with property such as real estate, stocks and bonds, bank accounts, etc., that must be passed on according to the laws of intestate succession. It's not necessary if a person leaves no will and only owns property of the sort that bypasses the law of intestate succession (like earlier mentioned jointly owned property, joint or "pay on death" bank accounts, insurance proceeds, Series E Bonds and death benefits like Social Security, VA and union benefits.) Legally, personal effects and clothing may be subject to probate, but in practice they're generally divided among family and friends.

When someone dies who has a will, the person named in it as executor or a lawyer versed in probate take it and a copy of the death certificate to the local court with probate jurisdiction and file for probate. The judge then decides if the will is valid. If someone dies without a will and there is property that doesn't bypass probate, the closest relative, friend or their lawyer takes the death certificate to the court and files to be named administrator. The judge decides who's the proper person for the job. Whoever is appointed may be required to post a bond to guarantee they'll do a good job and won't run off with the loot.

Once you file, the court issues **letters testamentary** if there's a will, or **letters of administration** if not. The 'letters' state that the executor accepts responsibility for collecting assets, paying debts and taxes, distributing the property and closing the estate.

The executor lists the assets collected, the debts, inheritance taxes and the share of each beneficiary. If there are no disputes, the property is distributed to the beneficiaries; they acknowledge receiving their share and the estate is closed. If there are disputes, the estate can be settled by written agreement among the disputing parties, or the executor and the people involved go before the judge for a decision. Upon proof of distribution, the estate can be closed.

TAXES

Depending on the size of the estate, state and/or federal taxes may have to be paid. Taxes vary from state to state. A few impose none.

As of 1987, a federal tax return must be filed on any **gross estate** that exceeds $600,000. **Gross estate** means everything someone owned, or retained some control over, and even includes some property such as insurance that bypass probate. The tax return must be filed and is due within 9 months of the death, although you can apply for an extension.

Federal estate tax laws are complicated to begin with, and they have recently undergone major revisions, so check with the IRS. If there is an estate of any size, you should consult an attorney or accountant.

What estate planning is really about, besides seeing that a person's property is well managed and properly distributed, is *saving money on taxes*. Tax accountants, bank trust officers and estate-planning lawyers are the people to consult if the finances involved warrant it. They know, for example, how to use trust, marital deductions and similar devices to 'split' an estate so that upon the death of the husband or wife, federal estate taxes will be at a lower rate or exempt from taxation. Many of us who aren't knowledgeable about taxes think owning everything in common when we're married is the loving way to handle property. However, for people with a large estate, joint ownership may be unwise because it increases the estate taxes that may be due in the future.

Two publications available at your local IRS office may be helpful: #559, *Tax Information for Survivors, Executors and Administrators*, and #448, *A Guide to Federal Estate and Gift Taxation*.

LIVING WILLS

Many people are now *remembering* that each of us has the right to determine the nature of our own death. Since 1976, all the states, except Kentucky, Massachusetts, Michigan, Minnesota, Nebraska, New Jersey, New York, Ohio, Pennsylvania, Rhode Island, South and North Dakota, have passed Living Will Laws—sometimes called Natural Death or Right to Die Laws. In 1986, all the excepted states, minus North Dakota, have proposed laws. These laws establish clear legal guidelines to protect our right to refuse medical procedures that serve only to prolong dying. They also protect doctors from liability for acting in accordance with our wishes.

The laws provide for a Living Will—a document we can sign in advance instructing that, in event of a terminal condition, life sustaining procedures be withheld or withdrawn. Later, when we're terminally ill, written verification of the terminal illness by one, sometimes two doctors is required.

It's encouraging that many people are reclaiming an age-old right that had been given away to doctors, lawyers and courts. None of them has the right to say how long a dying person or their family must suffer, or that a family potentially must go broke. A Living Will relieves both family and doctors of responsibility for making the ultimate decision about somebody else's life. By signing one, we perhaps give our loved ones a gift of peace of mind.

In a home dying, sustaining life artificially usually is not a problem. It might become one if a person had to go into a hospital for a specific treatment and their condition worsened or they went into a coma. Even if a person plans to die at home, making a Living Will can be useful.

I suggest making a Living Will even if you live in a state that has not yet passed a Living Will law. In the event of a legal, ethical or medical question about treatment, it serves as clear evidence of your wishes. It gives you a voice if you can't speak for yourself later. Doctors feel safer about not being sued for malpractice if there's a Living Will.

In states that do not yet have Living Will Laws, there have been court decisions affirming that these wills are legally enforceable under certain circumstances. There are a growing number of cases that affirm a patient's right to refuse treatment, whether or not this results in death. Some legal advisors believe that Living Wills are enforceable in all states under the common-law right to bodily self-determination and the constitutional right to privacy.

If you are Catholic, you may already be aware that the June 1980 Declaration of Euthanasia concluded: "When inevitable death is imminent, it is permitted in conscience to take the decision to refuse forms of treatment that would only secure a precarious and burdensome prolongation of life." The United Methodist Church says, "We assert the right of every person to die in dignity without efforts to prolong terminal illnesses merely because the technology is available to do so." The Central Conference of American Rabbis said, "The conclusion from the spirit of Jewish Law is that while you may not do anything to hasten death, you may, under special circumstances of suffering and helplessness allow death to come."

Concern for Dying, a non-profit educational council, researched what effect a Living Will might have on a life insurance policy. They reported that signing a Living Will would not invalidate any life insurance policy and would not be construed as an intent to commit suicide. Insurance companies stand to save lots of money if people are not kept alive artificially for months or years in hospitals or nursing homes.

States that have passed Living Will Laws prescribe a particular form for the will. To get your state's form, ask your lawyer or write to The Society for the Right to Die (SRD) or Concern for Dying. (See Appendix A for their addresses.)

If your state hasn't passed such a law, either group will send you a sample will like the ones shown here. Both groups have worked hard to protect our right to die with dignity. I encourage you to send a small contribution with your request.

Some state forms include space to name a proxy to make decisions for you when you're unable. (They're similar to the samples shown here.) If you don't have a durable power of attorney and your state form doesn't include naming a proxy, consider signing a Living Will like the samples. You could attach it to your state form as a further, although not legally binding, expression of your wishes.

The will must be witnessed by at least two adults unrelated to you and notarized to show the seriousness with which you regard it. Update the will every year by redating it and initialing the new date. Living wills can be revoked at any time you change your mind.

Once you sign a will, to be sure it's enforced, **let everyone close to you know how you feel.** Talk with your doctor or clergyperson and give him or her a copy. Tell your family and be sure they know where it's located. One elderly woman taped hers up on the bathroom wall and initialed it frequently to make sure she wouldn't be kept alive against her will. If you doubt that your family or doctor will follow your wishes, talk with a lawyer.

LIVING WILL DECLARATION

To My Family, Doctors, and All Those Concerned with My Care

I,_____, being of sound mind, make this statement as a directive to be followed if for any reason I become unable to participate in decisions regarding my medical care.

I direct that life-sustaining procedures should be withheld or withdrawn if I have an illness, disease or injury, or experience extreme mental deterioration, such that there is no reasonable expectation of recovering or regaining a meaningful quality of life.

These life-sustaining procedures that may be withheld or withdrawn include, but are not limited to:

SURGERY   ANTIBIOTICS   CARDIAC RESUSCITATION
RESPIRATORY SUPPORT   ARTIFICIALLY ADMINISTERED FEEDING AND FLUIDS

I further direct that treatment be limited to comfort measures only, even if they shorten my life.

You may delete any provision above by drawing a line through it and adding your initials.

Other personal instructions:

These directions express my legal right to refuse treatment. Therefore, I expect my family, doctors, and all those concerned with my care to regard themselves as legally and morally bound to act in accord with my wishes, and in so doing to be free from any liability for having followed my directions.

Signed_____Date_____

Witness_____ Witness_____

PROXY DESIGNATION CLAUSE

If you wish, you may use this section to designate someone to make treatment decisions if you are unable to do so. Your Living Will Declaration will be in effect even if you have not designated a proxy.

I authorize the following person to implement my Living Will Declaration by accepting, refusing and/or making decisions about treatment and hospitalization:

Name _____

Address _____

If the person I have named above is unable to act on my behalf, I authorize the following person to do so:

Name _____

Address _____

I have discussed my wishes with these persons and trust their judgment on my behalf.

Signed _____ Date _____

Witness _____ Witness _____

Courtesy of Society for the Right to Die, 250 West 57 Street, New York, NY 10107.

My Living Will
To My Family, My Physician, My Lawyer and All Others Whom It May Concern

Death is as much a reality as birth, growth, maturity and old age—it is the one certainty of life. If the time comes when I can no longer take part in decisions for my own future, let this statement stand as an expression of my wishes and directions, while I am still of sound mind.

If at such a time the situation should arise in which there is no reasonable expectation of my recovery from extreme physical or mental disability, I direct that I be allowed to die and not be kept alive by medications, artificial means or "heroic measures." I do, however, ask that medication be mercifully administered to me to alleviate suffering even though this may shorten my remaining life.

This statement is made after careful consideration and is in accordance with my strong convictions and beliefs. I want the wishes and directions here expressed carried out to the extent permitted by law. Insofar as they are not legally enforceable, I hope that those to whom this Will is addressed will regard themselves as morally bound by these provisions.

(Optional specific provisions to be made in this space)

DURABLE POWER OF ATTORNEY (optional)

I hereby designate _____ to serve as my attorney-in-fact for the purpose of making medical treatment decisions. This power of attorney shall remain effective in the event that I become incompetent or otherwise unable to make such decisions for myself.

Optional Notarization:

"Sworn and subscribed to

before me this _____ day

of _____, 19_____."

_____
Notary Public
(seal)

Signed _____

Date _____

Witness _____

_____
Address

Witness _____

_____
Address

Copies of this request have been given to _____

_____   _____

(Optional) My Living Will is registered with Concern for Dying (No._____)

Distributed by Concern for Dying, 250 West 57th Street, New York, NY 10107 (212) 246-6962

BODY DONATIONS

In recent years all states have enacted or revised Anatomical Gift Laws, which permit people to donate all or parts of their bodies to hospitals, research or educational institutions. If you or the dying person want to give your body or parts of it, tell your family, write a letter stating your wishes and fill out a Uniform Donor Card or other such document. Call a medical school or hospital to get exact details for your state and area. Ask if your age and physical condition are suitable. The presence of cancer or a communicable disease disqualify a transplant donor, except for corneas.

Uniform Donor Cards are available from some medical schools. A number of states include them on the backs of driver's licenses. (See Appendix A for other sources.)

UNIFORM DONOR CARD

OF _____

Print or type name of donor

In the hope that I may help others, I hereby make this anatomical gift, if medically acceptable, to take effect upon my death. The words and marks below indicate my desires.

I give: (a)_____ any needed organs or parts

          (b)_____ only the following organs or parts

_____

Specify the organs or parts

for the purposes of transplantation, therapy, medical research or education;

          (c)_____ my body for anatomical study if needed.

Limitations or special wishes, if any: _____

Signed by the donor and the following two witnesses in the presence of each other:

_____   _____
Signature of Donor   Date of Birth of Donor

_____   _____
Date Signed   City & State

_____   _____
Witness   Witness

This is a legal document under the Uniform Anatomical Gift Act or similar laws.

For further information consult your local memorial society or:

Continental Association of Funeral & Memorial Societies
1828 L Street, N.W. Washington, D.C. 20036

Nothing is more or less sacred than anything else.
Everything and everyone are equally divine.

—From a meditation on the Christ

CHAPTER 11

HEALING

At the core of healing lies a deep mystery that is to be respected. It is the mystery of transformation and regeneration and is different for each person. It is the mystery of balance and harmony, and at the core of this mystery lies the universal Heart.

—Satya Miriam
Healing is Transformation

I share with you my beliefs about the nature of our being, of disease and of healing. Throughout the world increasing numbers of people are coming to the same or similar realizations. They're departures from a lot of old assumptions.

Each of us is a whole composed of body, mind, feelings and soul. Body, mind and feelings are sometimes called the 'body', or personality of the soul. The word 'personality' comes from the Latin persona, which means 'mask'. Soul is consciousness, spirit, or God, individualized.

269

Disease (dis-ease) indicates a disharmony within the whole. The body is the last part of us in which dis-ease manifest. It appears first as a disharmony between the soul and mind or feelings. To heal, we have to understand and treat ourselves as whole beings within a physical and social environment.

At present, most medical doctors are trained to treat the symptoms of disease rather than to support an individual's own process of healing. Penicillin and aspirin, for example, are not going to heal a person's real dis-ease. At best they buy time by curing symptoms so one can discover and heal the real imbalance. Splints may help cure a leg broken in a car accident, but they won't heal the consciousness that caused the person to be in the accident. Curing symptoms and healing dis-ease aren't the same thing.

The more we've given away the responsibility for our health to doctors, the sicker we've become. It's not the doctors' fault. We're the ones who got addicted to the body as our main point of reference and mistakenly looked for the source of healing outside of ourselves. **The source of healing is within.** The work of medical doctors can be very valuable, but has limits because it works only on physical symptoms, or, in the case of psychiatrists, with mental and emotional symptoms. **Real healing must take place at ALL levels of our being.**

Healing, righting the energy balance within us, is a process that requires our active participation. Human beings are dense, somewhat solidified energy. And imbalance in this energy results in disharmony or disease. It can be a great adventure to find the source of the imbalance and to heal ourselves. The dying person you are supporting can certainly be healed — even if his or her body cannot be cured or saved. Sometimes the fundamental imbalance is healed and the body dies anyway.

Many people have lost faith in prayers (an important healing aid) when they prayed for someone to be healed and she or he died. Their prayer was heard. Perhaps they didn't recognize the answer. The disharmony may have been healed and it was time to leave an uninhabitable body. Prayer is useful if we avoid praying for what we want and pray instead for whatever is *the highest good* for ourselves and others. We're fortunate if we know the divine plan for ourselves, let alone for someone else.

We are either victims of our diseases or we are responsible for them. I believe we're responsible. This is much more hopeful and useful than thinking we're victims. If we're victims, disease is out of our control and we can't do anything about it except try to cure the symptoms. On the other hand, if we're responsible (accept our dis-ease as ours), it is possible to heal ourselves.

The principal pitfall when we begin to take responsibility for our dis-ease is guilt. Who needs to feel sick and guilty too? For many years my body was sick with one thing or another. For four of those years after I was introduced to holistic healing and began to take responsibility for my sickness, I felt like a spiritual leper. I didn't want to see anyone because I was sure they'd see I was sick and know something was wrong with me spiritually. I felt sick and guilty — and I was afraid to talk with anyone about it.

Spare yourself! There's *nothing* to feel guilty about. The body is a sacred vehicle and messenger. If the postman brought you a letter that contained information you didn't want to hear, you wouldn't berate the postman or feel guilty. When our bodies give us a message that something is not working, instead of berating ourselves, we can thank our bodies, send them love, take care of them in the way appropriate for us and start looking for the source of the imbalance.

Within each of us is soul and personality, man and woman, giver and receiver, pragmatist and visionary, do-er and be-er, father and mother, creator and inspiration, light and darkness, intellect and intuition, movement and rest, will and awareness. When we balance these polarities, we feel vibrant, alive and whole. If we neglect any of them, we cause an imbalance in the whole — dis-ease. We can balance them by accepting, nourishing and expressing them. **The marriage of the polarities within us is the most important marriage we make.** It opens our hearts and more.

To find the *source* of the imbalance, we must find the part or parts of ourselves that we're not loving unconditionally. When body, mind, feelings and soul are not in balance, we limit the amount of God (energy) we can express, and we're not aware of who we really are. If we accept only body, mind and feelings, we accept only half of ourselves, of God. If we accept only soul, we accept only half. When we accept both we are truly healthy, conscious of our God-self.

You may want to look at the polarities in your own being. Are you listening to both your visionary and your pragmatist? Are you using your intellect as well as your intuition? If you're a man, are you expressing the woman in you? If you're a woman, are you expressing the man in you? Are you allowing time for quiet and time for activity, time for creating and time for inspiration? Are you as good at receiving as you are at giving and vice-versa? Are you loving and accepting all of yourself?

Healing

When you make the two one, and when you make the inner as the outer, and the outer as the inner, and the above as the below, and when you make the male and the female into a single one, so that the male will not be male and the female not be female, then shall you enter the Kingdom.

> — Jesus Christ in
> *The Gospel According to Thomas*

We can recognize imbalances where we see sickness instead of health, fear instead of love, hate instead of compassion, separation instead of unity, war instead of peace. Imbalance exists when we don't see matter and spirit as equally sacred, and when we don't accept life as it is. Balance comes from changing what we can and leaving the rest to be transformed in its own time. An imbalance exists if we don't remember, "Not my will but Thine."

What can you do if you find you have a life-threatening disease? The following suggestions are adapted from an anonymous contributor to *New Age Magazine.*

1. Avoid medical paraphernalia and practice that treat only symptoms — unless, of course, you need to buy time to heal the source of the disease. (Chemotherapy and radiation don't heal cancer. In large amounts they destroy the immune system which must be strengthened in order to heal ourselves.

2. Sit down and center yourself. Begin reversing the self-irresponsibility pattern endorsed by the culture and ask yourself, 'How did I create this situation? Do I really want out? Of life, of the disease?' If you

decide it's life you want out of, acknowledge that cancer, for example, was the one-way ticket you purchased and it's OK. If you decide you want out of the disease, then accept that any condition you have created can be recreated. Any decision you have made can be reversed.

3. Take a holistic approach . . . A superior healer, to use the Chinese phrase, uses modalities that support the healing forces of the patient; the inferior healer uses modalities that fight disease. Locate a superior healer.

4. Use your experience as a learning and growth vehicle by extracting the principles involved . . . it's not enough to live. Survival as a life purpose is mockery. The body, like a fine musical instrument that must be kept in tune in order to be useful, might occasionally need repairing and tuning. When it no longer responds to repairing and tuning, it should be discarded as graciously and as soon as possible. Clutter diminishes the clarity of living.

You may want to consider healing possibilities you haven't tried before or you may want to stay with the familiar. Whether you prefer holistic or traditional medicine, get a second opinion and consider your alternatives. There are unskilled practitioners and charlatans in both groups. To discriminate which treatment forms are appropriate for you, research the alternatives, use your intuition and intellect and choose from the heart.

Barry Sultanoff, MD, offers these wise prescriptions for all of us 'suffering' with dis-ease.

Healing

1. Breathe. Quiet yourself, observe your breath, count your breath. Reflect on the marvelous process of breathing.

2. Ask for help and express your willingness to receive it. Ask a friend for a backrub. Ask God, your higher self, for healing on whatever level serves your highest good.

3. Forgive others and forgive yourself.

4. Listen to healing music.

5. Sing, hum, chant, yodel.

6. Laugh. Ask people to tell you jokes and funny stories.

7. Ask your 'inner child' what to do about your symptoms and what she or he needs from you. Take time to play.

8. Write to someone you feel "at odds with." Express your willingness to let go of positions or attitudes you held about them in the past. Ask what he or she wants from you. Or telephone instead.

9. Take a walk in nature. Observe and ask yourself, "What does nature have to teach me about how I can heal myself." Ask trees, flowers, birds or animals you meet along the way, "What can you tell me about . . . ?"

10. Hug as many people as possible, as often as possible. Say "I love you" to yourself and to others.

The following list includes additional tools you can use to create your unique path of healing. If some of these words aren't familiar, look for their definitions in Appendix F.

Allopathy	Homeopathy	NeoReichean work
Yoga	Do-in	Dancing
Herbs	Shiatsu	Drawing
Rolfing	Polarity therapy	Dreams
Feldenkrais	Psychic surgery	Rebirthing
Vitamins	Chiropractic	Bach flowers
Diet	Aikido	Meditation
Jogging	Biofeedback	Affirmations
Acupuncture	Gestalt therapy	Astrology
Massage	Encounter	Tarot
Color work	Psychosynthesis	Guided meditation
Sound	Aura balancing	Prayer
Music	Tai Chi	Spiritual healers

I've often observed people begin to experiment with alternative techniques and become discouraged when they didn't get the desired results. Either the person didn't work on **all** levels (body, mind, feelings, and soul) or didn't know that a person can be healed and no longer need a body. Healing as an intellectual pursuit alone doesn't work.

Two useful survey books on natural and holistic healing are *The Holistic Health Handbook*, by the Berkeley Holistic Health Center and *The Practical Encyclopedia of Natural Healing* by Mark Bricklin.

CALLING IN THE LIGHT

In my experience, a very effective healing technique is calling in the Light. Light is the energy that created and sustains us. It's another name for unconditional love, the Christ,

Buddha, etc. When we call in the Light (become conscious of it), we become it for as long as we remain focused in our hearts. The purpose of calling it in is to support healing.

If you want to support yourself or another, ask the Light to be present. I ask that "the Christ Spirit be present." Use words that suit you. There's no need to tell the Light what to do because it has perfect knowledge. Ask that it be used for the 'highest good' of whomever you're sending it to, so you don't interfere with their process or your own. You may feel it or see it as a light coming through the top of your head and filling your body. No effort is needed. When we exert ourselves, we have no place to receive. At first you may feel a little dizzy and uneasy. This passes as your body adjusts to the energy. You may feel nothing special at all and that doesn't mean it's not working.

"Holding the Light" means remaining focused in your heart, for whatever amount of time feels good. This may be a few minutes or a half hour. At the same time as you hold the Light for another, you are also being healed. I find holding the Light very supportive for dying people and continue to do it periodically during the first weeks after death.

LAWS FOR HEALING

Three universal laws for healing are: 'As above, so below', self-forgiveness, and 'As a man thinketh in his heart, so he is.'

As above, so below. If perfection exists in the universe, it exists in us as well. If there is love, beauty, health, peace and joy 'above', or anywhere else, they are in us as well. We have to lift the blinders that prevent us from seeing them. Simple and not easy.

The blinders are our judgements, our limited thinking. "This is good (or bad)." "This is right (or wrong)." Everything is energy and energy is neither right nor wrong. It just is. There is only one energy from which everything is created. It can be used skillfully or unskillfully, with love or with fear. We make judgements that make things seem separate and then we feel separate. A human being, table, flower, or bomb are all manifestations of the one energy. We have free will to use energy as we choose.

Self-forgiveness. God, or whatever you like to call this underlying energy, doesn't judge and so has nothing to forgive us for. We judge ourselves, so we must forgive ourselves. We need to forgive ourselves whenever we make judgements that make us feel separate or less than who we are. Perhaps that's many times a day. Each time we forgive ourselves, our hearts open wider. "I forgive myself for being afraid I don't know enough to write this book." "I forgive myself for thinking there's not enough money for my needs." "I forgive myself for not loving myself and others more." "I forgive myself for fearing fear."

Self forgiveness is an art we learn as we move toward loving ourselves and remembering who we are. If you need help with forgiving yourself, I recommend *Goodbye to Guilt, Releasing Fear through Forgiveness* by Gerald Jampolsky, or studying *A Course in Miracles*.

"As a man thinketh in his heart, so he is." This goes for women too! Energy follows thought. We create what we think or fear. If we think we're sick, we're sick. And we're free to change our thinking. If we think from our hearts, we're healthy. If we think from our hearts, we know love, joy, peace, beauty and abundance. Even if we just focus on these qualities with our minds we make room for them to develop in our lives. Each day we can *choose* what we think and whether to think from our limited minds or from our unlimited hearts. When I find myself running around my mind in negative circles, I say "God" to short-circuit it. It might work for you too.

If your body is sick, you might ask your friends to think of and visualize you as healthy, not sick. A lot of friends thinking of us as sick can hold us to old patterns and help us stay sick.

A person with cancer can visualize each cell working perfectly and any malfunctioning cells lifting up and out of the body. Again, remember to work at the feeling, body and soul levels as well. Carl Simonton, M.D. has worked extensively and successfully with nutrition and visualization techniques for cancer. Instruction tapes are available. (See Appendix A for address.)

A GUIDED MEDITATION

Guided meditation is another way to explore our inner experience and capacity for healing. Earlier I mentioned that a transcendent or mystical experience can eliminate or transform pain. Guided meditation is a simple method of helping someone get in touch with their own transformative energies, whether or not they're in pain.

Use the meditation below or create one that's right for the particular circumstances of the person you're guiding.

You may give or receive a guided meditation. Don't be upset if the person cries. People often do. Some people fall asleep and that's all right also. Both times I used this meditation with Mom and Dad they fell asleep about the time they got to the "top of the mountain" . . . and they woke up feeling great!

Ask the person to lie down or sit, making him or herself as comfortable as possible. Keep your voice soft and non-interfering. Leave time — long pauses — as you read for the person to get images and experience his or her feelings. The meditation:

> Close your eyes and breathe gently. With each breath gently move deeper inside yourself . . . Imagine that you're in a beautiful meadow . . . The sun is coming down in golden rays through you and around you. (If the person is in pain, suggest: As you feel the sun, allow its light to move through any place in your body that hurts . . . any place in your feelings that hurt . . . start relaxing the tension around the hurt . . . Imagine each cell around that area softening . . . opening . . . relaxing . . . Keep softening and opening and letting the light fill you . . . Then continue.)

> Open fully to the light and let it fill you . . . Relax and feel the richness around you and through you . . . Smell the air . . . Touch the earth and feel it in your hands . . . are there birds . . . or flowers . . . or animals . . . ? Be with them . . . You feel perfectly comfortable with everything . . . Is there a stream or brook? . . . If so, listen to the sound of the water. Are there any wild berries . . . wild strawberries or anything to eat? . . . If so, put

it in your mouth and really savor it . . . If there is
anything you want to do in this meadow, where
there are no limits, do it . . . explore . . . sing . . .
dance . . .

On the other side of the meadow is a beautiful
mountain . . . start walking toward it and climbing
up it . . . If you need help, imagine something to
help you . . . a bird, a person, an elevator. You can
imagine anything you want . . . You can see that
the light at the top of the mountain is incredibly
beautiful . . . As you climb, the light starts to fill
you. Soon you're at the top. If you need a rest,
invent a seat . . . An exquisite beam of light surrounds you and fills you . . . allow yourself to
really feel the light . . . Within the light, a figure or
form comes toward you that represents the highest
you know . . . You feel this being's love for you . . .
really let that love in . . . (allow plenty of time) . . .
You know that this person or energy has always
loved you and has never judged you or anything
you've done . . . Forgive yourself for all the times
you've judged yourself or other people . . . for all
the times you've felt unworthy . . . guilty . . .
fearful.

As you forgive yourself, feel your heart opening wider . . . Forgive yourself for all the judgements you made against your body . . . your feelings . . . your mind . . . Allow forgiveness and love
to fill every cell of your being . . . If you like, ask
the figure or energy any question you have about
anything . . . The figure or energy reaches out to
you and gives you a gift to take with you so you
can remember this experience . . . After you

receive the gift, say goodbye, knowing you can always return . . . From the top of the mountain take the light that fills you and radiate it to everyone . . . all the people you love . . . all the people, plants, animals . . . all the creatures of the earth . . . When you feel ready, slowly come down the mountain with your heart open, bringing this light energy with you . . . Take all the time you need; there's no hurry . . . When you feel ready, open your eyes, bringing the energy back into this room.

Allow yourself to receive and share whatever the person brings back.

Butterflies count not in months but in moments and have time enough.

— Rabindranath Tagore

CHAPTER 12

PREPARATION FOR DEATH AND AFTERWARD

For brief as water falling will be death.

—Conrad Aiken

SIGNS OF IMMINENT DEATH

As the moment of death approaches, a dying person usually wants more and more time alone, resting and sleeping, preparing internally for what is to come. Cells are dying at a greater rate than ever and the person has less and less physical energy. As you see the person less connected to the outer world, it's useful if there are fewer visitors and distractions.

You may find it nourishing at times to just sit quietly and watch the dying person. Silence is a living, healing energy that makes space for renewal and internal preparations. One friend said, "I know why I was sitting with my father. It was so my heart could open wider and I could feel his essence." Your intuition will tell you if gentle touching is a comfort to the person or an intrusion.

Don't misinterpret a dying person's seeming distance or lack of connectedness with you as a lack of love. Even as they love you dearly, they begin to move toward the new life. Share this with family members whose feelings might be hurt. While death is easy, dying can be hard work.

Dying people are often conscious until death. Some move into a coma. Although medically they're called unconscious, they're not. As I said before, a person in this state hears everything at some level. Talk in their presence as you would with a conscious person, not as if they were unconscious. We are alive and have consciousness even when very little or nothing is functioning outwardly.

If you have unfinished things to share with someone in a coma, talk to them and know they'll hear you. Questions may be fruitless because the person can't answer verbally. Although, if you listen with your heart, you may hear the answer. One way to understand a coma is as a kindly teaching that we're not just a body.

The dying person will take less and less food and liquid. Less urine will be eliminated. If she or he can no longer eat or drink, keep the mouth as moist and fresh as possible. As I mentioned before, ice chips or a wet washcloth to suck on are useful.

If the person is dehydrated or the air is very dry, mist the room with a plastic spray bottle filled with water — any empty spray bottle will do. Some people enjoy having their bodies sprayed with a water mist. Ask.

One sign of approaching death, but not necessarily imminent death, may be an odor coming from the person.

To me, it seems to be the smell of cells decaying. If there are lung complications, the odor may be particularly strong. With cancer, a strong odor is sometimes present earlier. In John's case the odor was so strong that some of us felt nauseous. Burning incense and putting Tiger Balm under our noses helped. Ben Gay or perfume works as well. In my father's case, by contrast, there was no odor.

A person in the last stages of dying may find massage soothing or an intrusion or interruption. Use your intuition. A very gentle massage may be one of the last outward ways of expressing your love. Dying people are sensitive to pressure. A person with cancer may be quite 'skeletal' by now, with very little fleshy protection for the bones. (Remember pillows and padding between the knees.) Because the skin is also sensitive, use a cream skin toughener if you have one. I've used Lanacane and an oil prepared by an herbologist containing Benzoin and myrrh. Sensitivity to light may be heightened. If you need a bright light to see by, warn the person so they're prepared for it.

As people approach death, their arms and legs may get colder and colder as circulation withdraws. Keep them warmly covered. Some people sweat profusely. If they do, lighten the covers. Don't tuck in the top sheet or covers, so the person can move about if able to. Put some pillows or folded blankets at the foot of the bed, under the sheets, to make a space for the feet to move easily. Again, you may be asked to turn the person frequently, which can be exhausting and may take two people. Most people close to death need less pain medication.

Other signs that death is probably near: the underside of the body becoming a darker color, the mouth hanging open, brown secretions in the mouth (possibly old blood from the stomach lining), the pupils of the eyes reacting less to changes in light. The person may have a glazed faraway look or stare into the distance without blinking. In sleep the eyes may shut only partially. If you take a pulse (a measure of the heartbeat) you may notice it's weak. The skin may be pale and waxy and the face drawn. Again, even if the person is showing few signs of life, talk in their presence as if they're present, because they are.

As a result of changes in body metabolism, the dying may experience increasing confusion about time, place and identity of family and friends. Reassure them by telling them the time, a person's name or who's in the room. Loosening connections here is part of the preparation for death. It's important not to insist that they pay attention to what's "real" for us, which may no longer be for them.

It's not uncommon for dying people to talk out loud with God or someone who's already died. Dad saw lights around him. Some people call this "hallucinating." The word suggests they're crazy or need sedation; they aren't and they don't. I believe they've just opened the door to another level of reality. On this level they may have a profound mystical or religious experience. The dying may also experience various degrees of age regression and relive important memories or review their entire lives. Respect these preparations. If their words seem garbled, listen carefully. You may discover unsuspected meanings that may help you meet a final need and/or comfort you.

As a person moves close to death, breathing usually becomes more and more labored. Secretions may build up in the lungs so that less oxygen is being exchanged for carbon dioxide, further weakening the person physically. You can help them by speaking gently and soothingly, or just by breathing gently and fully yourself. You might ask the person to remember how they breathed sitting or sleeping next to someone they love and suggest they breathe that way now.

Even closer to death the breathing pattern may change again. A drastic change in breathing doesn't necessarily mean the person is going to die immediately. A person may continue for a number of days to breathe in a way which we might guess each breath is the last. The breathing may seem bizarre and frightening if you're not used to hearing it. There may be a crescendo of breath and then no breathing for 10-30 seconds. Doctors call this Cheyne-Stokes or neurogenic breathing.

You may hear a rasping or gurgling sound at the back of the throat caused by oral secretions that the person can't cough up. For the sake of the family, hospices often use a Transderm Scop, a medicated bandaid placed behind the person's ear that eliminates the sound by drying up the secretions. You need a doctor's prescription for it. Elevating the person's head may help ease the effort of breathing.

If the breathing bothers you, take breaks out of the room. The breathing may not only sound strange, but can bother us because we feel helpless. Perhaps the deeper reason for our discomfort is that by now we're seeing the difference between the person we love and his or her body. When we see the body hanging on, we feel a sense of inappropriateness. Remember, you're watching the labor pains of the soul.

The symptoms of imminent death given here may not all appear at the same time and some not at all.

Dying people know at some level when they're going to die. Both Mary and Dad communicated that they knew. Using your intuition is one way to know when death will come. When John was dying, I meditated and prayed for guidance and was told he had four days. On the fourth day he died. Don't worry if you're 'off'. God's timetable is flexible.

Whether or not a person has accepted that they're dying, there is frequently a period of peace before death — perhaps it's that final surrender. It's interesting to note that according to Ruth Gray, a nurse and author of *Dealing with Death and Dying*, "a dying person always turns his head toward the light". Could it be that as we die we know we're going home to the Light even before we open the garden gate?

BEING WITH SOMEONE THE LAST FEW DAYS

A dying man needs to die, as a sleepy man needs to sleep.

— Stewart Alsop

The last few days it's most useful if your attitude is one of letting go and releasing the person. Both of you are working on surrender, trusting the moment. Suffering is caused if a person is ready to die and feels the family is hanging on. It creates a struggle. "I know I can't stay and I don't feel like I can leave." Let the person know you'll be OK and encourage him or her to go free.

At this point all we can be is present. Quiet. Loving. Open. Holding hands if that feels appropriate. Or hold the Light (page 276). Suggest she or he breathe as calmly as possible. I suggest (verbally or non-verbally) that the person move toward the Light, allowing him or herself to feel lighter and lighter, lifting up. See if the meditation that follows, or parts of it, is useful for you.

Two situations that may come up at the end of a dying process can generate a lot of guilt if we misunderstand them. The first is a feeling of irritation or anger that this process is taking so long. It's a natural feeling many experience, like a mother who loves her child yet is tired because she or he needs so much attention. Recognize the anger or irritation and forgive yourself. (See anger, page 239.) These feelings are signals that we need a rest, a change of scene, time away for ourselves. The person is still here because he or she has something to finish on some level. It'll be easier for you if you don't make assumptions about how long the process will take and continue to pace yourself.

The second situation occurs if the death happens while you're out of the house or room. If someone wants to feel badly because "I wasn't there", that's a choice. Not being present may also be a beautiful expression of love. Many dying people are so attached to people they love that it's easier for them to die when those people are not present. The energy of loved ones can hold us in a body we need to leave.

Perhaps you have to leave town before the actual death. We are no less loving or loved because of where we are. We can tell the person before leaving that we love them and know they love us. An appropriate expression of our love is to live the life we are given to live. Even if this never reaches words, we know that **love is not expressed only by sitting at the bedside.**

A PRACTICE MEDITATION FOR LEAVING THE BODY

Knowing ahead of time what death may be like alleviates fear for some people. The following meditation may be useful before the actual time of death. At the moment of death, silence may be more appropriate. Read the meditation to yourself first. If it feels right in your heart, ask if the dying person wants to try it. Sometimes it's clearly inappropriate.

It's not probable that a person will leave their body during the meditation, but it's possible. If the body dies, it's because it's time. Remember, the vehicle does not die until after the soul decides to withdraw its energy. This meditation may be used as is, or you may be inspired to create your own:

(The person's name), *we love you and we're ready to let you go. Feel a lighter body within your heavy physical body . . . move into your Light body. You don't need the old one anymore . . . Trust each moment . . . Let go of any distractions or anything that's holding you here. Softly and lightly. We're OK. God is within us and within you. Surrender to who you are. Feel our love . . . God's love. We are love. If there is anything you haven't forgiven yourself for, forgive yourself now.* (pause) *We are One and we can never be separated . . . Move into the Light . . . Just keep moving into the clear Light . . . Nothing to hang on to . . .*

Whenever it feels right, just lift up and dissolve into the Light. There's no pain, only Light. Anything you see is a projection of your mind. Think

*God. See Light. 'Be not afraid for I am with you
even in the shadow of death.' Move from the
shadow into the Light . . . You will see and hear us.
Don't be surprised if we can't hear you when it's
your time to leave. The veil will not yet have lifted
for us. You'll be met and welcomed on the other
side and God will comfort us. You may review
your life so that the lessons are clear . . . There is
no punishment. Only unconditional love.*

*You're going Home . . . Home is the brightest
Light. Move into the brightest Light. Know we
love you and rejoice that you are God . . . You are
free . . . Home to the one heart . . . total understanding . . . beauty . . . joy . . . We are One.*

THE MOMENT OF DEATH

We use the phrase "moment of death" because that's how
long death lasts. Just a moment.

The sound of silence may be the most loving gift right
before the moment of death. At this moment, people of the
Jewish faith say, "Baruch Dayan Ha-emet" (Blessed is Judge
of Truth); others say "Glory to God," or chant "Om." Others are silent.

At the moment of death the final thread holding the life
force to the body releases. There is no pain. Consciousness
leaves the dead body. I've experienced the life force lifting
up out of the body through the solar plexus, the heart, or
the crown of the head. If you place your hand over these

places at the moment of death, you may feel the energy going out. Your hand will tingle or feel different.

IMMEDIATELY AFTER DEATH

Do whatever is right for you. Be who you are. Be your heart. Share your hearts.

Pray from your heart . . . perhaps for God to help _____ to his (her) new life . . .

Close your eyes and see what you see. Close your ears and hear what you hear.

Allow your tears, your grieving.

Breathe deeply, exhale deeply.

Hold someone who needs holding. Be held.

Send your blessing with the newly free.

Send love to all around you.

Chant or sing a prayer.

Does anyone need extra help?

Make a circle holding hands and linking hearts.

Make a forgiveness circle. Each in turn in the words of each heart:

I forgive myself for each time in my life I have been less than loving with _____ (the one who's free). I forgive myself for each time in my life I have been less than loving with myself. I forgive myself for each time I have been less than loving with any of you. I accept my forgiveness. I accept your forgiveness. I accept that God has never judged me.

LAYING OUT THE BODY

Treat the body with respect, knowing however that it's only a body. What you do with it in terms of cleaning and dressing has to do with your needs, not those of the soul now free. Dressing the body is easier in the first hour, before it starts to stiffen. Unless you want to, it's not necessary to dress a body for cremation, for going to a hospital for examination, or to a funeral home. We dressed Mary and John ourselves and didn't find it gruesome—just another task to be completed with love. Dad had promised the doctors at the VA hospital that they could examine his body so we didn't dress it.

In choosing clothes, think of what the person enjoyed wearing and how they'd like to be last seen. If a man was not a coat-and-tie type, it adds a jarring note to see him decked out like a Wall Street businessman or like an attendant at someone else's funeral. It doesn't matter what some relatives or friends may think. They can do it their way when it's their turn.

If it bothers you to see the eyes open, close them shortly after death. If the aesthetics of an open mouth bother you, tape it closed and leave it taped a few hours until the jaw sets closed.

After death, the body may involuntarily empty its bladder or bowels. Remember, it's a function of the body that is no longer related to the person. It doesn't always happen.

A short time after death, the faces of John, Mary and Dad looked more relaxed peaceful and younger than while they were dying. All signs of the effort of leaving had gone.

There's no need to spend a lot of time with a body. Yet I recommend spending enough time so you really know it's only a cocoon. Go into the room where the body lies as often as feels right and perhaps talk with the soul, encouraging it to go free.

When you feel ready, call the funeral home, if you're using one, to remove the body.

GETTING A DEATH CERTIFICATE

To prevent legal complications, you'll need a death certificate signed by a physician, medical examiner, or coroner. If a doctor is present at the death and has the certificate, he or she can sign it right away.

If a doctor is not present, call the one you've been working with. If you don't have one, call the medical examiner or coroner. A doctor usually has to see the body before signing a death certificate. If it's the middle of the night, wait until morning.

If you're working with a hospice, they'll help you get the death certificate. In many places, a hospice nurse can pronounce someone dead. Then the funeral home picks up the body, sends a death certificate to the doctor and returns it to you.

You will need copies of the death certificate for the state, banks, insurance companies, etc. **Keep the original.**

ADVISING RELATIVES AND FRIENDS

Advising relatives and friends of the death and burial plans should be done promptly in case they need time to get there. It's helpful to have a list with phone numbers and addresses ready. Some people want to call themselves; others are very grateful for a volunteer. However, if no one has had any sleep, all this can wait until the next day. Sleep.

A CHECKLIST OF THINGS TO DO

The checklist shared here is adapted from *A Manual of Death Education and Simple Burial* by Ernest Morgan. Some of these things need to be done shortly after the death and others may be done by you or friends and relatives in the weeks to come. Not all will apply to you.

_____Decide on time and place of funeral or memorial services.

_____Notify immediate family, close friends and employer or business colleagues.

_____Arrange for members of family or close friends to take turns answering the door or phone, keeping careful record of calls.

_____Arrange appropriate child care.

_____Coordinate the supplying of food for the next few days.

_____If flowers are to be omitted, decide on appropriate memorial or charity to which gifts may be made.

_____Write obituary. Include age, place of birth, cause of death, occupation, college degrees, memberships held, military service, outstanding work, list of survivors in immediate family. Give time and place of memorial services. Deliver in person or by phone to newspapers.

_____Notify insurance companies, including automobile insurance for immediate cancellation and refund of premium.

_____Consider special needs of the household, such as cleaning, etc., which might be done by friends.

_____Arrange hospitality for visiting relatives and friends.

_____Select pall bearers and notify. (Avoid men with heart or back difficulties, or make them honorary pall bearers.)

_____Notify lawyer and personal representative (executor).

_____Plan for disposition of flowers after funeral (give to hospital or rest home?)

_____Prepare list of persons living at a distance to be notified by letter or printed notice, and decide which to send to each.

_____Prepare the message or printed notice if one is wanted.

_____Prepare list of persons to receive acknowledgements of flowers, calls, etc. Send appropriate acknowledgements. (May be written notes, printed acknowledgements, or some of each.)

Preparation For Death And Afterward

_____Check carefully all life and casualty insurance policies and death benefits including Social Security, credit union, trade union, fraternal, military, etc. Check also on income for survivors from these sources.

_____Check promptly on all debts, mortgages, and install-ment payments. Some may carry life insurance clauses that will cancel the debt. If there is to be a delay in meeting payments, consult with creditors and ask for more time before the payments are due.

_____If deceased was living alone, notify utilities and land-lord and tell post office where to send mail. Take precautions against thieves.

Bury me if you can catch me.

— Socrates

CHAPTER 13

PLANNING A BURIAL AND SERVICE

A simple analogy for death that appeals to me is the butterfly leaving the cocoon. In a burial and memorial service, consider focusing on the beauty of the living butterfly instead of on the cocoon.

If possible, make burial plans **ahead of time.** It may be more difficult to make practical decisions after the death than before. If you're feeling less than calm, you're more likely to let others—like the funeral industry, friends, clergy, etc.—take responsibility for arrangements. If you can't plan ahead, don't worry. You'll be surprised how everything will fall naturally into place.

Find out your state's law about how a body can be disposed of. Call the county coroner, State Board of Medical Examiners or a local memorial society (see page 92) for this information. In John's and Mary's cases all we knew ahead of time was that our state law permitted burial on private property.

When Dad was dying, we talked with him and without him about plans, and my mother visited several funeral homes. I called the San Antonio city coroner to find out the Texas laws. Embalming was not legally required so we planned to have his body refrigerated, the coffin closed, and no visitors to the funeral home.

My parent's home is in a little incorporated city within San Antonio so I also called the local courthouse. The chief of police said they had to investigate any death at home but because they knew Dad and what we planned, it wouldn't be necessary. A simple call avoided a police visit.

Police are required by law to investigate a "medically unattended death." In many places they also investigate a natural home death attended by a doctor. Having police come into your home right after the death of someone you love is emotionally jarring so preventing it, if possible, is worth a try. Again, find out the legal requirements in your area.

In some places a police visit after such a death is a *tradition*, not a legal requirement. In those places, you might avoid one by calling, ahead of the death, the police and/or medical examiner (coroner). Let them know what you're doing—preparing for a natural expected death at home attended by a doctor—and ask their advice about preventing a police visit. You might ask your doctor, hospice or funeral home director to make the call for you. If a natural expected death at home is not under the jurisdiction of the police or medical examiner, simply don't call them or the Emergency Medical Service (EMS) after the death.

If a police visit is unavoidable, ask the person most able to handle such a visit to answer the questions the police are required to ask.

Let's look at the purpose of a burial service, to enable you to create a meaningful one that nourishes you and fulfills the purpose.

1. To dispose of a cocoon.

2. To facilitate the process of grieving by allowing family and friends to express their love for the living spirit of the cocoon and for one another.

TO DISPOSE OF A COCOON

Only when the earth shall claim your limbs, then shall you truly dance.

— Kahlil Gibran

Find out what the dying person wants and, if possible, meet his or her wishes. If you don't feel comfortable with these wishes, for example, the dying person wants cremation and you find it horrifying, discuss your feelings with him or her. Unnecessary pain is caused after a death if we feel torn between wanting to follow a loved one's wishes and our distaste for their choice. What dying person would want additional pain for you if they were aware of your feelings? As we become more comfortable talking about dying and its aftermath, hopefully more dying people will say, "I prefer _____ and I want you to do what feels best to you."

The choices for disposal of the body are cremation, burial, or bequeathal to science.

Unless you plan to bury the body yourself, I suggest you check first with a memorial society. A memorial society is a non-profit group of consumers who help members make pre-arrangements for a simple, economical burial. Because they're non-profit, they'll give you straight information about legal requirements, costs and arrangements. There are now about 200 memorial societies in the U.S. and Canada. Look in the white pages of your telephone book under Memorial Society or Funeral Society. If you don't find a listing, See Appendix A. Membership runs $10 to $25 and anyone can join. If you're quoted a higher membership price, it's probably not a real memorial society.

Memorial Societies do what we often don't—shop around and compare services and prices. They generally act in an advisory capacity, not offering services themselves but providing information about local services. In my experience they're fine people who know what's happening in the community and are very helpful.

One of the finest books about death and dying, Ernest Morgan's *A Manual of Death Education and Simple Burial* is available from Memorial Societies or from the Continental Association of Funeral and Memorial Societies. (See Appendix A for addresses.)

CREMATION

Burning a body until only ashes remain is a simple, clean, economical way of returning earth to earth. Actual cremation costs about $150 to $200. You can take the body to a crematory yourself or have a funeral home take it.

Most people prefer to have a funeral home make cremation arrangements. If that's your choice, call them when you're ready to have the body removed. They'll pick it up, refrigerate it for the 48 hour waiting period required by law, do the paperwork, have the body cremated and return the ashes to you. Funeral homes call this "direct cremation." The cost varies for $500 to $1500—not including a service, urn or niche in the cemetery. Some states have a new service called "direct disposal" which do this service at a low cost.

Crematories require a suitable container for the body, such as a simple wood or heavy card-board box. **A casket or embalming are not legally required for cremation.** The funeral home will give you the ashes in a cardboard box. You can scatter them where you choose, except in Indiana, keep them at home or in a cemetery niche ($400 - $900). Scattering the ashes helps us focus on a living spirit instead of on a cocoon.

Overseeing a cremation yourselves is hard work when you're emotionally and/or physically exhausted and it can be very satisfying. Anybody can take a body to a crematory without the services of a funeral director **as long as the legal requirements are met.** These include getting the death certificate, transit permit, authorization to cremate, filing with any other authorities, refrigerating the body for 48 hours at the crematory or funeral home and a proper body container. You can build your own wood box or buy a cardboard one from the crematory. If you choose to handle arrangements yourself, check with the coroner or medical examiner to determine exact legal requirements. You may run into opposition along the way, not because what you're doing is illegal but because it's unusual.

EARTH BURIAL

In our country earth burial is the most common form of disposing of a cocoon. It has become extremely costly unless you live in a state that permits burial on private property or the person is eligible to be buried in a National Cemetery. (see page 90 for eligibility.)

If your state permits burial on private property, it can be very satisfying to do the burial yourself. **Plan ahead.** You will need to present the death certificate to the local registrar of vital statistics or appropriate agency to obtain a burial or transit permit. A professional carpenter or friend can build the coffin. For an adult, the box should be 6 inches to 1 foot longer than the person, about 1 foot to $1\frac{1}{2}$ feet deep, and 2 feet to 3 feet wide. It should have a separate top that can be put on later. Line the box and decorate the outside if you wish. Use the box to transport the body to the chosen burial place, where you'll probably want to have a service. For digging, you need shovels and picks.

Home burials cost almost nothing. John's burial cost $150. This included two trees to start the orchard and food and drink for the celebration. Mary's funeral cost $44, which included wood for the coffin, gasoline for two trucks and beer for the diggers.

Planning A Burial And Service

If the laws in your state don't permit burial on private property or you don't want to handle arrangements yourself, you'll need to make them, if you haven't already, with a funeral home and cemetery. Added to the cost of funeral home service are cemetery expenses. They include:

Buying a plot	$300 – $15,000
Digging the hole and closing it	$300 – $400
A concrete liner	$250 – $400
or a vault	$300 – $15,000
A simple grave marker	$250 – $500

Cemeteries require a casket to be placed in a concrete liner or a vault to prevent the ground above the grave from sinking. Sometimes moisture proof vaults are recommended as a way to preserve the body. A body in a $15,000 vault will decay just like one in a concrete liner or a blanket, as Native Americans traditionally use . . . perhaps faster. "Traditional" cemeteries allow you to choose any gravestone you like. In "memorial parks", markers must be level with the ground.

FUNERAL HOMES

The dollars spent for a funeral don't say anything.

—A funeral director

In 1987, the average cost of an American funeral was $3600, according to the National Association of Funeral Directors. Not included in this cost are cemetery fees.

After a home and car, a funeral is the third largest purchase most Americans make. Unlike for the first two major purchases, we don't shop around when it comes to funerals. We usually use a funeral home because "My family's always used them." The funeral industry took advantage of our vulnerability and failure to comparison shop and took us for a financial ride. They're not solely responsible — we played victim.

Funeral industry practices got so outrageous that the Federal Trade Commission stepped in and passed the 1984 Funeral Rule. This law requires, among other things, that funeral homes provide prices of individual services over the telephone. They are also required to give you a written price list of goods and services when you visit to enquire about services. The law makes it possible for you to buy individual items as well as package service and goods.

If you're not emotionally up to comparison shopping, ask someone to call for you and then make your choices. There's still wide disparity in prices.

The Funeral Rule makes it illegal for funeral homes to represent to you that embalming is a legal requirement when it's not. In most places embalming is not required unless a body is to be transported across state lines, preserved beyond a certain time limit or unless death was caused by a communicable disease. Embalming is not a religious requirement. It's expressly forbidden, and considered a desecration of the body, by the Jewish Orthodox faith.

Instead of being embalmed a body can be refrigerated until a service, burial or cremation, or disposed of within 24 hours. To rationalize embalming, funeral directors sometimes say that viewing the body aids families in their grieving process. It's true that viewing the body is important; it seems to cauterize the emotional wound. But, even in a sudden death, the body may be viewed on the spot or in the hospital emergency room. In a home death you've had time to experience the physical reality of death and there's usually no need for "viewing the body." If there is a need, it can be viewed refrigerated.

Caskets are generally the most expensive funeral item. No state law has explicit casket requirements. Consider having a service without a casket, without the body present, or if you want it present, consider a simple wood box or cardboard container. The least expensive casket may not be shown in the funeral home showroom because funeral directors get commissions on caskets. Feel free to ask to see it. Don't believe anyone who tells you a $150 casket doesn't show the respect of a $2,000 one. **Respect is an attitude, not a coffin.** The dying person may already have expressed definite preferences on this subject.

A fancy funeral or casket is not an effective way to deal with grief or guilt. If you like a big show, why not have a super party? Why finance your funeral director's party? Or, you might want to give the money you'd have spent to a person or group who needs it, perhaps one favored by the person who died.

Many funeral directors are fine responsible people. Don't be manipulated into spending more on a funeral than you want and can afford by one who's not. Statements such as "He deserves the best," "This is the last thing you can do for your mother," "That's the welfare funeral," or "Spend enough to do the deceased credit" are guilt causing baloney!

The Consumer Guide to the Federal Trade Commission Funeral Rule is in Appendix J. It includes to whom you report a complaint about a funeral home.

BEQUEATHAL OF THE BODY

Bequeathal of the body to science is another way to dispose of a cocoon (see page 266). If the person has signed a Uniform Donor's Card, find it and call the closest medical school. Some schools have more bodies than they need, others not enough. They'll generally pick up the body. If you live a great distance from the school, however, you may have to pay part of the transportation costs. Ask them while you're on the phone. Their release form includes what you want done with the body after it's served its usefulness to the medical profession.

RITUALS AND CELEBRATIONS

A ritual or celebration facilitates the process of grieving by allowing family and friends to express their love for the living spirit and for each other.

Leaving a physical vehicle (the body) is an important rite of passage for both the person doing it and for the family and friends. A ritual marking this change helps us express our sadness and loss with others before we face our changed reality sometimes seemingly alone.

The ritual you create can be a celebration of life. We can celebrate the life completed, and through it, all of life. We can celebrate Love. We can celebrate the joy of sharing time together. We can share love and support for each other. The celebration can also help us express our grief, sadness and perhaps anger that we're left to take care of daily business.

Planning A Burial And Service

Jewish shivas, Irish and Polish wakes, and Hispanic *veladas* (candlelight watches) have long been useful forms for exploring and sharing loss and renewing old relationships.

You might use an old form or create a new one. A memorial service is a service generally held 2 or 3 days after the death without the body present. In a funeral service the body is present in a casket. A commital service is a brief service held at a graveside, in the chapel of a crematory or wherever the ashes are scattered.

Allow a celebration to grow in whatever way feels appropriate for you. Choose a place that's meaningful — indoors or out in nature. Does it matter if the body is present or not? Do you, the people involved, want to speak about your feelings? Would you rather be silent? Do you want someone to lead the ceremony or can each person share in their own way? Do you want clergy or do you want to be your own ministers and celebrants? Do you want flowers, music, poetry? Do you want to share food or dancing or song? What about a prayer circle, a hug or holding circle? Even digging can be part of the ritual. You may want to use the 'Forgiveness Circle' (page 294).

Anything is possible in a service as long as it meets your needs.

In a ritual, I believe we need to focus on releasing the soul even if it is difficult for us. If we cling to it, the soul's love for us makes it difficult for it to move away from family, friends and the familiar physical world and on to its new life. We're accustomed to thinking there is nothing further we can do for someone after he or she dies. We speak at our services as if they weren't there. I believe they are there and that we can still help. We can talk with the person, let

311

them know we're OK and encourage them to go free. We can offer prayers of thanksgiving for life that never ends and we can continue to share our hearts.

WORKING WITH CLERGY

If your spiritual understanding and practices have been related to a particular religious group, you may want to ask your minister, rabbi or priest for help in planning a service. The clergy have shared their knowledge and compassion many times with dying people and their families. They do have a commitment to do things in the manner prescribed by their particular faith. Check within yourself to see if their suggestions meet the earlier wishes of the person as well as your own sense of rightness. **Everyone has equal access to God.**

WHAT TO WEAR

Darn, I don't have a black dress or suit. Will navy blue do?

What to wear for a funeral is still an issue for many people.

Some people don't own black clothing because they don't like black. It makes me feel locked in, constricted, as though I can't express myself. Wearing black forms a shield around the body that retards energy going in or out and protects us when we're emotionally weak. But the price of this protection is high. Black locks in energy, including sadness, grief and love. In countries where it's the custom to wear black for a long mourning period, holding in feelings frequently becomes a way of life. In my view, wearing black is like a heavy casket — it keeps things in. Can you remember anyone wearing black in all those paintings of the death of Jesus Christ. No, they wore white or light colors. White is expansive and reflects energy. Wear a color you like or one you know the butterfly liked.

We can reflect the rainbow. Respect is an attitude, not a color.

A LIFE CELEBRATION TO SHARE LATER

Death is not extinguishing the light but putting out the candle because the dawn has come.

— Rabindranath Tagore

The blessing of having shared time and love with someone doesn't end just because they're no longer here in a body.

In the months to come, you might want to create something to celebrate their life . . . and your life: a garden, an orchard, a carved cross, or whatever. Making a card or writing a story or poem can be a healing way to share someone's movement from life to life, particularly with friends who weren't present for the death or burial. Months after John died, a friend hauled a rock down off a mesa, carved it and set it on John's grave.

Many people expect the anniversary of physical death or the person's birthday to be a day of sadness. If we expect them to be sad that is what we'll create. We can make them days to celebrate the joy of having loved them as well. Consider putting flowers in your living room that you might have put on the grave to remind you of that joy.

I was deeply moved by celebrations for two women I never met, Jean Lake and Gloria Weatherby.

Before she died of cancer, Jean dreamed of publishing a book of her paintings of rural life in Alabama and simple sayings she'd found helpful in her life. One day after she died, one of her young children was talking with a family friend and mentioned her mother's dream. The dream touched her friend's heart. She resolved to publish the book, whatever it took, and give the proceeds for an art scholarship at a local college. In the process of completing the book she married her friend's husband. So, the dream of the first wife was carried out by the second wife. To order this delightful book, *Seeds to Sow*, see Appendix A.

During the first year after his wife, Gloria, died, Peter Weatherby wrote the story of her dying and death at home and his own spiritual journey. He calls this beautiful love story, *The Pilgrim Soul*.

Weeping may endure for a night, but joy cometh in the morning.

— Psalms 30:5

CHAPTER 14

GRIEVING

Perhaps the most important reason for 'lamenting'
is that it helps us to realize our oneness with all
things, to know that all things are our relatives . . .

— Black Elk

If you know in your heart that your loved one is alive although alive in a different way, you may feel joy as well as sadness. Allow joy. Allow relief. If your relationship with the person wasn't central to your life, you probably won't feel sad. That's fine. No need to pretend to grieve. But if the relationship was close to your heart and you hurt, you need to express the pain so you don't suffer later.

Allow yourself your grieving. Allow it to express in whatever way feels right to you. Grieving is the way we heal the loss we feel for someone we love. You're not crazy. A deep bursting sorrow is one reflection of the value in your life of this close relationship that has now changed form.

You may have feelings similar to those the person had while dying: denial, isolation, guilt, anger, bargaining, depression and acceptance.

Cry those oceans if they're there. Yell. Be sad, be lonely, be helpless, be out of control, be angry. Move your body. Don't let anyone tell you to be quieter—they can do it their way when it's their turn to grieve. Yell at "John the Bastard" for leaving you. Yell at "God the Merciless" for taking your loved one away. God can take it. Let it spill out of all the nooks and crannies of your being. Cry for all those things you didn't cry about in the past. Clean out old sadness.

At one time or another the emptiness comes. Know this space. It may be with you for a time and it may be one of the most important spaces in your life. It's in this quiet after the outward grieving that the seeds for your new life begin to grow. Some people call this emptiness the "Dark Night of the Soul." You've let go of something precious and familiar and the new meaning is not yet known. It takes a lot of courage to be alive in this emptiness. Just be with it. Pay attention to what is trying to grow . . . new qualities or ways of being, new ideas about life, work, whatever.

There is an old Zen saying, "You can't fill a teacup that is already full." If we allow the emptiness, we can move to a new fullness.

As you begin to understand what is trying to grow, and if you're willing, make it a choice to nourish these tiny seedlings. If you panic, you may stomp down little new beginnings. A lot of people panic. I have. Because this emptiness is often unknown and frightening, we rush to fill the void with busy-ness or suffering—perhaps the closest, most familiar thing at this moment. Maybe we say to ourselves,

"Better to feel something, even if it's suffering, than nothing at all." It's true a vacuum looks to be filled. And we have a choice what we fill it with. We have a choice! You can use this quiet space instead of it using you. Catch up on sleep, eat balanced meals, pray, meditate, take long walks, work in the garden . . . prepare your soil. If possible, if the death was someone very close to you, put off major decisions for at least a year.

When our hearts break, they break open, making more room for everybody and everything — more love, more joy, more compassion. We can stay open to the loneliness and pain, knowing it's moving us to a new fullness. Or we can shut down. A heart that has broken open, doesn't close unless we close it. We make the choice.

Part of grieving is fear. We're afraid we've lost our love, that somehow it's gone with the physical body of the person. Without the soul that shone through that person we probably wouldn't have loved him or her in the first place. And the soul is not gone. We don't have to stop thinking about or stop loving the person. I believe it's inaccurate to assume that the *object* of our love is our love. We are love, so we can never lose it.

We can expand our love, which may recently have been focused almost exclusively on one person, to include more and more people. Give your love to yourself. **Loving yourself is the greatest gift you can give to the people you love, present in a body or not.** When you feel able, give love to the people around you. If there aren't any, find new people and situations in which you can share love. When you give it away, it always returns to you increased.

If we don't express our feelings, including our love, we feel depressed. Our love backs up on us and poisons our lives instead of illuminating them. I don't remember having felt depressed around people I love while they were dying. Depression often comes afterwards, when suddenly there's no longer a clear focus for our love and energy . . . no one to care for . . . no obvious way of expressing love. The solution is to find new ways to express it . . . not too difficult really. It's needed everywhere. The teenager who bags your groceries needs it, the gas station attendant needs it, your neighbors need it, babies need it, old people need it, prisoners need it . . . Don't be put off if they're not yet skilled receivers of love—perhaps you know what that's like yourself.

I've observed, and experienced, two kinds of grieving: grieving for *cleansing* and *healing* and grieving as a *habit of suffering*. The first is essential for growth; the second offers no movement. Treading water. Who wants to tread water for the rest of their lives? It's tiring . . . and boring. Cleansing and healing provide space for delicate, and perhaps exciting, new growth.

If you feel stuck in suffering, get help. Find a friend or counselor. Someone who works with Gestalt or other techniques that focus on releasing stuck feelings may be useful. Some cultures meet the need for grieving with wailing, dancing, chanting—all ways of releasing pent-up energies. However, in our culture we tend to find such releases embarrassing, so sometimes we need counselors. We probably won't need them anymore when we stop making judgements against our feelings, appreciating instead the help expressing them gives us in adjusting to life's great changes.

Avoid drugs and alcohol. They may temporarily ease your pain but will delay or stop the necessary grieving process. If you're alone at home, have already let out the tears, and the pain still feels too heavy, send love to the part of you that hurts. Try compressing time. Imagine yourself a year from now: How are you feeling? Is there more space around the pain? Write your feelings on paper. Talk, perhaps out loud, to the person you're missing. She or he can still hear you. Dr. Moody, Dr. Kübler-Ross and many others confirm this.

During your grieving, allow friends the opportunity to share with you. Improve your skill at receiving and allow friends to have the joy of giving. They'll feel privileged that you chose to talk with them about your feelings, about the person you love. Sometimes they can help you recognize the new seeds sprouting. And they can hold you when you need it. Ask. Often, friends want to share their love and don't know how. Tell them what you need. It's after the first month or first year, when the shock and numbness are wearing off, that we particularly need their support.

In the jungles of Mexico they have a useful custom. After someone dies, each person who comes to the funeral or to visit asks the mourner to recount the story of how the death happened. The visitors probably already know, but the point is to keep the mourner repeating and repeating the story until the shock lessens and he or she begins to accept what's happened. Friends can do the same for us . . . listen . . . and listen . . . and listen. Share your story. It will help you and others will benefit as well.

In addition to sharing with friends, it's healing to share with people who've had similar experiences. To locate a support group if your husband or wife died, call your hospice, church or the social service office of a hospital. If your child died, Compassionate Friends can be very helpful. It's a national organization with about 500 local support groups. (See Appendix A for their address and phone number.) See

Appendix K for a parent's suggestion on healing your grief by writing your child's story.

Books with practical ideas to help us mend an injured or broken heart can also be helpful. I recommend, *How to Survive the Loss of Love*, Bantam Books; *Don't Take my Grief Away*, Doug Manning, Harper and Row; *The Bereaved Parent*, Harriet Schiff, Penguin Books; and *Learning to Say Goodbye*, Eda Leshan, MacMillan. If you want a reminder about joy, I highly recommend *To Hear the Angels Sing*, Dorothy Maclean, Lorian Press.

Take time to appreciate yourself. You are the same person who began this experience and you aren't. You have changed and grown in immeasureable ways.

In case it would happen to slip your mind, remember,

Spring has always come and it always will.

Grieving

Death is nothing at all. I have only slipped away into the next room. I am I and you are you: Whatever we were to each other, that we are still. Call me by my old familiar name. Speak to me in the easy way you always used. Put no difference into your tone; wear no forced air of solemnity or sorrow. Laugh as we always laughed at the little jokes we enjoyed together. Play, smile, think of me, pray for me. Let my name be ever the household word that it always was. Let it be spoken without effort, without the ghost of a shadow on it.

Life means all that it ever meant.

It is the same as it ever was; there is absolute unbroken continuity. What is death but a negligible accident?

I am waiting for you, for an interval, somewhere very near, just around the corner. All is well.
— Canon Scott Holland
Facts of Faith

And let us, above all things, never forget that in due course the dead will come back, and we never know when we shall see looking out at us from the eyes of a little child a soul we have known. Let us therefore, making expression for the love that now may have no earthly outlet, turn it to the endeavor of making the world a better place for the return of those we love.

—Dion Fortune
Through the Gates of Death

CHAPTER 15

LIFE AFTER DEATH

People sleep and when they die they awake.

—Mohammad

Your own heart is the best source of knowing about life after death.

I can share with you my reality and how I arrived at it. I can tell you about recent studies and writings across the ages. All of these are just footnotes to your own knowing.

If you're willing, try this:

Find a quiet place and close your eyes. Breathe gently inside and let go of any ideas you have about life after death. Become 'empty'. If thoughts come up, don't get caught up in them . . . just watch them. Breathe into your heart and from this place ask for guidance . . . Ask if death exists other than as a change in form. Ask if we're born again

325

and again. Trust what you hear, especially if it's a calm gentle inner voice. If nothing comes, that's OK too.

My own sense is that life after death and rebirth are two of the best-kept secrets in the West. Working with dying people I've found that most have had hints or visions that life continues and/or that they've lived before and will again. When they felt that I wouldn't judge them crazy or senile, many dying people shared experiences they'd not shared before. We learn a lot about our common human experience when people feel free to share their experiences without fear of being ridiculed.

One of the glorious things about being alive in our time is that mystics and scientists are finally beginning to say the same things. Mystics have always believed life continues after death. Some scientists are beginning to say, "Well, maybe." To mystics the one family of humankind has always been a reality. Now scientists, in particular biochemists at the University of California, have proven genetically that all the humans alive today had **the same mother**. Their study used a part of the cell inherited only from the mother, so they haven't yet announced who our father was. We're beginning to realize that the mystic and scientific paths are both valid ways to approach truth.

Elisabeth Kübler-Ross, M.D. has said, "I don't have a shadow of doubt death (as an end) doesn't really exist . . . If they hang me up by my toes, I won't stop exploring life after death."

Raymond Moody, M.D., in his popular book *Life After Death*, reports the experiences of people who 'officially died' and were resuscitated. Since his book, numerous books and articles on "near-death experiences" have been published. Many are by medical doctors who received first-hand reports from patients and by ordinary people who've had the experience themselves.

What Dr. Moody reports basically agrees with what dying people have told me. From his interviews with people who died and were resuscitated, Dr. Moody reports:

1. When the 'officially dead' persons heard someone say they were dead, they felt surprised and afraid.

2. After the initial fear, they felt incredibly peaceful.

3. Some reported hearing noises, buzzing, ringing, roaring, chimes or bells.

4. Most experienced a dark space, often described as a tunnel, which they moved through quickly.

5. Many then experienced being outside of their bodies and looking down, surprised at the efforts being made to revive them. Seeing and vision seemed enhanced.

6. Most reported reunions with relatives and friends who'd died earlier, a sort of greeting committee.

7. Nearly all experienced a beautiful luminous light or 'light being' who felt enormously loving. The identification of this light being was determined by their experience before death. (Dr. Karlis Osis and Erlendur Haraldsson made a cross-cultural study between the U.S. and India. They found that Christians interpreted the light being as Christ and Hindus interpreted it as a Hindu deity. Both Asians and Americans saw the dark passage, brilliant light and 'dead' relatives.

8. The light being often suggested that the person review their life. No one reported feeling this was punitive, only instructive.

9. The person reached a barrier or limit where they felt they must choose whether or not to return to life. Most found 'being dead' so beautiful that returning was a hard decision. Many decided to return only because of their great love for their children or spouse.

10. After the experience, most felt they wouldn't be afraid to die again. And their experience of life was greatly enhanced.

What about heaven and hell? Each of us defines them in our way. To me, they're states of consciousness rather than places. Heaven is consciousness of union with everything, with God. Hell is consciousness of separation. Heaven is remembering who we are. Hell is forgetting—believing we're separate and alone. Heaven is love. Hell is fear.

There is only one time-space, so after we die we all go to the same 'place'. If we got what we deserved based on some of our unkind behavior in life, there probably would be a hell. I believe we get what we deserve based on who we most profoundly are, no matter what the outward appearances—love. And love is the reward for love. So I believe in a heaven, a 'place' of love, after physical death.

I also believe as surely as hell has existed on earth, so does heaven exist on earth. To experience heaven on earth, we have to heal the eye of the heart so we see life through the lens of love instead of the lens of fear. Then we see the beauty, courage and nobility of our human family and the exquisite natural beauty of the earth. When we're in love, we experience heaven on earth. That's why we long for that experience. Through our much disparaged "rose colored glasses", we see the truth. Heaven is already on earth. We don't have to wait until we die.

To me, hell is all the things we create when we see life through the lens of fear. Hell is punishment. If life is a school for remembering love, as I like to think, would God punish us because we stumble and fall? Seems unlikely to me. I imagine that each time we fall, the God in us picks us up, dusts us off, says "I love you", and we start again. No one punishes us except ourselves.

Evidently, after we die, we review our lives so we can learn from our experience. Perhaps this review is what some call hell or purgatory. Re-experiencing some of the unloving things we've done can be awful. Once my whole life flashed before me and I felt enormous pain just witnessing myself turning my back on someone whose eyes were asking me for love or help. I hate to think how I'd have felt if I'd killed someone. But perhaps in terms of unconditional love, killing someone physically and withholding love, killing someone emotionally, are of equal weight.

What about sin and evil? To me, they're energy we haven't looked into deeply enough to fully understand. Sin and evil are a lack of love. So they are healed by love, not punishment, which is just more lack of love. At times we may have to physically segregate someone so they won't hurt us while they're learning to love. Prisons won't be effective deterrents until they teach love.

Punishment is a form of manipulation. It's a way to control people with fear. Perhaps hell, major punishment, was invented so some groups could control their members with fear. Many organized religions suggest that *their* way is the *only* way to God. Follow instructions or be punished! This is not to deny the beauty of organized religions, but only to point out that they are made up of people like you and me who have free will and are, therefore, fallible.

I believe we can't give the responsibility for our relationship with God, with life, to anyone else. We are each ultimately responsible.

Until the Second Council of Constantinople in A.D. 553, reincarnation, which teaches that we're responsible, was included in the Bible. Jesus himself indicated his belief in reincarnation when he said that John the Baptist was Elijah, the dead prophet returned. (Matthew 11:14)

For more than 500 years, reincarnation, "the **mystical** doctrine", was widely accepted by Christians including the most eminent church fathers. The Council, presided over by the Emperor Augustinian, declared it heresy. They called it "the **mythical** doctrine" and deleted it from the Bible by a vote of 3 to 2. Perhaps it was politically expedient for the Church for people *not* to know that they had more than one chance to get to heaven, or that eventually everyone gets there no matter what their religious path.* Reincarnation is still found in St. Augustine's writings, a man who inspires both Catholics and non-Catholics.

The fundamental premise of reincarnation is that everyone is in the process of returning home to God or

---

* The edict of the Second Council of Constantinople said: "Whosoever shall support the mythical doctrine or the preexistence of the soul and the consequent wonderful opinion of its return, let him be anathema."

Pope Vigilius never authorized the "anathema" but it was generally believed that he had. Because the Church never made an 'official' statement against reincarnation, perhaps it's possible for practicing Catholics to believe in reincarnation without being in technical disagreement with Church doctrine.

growing to godhood. And we are born again and again until we reach that union. Each soul is created equal to every other soul. Each soul has free will to remember its true nature in its *own* way and its *own* time. **No time or way is better than another.** The paths home are as many as the people on the earth. Nothing can stop our homeward journey. Any delays we might experience are just opportunities to deepen our understanding.

Reincarnation teaches that we choose when and to whom we will be born. We choose our parents, the ones most suitable to provide the environment we need to complete any unlearned lessons. As a soul, we enter the physical child conceived by the chosen parents. We reincarnate in groups, so we see again and again people we've loved and helped as well and those we've hated and hurt. According to this belief system, our coming together as families and friends is no accident.

We also choose when we will die. When the soul sees that the body is no longer in condition to support our continued learning, it gives a signal for the dying process to begin. Sometimes the soul leaves the body **before** the body stops functioning. This may explain a feeling commonly reported by people on deathbed watches. They sense the person has already gone.

According to the belief in reincarnation, we create, allow, or tolerate everything we experience in our lives in order to help us learn, or remember. We don't always get what we *consciously* want in life; we get what we believe or what we fear. No one is a victim. Assuming we're victims is a way we avoid taking responsibility for what we create. Once we remember who we really are and become responsible co-creators, we aren't born again, unless we choose to return to serve our fellow human beings.

"Whatsoever a man sows, that shall he also reap."
(Galatians 6:7) The cause and effect of our actions is sometimes called the **Law of Karma.** The law is simply a description of how energy works. Plant a carrot, reap a carrot.
Give love, receive love. Karma may also be understood as
our unlearned lessons and/or as judgements we make that
keep us feeling separate.

Karma means we're responsible and accountable for all
past choices and actions *no matter how small.* We reap the
blessings and the teachings. Being sick, having a car accident or going to jail are not punishments or 'bad karma.'
They're opportunities *we've created* to help us remember or
learn so we can change our lives and live more joyfully.

There's also group karma. I believe, for example, it's
the karma of the human race and individuals to learn to live
together in peace. World War II, for example, was a
reminder we created that we weren't doing too well. It was
group karma, but no one chose to be alive at that time who
didn't have the individual karma to learn from it.

Unconditional love doesn't create karma. If in any situation my intention was love, I am responsible for love. If
hate was my intention, I'm responsible for hate, and karma
is created. "Working out karma"—being responsible for
what we feel, think, say and do—teaches love and compassion. It helps us move beyond separation to the truth of
unity.

Unconditional love transcends karma. Another way of
saying that is "Divine will transcends the cause and effect of
human will." Sometimes this is called the **Law of Grace.
Grace is the teaching of compassion that Jesus Christ added
to the older Hindu and Buddhist teaching of divine justice,
karma.**

Life After Death

For example, if I become a different person from the one I was when I created the karma (by changing, transforming, repenting, re-thinking, etc.), I'm free of it. Karma is education, not punishment and I've learned my lesson.

Justice is the great teaching of the mind; love, compassion and freedom are the perhaps greater teachings of the heart.

Unconditional love heals, completes, finishes karma. At any time we can break the cycle of birth, death and rebirth, by loving unconditionally. It may take many lifetimes. Or, it's possible for you and I to do it right now.

In a very real sense, helping others love the God within them is helping ourselves, for . . .

No man is an island . . . (each) is a piece of the continent, a part of the main . . . any man's death diminishes me, because I am involved in mankind, and therefore never send to know for whom the bell tolls; **it tolls for you.**

—John Donne, 1623

Perhaps our work is to love, to serve and to remember.

When we see all of nature working in cycles, I often wonder why we don't envision the same for ourselves. Is it arrogance or is it fear that we'll lose our individuality, our specialness, if we're part of some larger whole? Are we confusing uniformity with unity? Each flower, tree, sunset and human being gives its unique gift to the whole. We see a seed planted, growing to maturity, bearing fruit, decaying, dying and releasing seeds that sprout anew. Over and over we see the cycle of birth, death and rebirth.

333

Coming Home

Are we not too part of the cyclical process of nature? Does not the seed-core in us continue to grow after our bodies die?

* * * * *

I'd like to share with you how my understanding of the continuity of life grew.

As a child, when I was still closely connected to my heart-knowing, I knew that life didn't end. But everyone said it ended with death and they were bigger than me, and I wanted their approval. (Interestingly, Dr. Kübler-Ross reports that children up to five years old believe death is reversible.) It didn't make sense to me that we came into the world, did this little dance and were snuffed out.

I heard a lot of talk about justice, loving our brothers, freedom and perfection that didn't make sense in terms of what I saw around me. "Why are they starving?" "Why was their son killed in an accident?" "Why are we so lucky?" "Why is his wife so mean to him?" "Why is she dying of cancer? She's such a good person."

It seems unfair! It looks like chaos!

Then I noticed there were some things I really loved and some I hated and most of the time I didn't know why. Not so long ago I loved everything Black American, Native American, Persian and Tibetan and hated everything German. I didn't think I was a racist . . . so why hate Germans? Out of ten years living in Europe, I spent *one night* in Germany. That night I was so terrified that I barricaded my hotel room door with a dresser and chairs. Definitely not rational!

334

First with the help of friends guiding me and then alone, I slowly began to remember what I call past lives. Others may prefer to call them personal archetypes.

I remembered having been a German Jew who died at Buchenwald. After remembering, slowly I began to understand. I was judging Germans as they had judged me. They made Jews separate. I made Germans separate. There is a 'Hitler' in me — the part of me that judges. I forgave myself for making that separation and now love Germans as I would anyone else.

There is a 'Hitler' in each of us. It's the part that keeps us separate from each other, from our kinship with all of life.

Perhaps the Jews and Germans sacrificed to remind us of our common humanity — to give us another chance to remember to love. Will we listen to the gentle teaching of love, or will we create something horrible to remind us again? It's our choice. At each moment of our lives, you and I must choose between love and fear. If we don't choose love **consciously**, fear wins by default.

Gradually I began to experience life as a wave of energy, now cresting in form, now dissolving into formlessness. The unconditional love, justice, freedom, peace and joy we dream of are possible for everyone if we're moving toward realizing them over a number of lifetimes. I began to understand that what I'd interpreted as chaos were opportunities to learn.

I began to understand that all our concepts and beliefs about life, including my own, are not to be taken too seriously. They're helpful, if limited frames of reference that give us a sense of purpose and direction. They point us toward experiencing everything as one. They aren't the experience. They too dissolve in the union with all that is. So one set of beliefs is temporarily as useful as another as long as it makes the heart glad and leaves room for the beliefs of those who differ.

I know again in my heart that death is just a word we invented to describe leaving a body we no longer need. Life is endless . . . only the form changes.

APPENDIX A

USEFUL ADDRESSES

Compassionate Friends

This is a national organization with about 500 local support groups for patients of children who've died.

Compassionate Friends
P.O. Box 3969
Oak Brook, IL 60522
(312) 990-0010

Center for Attitudinal Healing

This group provides support for children with life-threatening diseases and their parents. They have excellent educational materials.

The Center for Attitudinal Healing
19 Main St.
Tiburon, CA 94920
(415) 435-5022

Elisabeth Kübler-Ross Center

Provides educational materials about death and dying. Gives workshops around the U.S., Eurpoe and Australia for people in transition.

The Elisabeth Kübler-Ross Center
South Rte. 616
Head Waters, VA 24442
(703) 396-3441

Funeral and Memorial Societies

These groups can provide information about funeral arrangements in your community. To find a local chapter write:

The Continental Association of Funeral
and Memorial Societies
2001 S St., N.W., Suite 530
Washington, D.C. 20009
(202) 745-0634

Hospices

To locate a hospice, call your local hospital, visiting nurse service or contact the National Hospice Organization.

Appendix A

National Hospice Organization
1901 Ft. Myer Drive
Arlingtoon, VA 22209
(703) 243-5900

Medic Publishing Company

They publish the booklets *Healing a Father's Grief* and *Is there Anything I can do to Help*. Send $1.35 each.

Medic Publishing Company
P.O. Box 89
Redmond, WA 98073-0089
(206) 881-2883

Seeds to Sow

This book is available for $25 from:

Trigger and Barbara Lake
P.O. Box 203
Troy, Alabama 36081

Silent Unity

Silent Unity is the headquarters of the Unity Churches. They provide spiritual support. The name of someone who requests prayer is placed in what they call a Room of Light for 30 days. Someone remains in the room 24 hours a day praying.

Silent Unity
Unity Village, MO 64065
(816) 524-3550
(800) 821-2935 (toll free)

Simonton Cancer Center

This center does counseling based on the work of Dr. Carl Simonton. Their approach combines meditation, progressive relaxation, visual imagery and nutrition for treating cancer.

Simonton Cancer Center
P.O. Box 1055
Azle, TX 76020
(817) 444-4073

The Society for The Right to Die and Concern For Dying

Both societies are educational councils who work for the recognition of the individual's right to die with dignity. Write to them for Living Will Declarations and the appropriate documents authorized by state right-to-die laws.

Society for the Right to Die
250 W. 57th St.
NYC, NY 10107
(212) 246-6973

Concern for Dying
(same address)
(212) 246-6962

Southwestern College of Life Sciences

This college offers degrees in transformational counseling and seminars in working with different levels of consciousness. They also do aura balancings. I studied with them for years and found their work excellent.

Southwestern College of Life Sciences
P.O. Box 4711
Sante Fe, NM 87502
(505) 471-5756

Appendix A

Uniform Donor Card Sources

Living Bank
P.O. Box 6725
Houston, TX 77005

American Medical Association
535 N. Dearborn St.
Chicago, IL 60610

Eye Bank Association of America
1511 K. St. N.W. Suite 830
Washington, D.C. 20005-1401

Medic Alert
P.O. Box 1009
Turlock, CA 95380

National Pituitary Agency
Suite 503-7
210 West Fayetter St.
Baltimore, MD 21201

National Kidney Foundation
116 East 27th St.
New York, NY 10016

APPENDIX B

STANDING ORDERS
TERMINALLY ILL PATIENTS

1. Do not resuscitate.

2. Family conference whenever possible.

3. Social Service and Pastoral Care to see patient. OT and PT prn.

4. DIET: As tol. May have wine, beer, alcohol ad lib.

5. ACTIVITY: As tol. Posey belt prn, up with assistance.

6. SLEEP: Halcion 0.25 mg. (po), may repeat × 1; or Chloral Hydrate 500 mg. (po) or L-Tryptophan 2000 to 3000 mg @ HS prn — give 8:00 p.m.

7. DYSPNEA: O_2 nasal cannula @ 2 L prn c̄ chronic lung disease.

O$_2$ nasal cannula @ 4-6 L prn s̄ chronic lung disease.

2-4 mg. oral or rectal Morphine Sulfate q 4 h. prn dyspnea, for malignant chest disease. In chronic lung disease make sure bronchospasm has been adequately treated.

For wheezing: Ventolin Inhaler 2 puffs qid.

8. COPIUS SECRETIONS: Atropine 0.4 to 1.0 mg.

9. COUGH: Robitussin DAC 1 tsp. q 4 h. prn (contains codeine).

   Honey and lemon juice prn.

   Tesalon Perles 100 mg tid.

10. NAUSEA AND VOMITING:

Mild-intermittent

- Haldol 1.0 mg HS po or
- Torecan 10 mg (po/IM/supp) q 3-4 h. prn or
- Compazine spansules 10 to 15 mg. q 10 to 12 hrs. or
- Compazine 5 to 10 mg. po/IM q 4 hr. prn or
- Compazine 12.5 to 25 mg. PR q 6 h. prn, do not exceed 100 mgm. in 24°.
- Marazine 50 to 100 mg. IM or po q 4 to 6 hrs.

Moderate (Nausea continuous, vomiting intermittent and not controlled by above)

- D.C. Torecan, Compazine, Marazine
- Haldol 1 mg. q 6 h. po or Sub Q 6 h. NOT PRN

Increase by increments of 1 mg. q 3–6 h. until N/V controlled or until top dose of 4 mg. q 6 h. is reached. If no symptoms for 24 hrs., begin incremental decrease in Haldol of 1 mg. q 12 hrs. Attempt to decrease completely. If not possible, lower dose to lower dose compatible with control.

Severe

• Inapsine 1.25 mg IV every 2 hrs. prn.

Nausea due to Squashed Stomach Syndrome:

1. 6 small meals per day.

2. Simethecone (mylicon) 80 mg. po with meals.

   Maalox II 10 cc. after meals and HS, liquids or tablets.

3. Reglan 10 to 20 mg. po/IV q 6 h., 1/2 h. AC and HS.

Nausea due to motion

Add transderm Scopalamine 1 patch q 3 days.

11. INDIGESTION: Maalox TC 15 cc. prn.

    (15 cc. TC = 30 cc. other antacids)

12. ANXIETY: Xanax .25 to .5 tid.

    Use lower dose if elderly.

    Re-evaluate in 24-hours and call physician.

13. DEPRESSION: Call physician for consideration of tricyclic antidepressant.

14. ACUTE SEVERE AGITATION:

Valium 10 to 20 mg. IM. If no effect in 30-minutes, give initial dose plus increment of 5 mg.

If this method has to be used more than once in 72-hours, introduction of major tranquilizer needed.

Haldol 1 to 3 mg. po or IM q 4 h. prn.

15. ORAL CARE: Frequent mouth cleansing, vaseline to lips prn, suction prn.

(Do not use lemon-glycerine swabs)

Cepacol lozenges, Moi-Stir spray or artificial saliva 1–2 tsp. 4 h. prn.

Mycostatin Oral Suspension (S & S) 5 cc. qid or

Nizoral 200 mg. (po) qd. for Monilia infection.

16. EYE CARE: Isopto Tears prn or Lactilube ointment prn.

17. ELIMINATION:

When morphine or belladonna is in patient's regimen:

c̄ MS 10 to 15 mg. — Use Senokot-S 2 tabs HS.

c̄ MS 16 to 100 mg. — Use Senokot-S 3 tabs HS.

c̄ MS over 100 mg. — Use Senokot-S 4 tabs HS.

(may use tablets, flakes or liquid Senokot-S — if liquid is necessary use 1 tsp. of Senokot-S Syrup + 1 tsp. of liquid Docusate to equal 1 tablet Senokot-S.

Dulcolax tab 1–2 prn.

M. O. M. 30 cc HS or M. O. M. c̄ Cascara 30 cc. HS prn.

Dulcolax supp. 10 mg. prn. Fleet/KY/oil retention/ Castile soap suds enema prn.

18. BLADDER:

Foley catheter prn, replace q month, Caude Catheter if needed. Irrigate c̄ Saline prn.

Thorough Peri care bid.

For Bladder spasms—B and O supp. $1/2$ or full strength q 4 h. prn or

Cystopaz—1 to 2 tablets qid. (contraindicated in bladder outlet obstruction)

Neosporin to tip of penis prn.

19. SKIN

Eggcrate mattress/floatation pad prn.

Observe skin carefully for impending skin breakdown or irritated skin.

Tegaderm prn. Duoderm prn. Caldesene powder. Sween cream.

Cortaide or Neosporin prn for macerated skin.

20. FEVER:

Greater than 101° (R) Tylenol or Aspirin 650 mg. (po/supp) q 4 h.

21. PAIN:

Mild:

- Tylenol
- Mortrin 600 mg. q 6 h.
- Trilisate liquid (500 mg./5 cc. or 500 mg. tablets) 1500 mg. q 12 h.
- Arthropan Liquid 870 mg. po q 4 h.
- Feldene 20 mg. qd.

- Naprosyn 500 mg. qid.

Moderate Chronic:

- Tylenol #3 or #4 1 to 2 tab q 3–4 h. not prn.
- Emperin #3 or #4 1 to 2 tab q 3–4 h. not prn.
- Darvon 65 mg. Plain q 4 hr. not prn.
- Darvocet N 100 q 4 h. not prn.

Moderate to severe:

- Plain oxycodone 5 to 10 mg. q 4 h. not prn.
- Dilaudid 2 to 4 mg. q r h. po/IM not prn.
- Dilaudid Supp. 3 mg. q 4 h. not prn.
- Oral Morphine 5 to 10 mg. q 4 h. *NOT PRN*

Method of titration: Initiate dose according to estimation of level of pain. Assess in 2 hours (peak serum level), if patient still in pain give additional bolus of $\frac{1}{2}$ initial dose. At four hours from initial dose, if patient comfortable, the dose will be the initial dose plus bolus dose. If at 4 hours patient still uncomfortable, increase by 25% of total dose.

Severe Pain:

OMS 40 mg. q 4 h. not prn. Increase up to 80 mg. in the same manner as above.

Check with physician for levels over 80.

Alternate routes: May use morphine supp., instant release tablets — Sub Lingual tablets or buccal.

MS Contin 30 mg. tablets: Titrate dose first with OMS — then calculate 24 h. dose, dividing in 2, give q 12 h.

Appendix B

Long acting Morphine Tablets:

- MS Contin q 12 h.

- Roxanol SR q 8 h.

For IV drip of Subcutaneous pump: Check with physician and be certain to calculate equal analgesic doses.

Bone Pain:

Add ASA gr. X po or Supp. q 4 h.

Motrin 600 mg. q 6 h.

Feldene 20 mg. qd.

Trilisate liquid or tablets 1500 mg. q 12 h.

Arthropan 870 mg. po q 4 h.

Indomethecin Suppository 50 mg. tid.

Voluntary Muscle Spasm:

Flexaril 10 mg. tid or

Valium 5 mg. q 12 h.

Involuntary Muscle Spasm:

Cystospaz 1 or 2 q 6 h. (contraindicated in bladder outlet obstruction)

Atropine 0.4–0.6 IM/Sub Q

B. O. Suppositories ½ to full strength q 4 h.

Itching:

Benadryl 25 to 50 mg. po or IM q 6 h.

Seldane 60 mg. bid po

Periaction 4 mg. q 4 h. prn

Skin:

Alpha Keri lotion or oil prn.

22. AGONAL RESPIRATORY DISTRESS: IV Valium 2 to 5 mg. IV q 30-minutes.

23. AGONAL TWITCHING: IV Valium 2 to 5 mg. IV q 4 h.

24. AGONAL AGITATION: Thorazine 25 mg. (R) q 4 h.

Provided by the North Hospice, North Memorial Medical Center, Robbinsdale, Minnesota.

APPENDIX C

AMERICAN MEDICAL ASSOCIATION
Statement of the Council
on Ethical and Judicial Affairs

WITHHOLDING OR WITHDRAWING
LIFE PROLONGING MEDICAL TREATMENT

The social commitment of the physician is to sustain life and relieve suffering. Where the performance of one duty conflicts with the other, the choice of the patient, or his family or legal representative if the patient is incompetent to act in his own behalf, should prevail. In the absence of the patient's choice or an authorized proxy, the physician must act in the best interest of the patient.

For humane reasons, with informed consent, a physician may do what is medically necessary to alleviate severe pain, or cease or omit treatment to permit a terminally ill patient whose death is imminent to die. However, he should not intentionally cause death. In deciding whether the administration of potentially life-prolonging medical treatment is in the best interest of the patient who is incompetent to act in his own behalf, the physician should determine what the possibility is for extending life under humane and comfortable conditions and what are the prior expressed wishes of the patient and attitudes of the family or those who have responsibility for the custody of the patient.

Even if death is not imminent but a patient's coma is beyond doubt irreversible and there are adequate safeguards to confirm the accuracy of the diagnosis and with the concurrence of those who have responsibility for the care of the patient, it is not unethical to discontinue all means of life prolonging medical treatment.

Life prolonging treatment includes medication and artificially or technologically supplied respiration, nutrition or hydration. In treating a terminally ill or irreversibly comatose patient, the physician should determine whether the benefits of treatment outweigh its burdens. At all times, the dignity of the patient should be maintained.

March 15, 1986

APPENDIX D

GUIDELINES FOR HOME CARE OF PERSONS INFECTED BY THE VIRUS THAT CAUSES AIDS

These guidelines developed by The Department of Nursing Services, The Infection Control Program, and Home Health Services of the University of Minnesota Hospitals & Clinics.

I would like to add that people who have AIDS are our brothers, our sisters and our babies. They are presently our best teachers about love and compassion. Much of the information in this book will be useful in caring for them.

"This pamphlet was written for persons who will assist in the care of a patient infected by the virus which causes AIDS (acquired immune deficiency syndrome). It describes how the AIDS virus is transmitted and describes precautions that should be taken in the household to protect the person with AIDS as well as other household members. **Transmis-**

352

sion of the AIDS virus to caregivers at home has never been demonstrated. Nevertheless, there are certain hygienic measures that seem prudent to follow.

TRANSMISSION OF THE AIDS VIRUS

Aids is caused by a new virus which is most often called the HTLV-III virus. The virus itself can cause weakness, tiredness, fever, sweating episodes, chronic diarrhea, and alterations in mood and mental processes. In severely affected persons, this virus creates a defect in the immune system. People with this defect are susceptible to infection by a group of unusual germs ('opportunistic pathogens').

The major groups at risk for AIDS are homosexual and bisexual men, intravenous drug abusers, hemophilia patients, persons who have resided in Haiti or Central Africa, sexual partners of the persons mentioned above and offspring of women infected before delivery. Most of the people who have been infected by the virus causing AIDS do not currently have any symptoms from their infection. In the first five years about one to five percent of the people infected by this virus will develop AIDS. How many of the remaining people will ultimately develop AIDS is unknown.

Transmission of the virus which causes AIDS occurs during sexual contact and from sharing unsterilized needles. Transmission sometimes occurs during pregnancy from the mother to the unborn child. Blood products previously transmitted the virus. Screening of donated blood and heat treatment of certain blood products has greatly reduced this mechanism of transmission of the virus. **Transmission of**

the virus has occurred to health care workers when blood is accidently inoculated through their skin, for example, from a needlestick, and from nursing mothers to their babies.*

Transmission by non-sexual contact, even if intimate and prolonged, has never been demonstrated and therefore, if it occurs at all, must be very rare. Several hundred household contacts of AIDS patients, including parents who did not know their babies were infected, have been investigated. Not a single transmission of the AIDS virus was found. Nevertheless, **it is impossible to be certain that non-sexual contact will never result in transmission**. In light of this, the measures described in the next sections seem prudent. Most of them reflect basic hygienic practice and are reasonable in all situations.

PREVENTING TRANSMISSION
GENERAL PRECAUTIONS

The main focus of prevention of non-sexual AIDS virus transmission should be the avoidance of blood and body fluid contact with new cuts or fresh abrasions. It is extremely unlikely that the AIDS virus penetrates intact skin. It is prudent to **avoid transfer of blood and body fluids to the mouth, eyes and nose.** Handshaking, ordinary

---

* It was first reported in May 1987 that three professional caregivers working with Aids patients contacted the Aids virus by exposure to blood, without a needle prick. Breaks in their skin (such as abrasions, cuts, burns, chapped areas) and accidentally receiving blood in the mouth apparently allowed the virus to enter their bodies. **If you have skin breaks, use extreme caution to protect yourself from the blood or other body fluids of an infected person.**

social contact and touching dry skin are thought to be safe. Simple gestures of affection such as hugging and kissing dry skin are equally safe.

Precautions taken in the household are for the protection of the person with AIDS as well as the other household members. Fungal disease sometimes occurs in persons with AIDS. Therefore, the person with AIDS should avoid activities which involve major exposure to decaying organic debris such as a compost heap or hay barns. Roosting areas for birds such as pigeons should also be avoided. If there is a cat in the household, the litter box should be changed weekly by a friend. This activity should be done out of doors.

CARE GIVING TECHNIQUES

Gloves are to be worn when doing wound care or handling intravascular devices such as the Hickman catheter or IV line. The gloves are worn to protect the patient. In addition, it prevents the caregiver from potential contact with the person's blood and body fluids.

Caregivers administering medication utilizing a needle should take precautions to avoid puncturing themselves with the used needle. To avoid puncture do not break or resheath needles after use. Dispose of needles in a securely covered metal container (such as a coffee can). Dispose of the can by placing in the outside garbage on the day of pick up.

A gown or full apron and gloves are to be worn only when you give personal care that involves contact with body secretions. This may occur when changing linens of a person who has had an involuntary bowel movement. Following care, the gloves may be discarded and the gown or apron washed. (Refer to Housekeeping Section.) A mask and goggles are rarely indicated for procedures in the hospital and are almost never needed in the home. The virus does not spread through the air.

Kleenex rather than cloth handkerchiefs should be used and disposed of in plastic bags. Any other disposable items should be handled in this manner.

Toothbrushes, razors, nail files, tweezers and other personal care items are to be kept separate and not shared.

Pregnant individuals may visit or care for the patient using the same technique recommended for others.

HOUSEKEEPING MEASURES

Bed linen and pajamas soiled with blood, vomitus or stool should be collected separately in a disposable container such as a plastic bag. The linen and clothing should be washed as soon as possible. Always use the maximum water level in the washing machine. Set the water heater at a high level temperature (about 140°) for 15 or 20 minutes before washing the soiled clothing. If the water cannot reach this temperature be sure to use maximum water level with the detergent to dilute the soil in the linen. Permit the machine to agitate until linen and detergent have been thoroughly combined. Stop the cycle and permit the load to soak 20 minutes. After the soak add one half cup bleach and permit the machine to run the full wash, rinse, spin cycle.

Clothing not soiled with blood, vomitus or stool may be washed with detergent only.

During a meal there should be no sharing of food, eating utensils or cups.

Machine or handwashed dishes are to be washed in hot water and detergent, followed by a hot water rinse.

Tubs should be cleaned between use with a cleanser containing bleach. Toilets, sinks and showers should be washed with a bleach solution when soiled with vomitus, blood or diarrhea. Prepare the bleach solution by adding 6 tablespoons of bleach (sodium hypochlorite) to one quart of water.

Items which cannot be washed should be protected if there is the risk of contact with body fluids. For example, the mattress should be covered with a plastic mattress pad.

SOCIALIZING

Children in the home may visit the person infected with the virus that causes AIDS and participate in social activities such as playing games, listening to records, watching TV, etc. Children may be held by the person infected with the virus that causes AIDS. Affection may be shown by hugs and dry kisses, however, not near the eyes, nose or mouth. Infants should be restrained from placing their hands into the nose, mouth and eyes of the person infected with the virus that causes AIDS. Babies may be fed by that person. Efforts should be made to avoid any oral ingestion of the person's saliva of other secretions by the infant. For

357

instance, the person should not taste food fed to the infant or touch the nipple of a bottle-fed child.

Visitors with infections should be sure that infected secretions do not reach the person infected with the virus that causes AIDS. Those with respiratory tract infections should wear a mask while in that person's house. If the person infected with the virus that causes AIDS has not had chickenpox, visitors with chickenpox or shingles should not enter the house.

Transmission of AIDS by sexual contact raises an important concern as sexual expression is important and needed by a person infected with the virus that causes AIDS. 'Safer' practices can be used that do not permit exchange of body fluids (semen, blood or saliva.)

* * * * *

This guideline represents the best available information as of June, 1987. Because our knowledge about Aids has been increasing rapidly, I encourage you to contact your local city or state department for updated or further information. They receive regular updates from the Center for Disease Control in Atlanta.

APPENDIX E

DIRECTIVE TO PHYSICIANS

Sample From Texas

Directive made this _____ day of _____ (month, year). I, _____, being of sound mind, wilfully and voluntarily make known my desire that my life shall not be artificially prolonged under the circumstances set forth below, and do hereby declare:

If at any time I should have an incurable condition caused by injury, disease, or illness certified to be a terminal condition by two physicians, and where the application of life-sustaining procedures would serve only to artificially prolong the moment of my death and where my attending physician determines that my death is imminent whether or not life-sustaining procedures are utilized, I direct that such procedures be withheld or withdrawn, and that I be permitted to die naturally.

Coming Home

In the absence of my ability to give directions regarding the use of such life-sustaining procedures it is my intention that this directive shall be honored by my family and physicians as the final expression of my legal right to refuse medical or surgical treatment and accept the consequences from such refusal.

If I have been diagnosed as pregnant and that diagnosis is known to my physician, this directive shall have no force or effect during the course of my pregnancy.

Other direction: *[See reverse side for suggested Proxy Designation form]*

This directive shall be in effect until it is revoked.

I understand the full import of this directive and I am emotionally and mentally competent to make this directive.

I understand that I may revoke this directive at any time.

Signed _____

City, County, and State of Residence _____

The declarant has been personally known to me and I believe him/her to be of sound mind. I am not related to the declarant by blood or marriage, nor would I be entitled to any portion of the declarant's estate on his/her decease, nor am I the attending physician of the declarant or an employee of the attending physician or a health facility in

Appendix E

which the declarant is a patient, or a patient in the health care facility in which the declarant is a patient, or any person who has a claim against any portion of the estate of the declarant upon his/her decease.

Witness _____   Witness _____

This Directive complies with the Natural Death Act, Tex. Stat. Ann. art 4590h (1977, amend. 1985).

Courtesy of Society for the Right to Die, 250 West 57 Street, New York, NY 10107.

PROXY DESIGNATION CLAUSE

If you wish, you may use this section to designate someone to make treatment decisions if you are unable to do so. Your Directive to Physicians will be given effect even if you have not designated a proxy.

I authorize the following person to implement my Directive to Physicians by accepting, refusing and/or making decisions about treatment and hospitalization:

Name _____

Address _____

If the person I have named above is unable to act on my behalf, I authorize the following person to do so:

Name _____

Address _____

I have discussed my wishes with these persons and trust their judgment on my behalf.

Signed _____ Date _____

Witness _____ Witness_____

APPENDIX F

The American Hospital Association presents a Patient's Bill of Rights with the expectation that observance of these rights will contribute to more effective patient care and greater satisfaction for the patient, his physician, and the hospital organization. Further, the Association presents these rights in the expectation that they will be supported by the hospital on behalf of its patients, as an integral part of the healing process. It is recognized that a personal relationship between the physician and the patient is essential for the provision of proper medical care. The traditional physician-patient relationship takes on a new dimension when care is rendered within an organizational structure. Legal precedent has established that the institution itself also has a responsibility to the patient. It is in recognition of these factors that these rights are affirmed.

PATIENT'S BILL OF RIGHTS

1. The patient has the right to considerate and respectful care.

2. The patient has the right to obtain from his physician complete current information concerning his diagnosis, treatment, and prognosis in terms the patient can be reasonably expected to understand. When it is not medically advisable to give such information to the patient, the information should be made available to an appropriate person in his behalf. He has the right to know, by name, the physician responsible for coordinating his care.

3. The patient has the right to receive from his physician information necessary to give informed consent prior to the start of any procedure and/or treatment. Except in emergencies, such information for informed consent, should include but not necessarily be limited to the specific procedure and/or treatment, the medically significant risks involved, and the probable duration of incapacitation. Where medically significant alternatives for care or treatment exist, or when the patient requests information concerning medical alternatives, the patient has the right to such information. The patient also has the right to know the name of the person responsible for the procedures and/or treatment.

4. The patient has the right to refuse treatment to the extent permitted by law, and to be informed of the medical consequences of his action.

5. The patient has the right to every consideration of his privacy concerning his own medical care program. Case discussion, consultation, examination, and treatment

are confidential and should be conducted discreetly. Those not directly involved in his care must have the permission of the patient to be present.

6. The patient has the right to expect that all communications and records pertaining to his care should be treated as confidential.

7. The patient has the right to expect that within its capacity a hospital must make reasonable response to the request of a patient for services. The hospital must provide evaluation, service, and/or referral as indicated by the urgency of the case. When medically permissible, a patient may be transferred to another facility only after he has received complete information and explanation concerning the needs for and alternatives to such a transfer. The institution to which the patient is to be transferred must first have accepted the patient for transfer.

8. The patient has the right to obtain information as to any relationship of his hospital to other health care and educational institutions insofar as his care is concerned. The patient has the right to obtain information as to the existence of any professional relationships among individuals, by name, who are treating him.

9. The patient has the right to be advised if the hospital proposes to engage in or perform human experimentation affecting his care or treatment. The patient has the right to refuse to participate in such research projects.

10. The patient has the right to expect reasonable continuity of care. He has the right to know in advance what appointment times and physicians are available and where. The patient has the right to expect that the hospital will provide a mechanism whereby he is informed

by his physician or a delegate of the physician of the patient's continuing health care requirements following discharge.

11. The patient has the right to examine and receive an explanation of his bill regardless of source of payment.

12. The patient has the right to know what hospital rules and regulations apply to his conduct as a patient.

No catalog of rights can guarantee for the patient the kind of treatment he has a right to expect. A hospital has many functions to perform, including the prevention and treatment of disease, the education of both health professionals and patients, and the conduct of clinical research. All these activities must be conducted with an overriding concern for the patient, and above all, the recognition of his dignity as a human being. Success in achieving this recognition assures success in the defense of the rights of the patient.

APPENDIX G

TAKING A DYING PERSON HOME
FROM THE HOSPITAL
WHEN THE STAFF OBJECTS

If the dying person has expressed a wish, either now or earlier, to die at home and the hospital staff objects, here are some suggestions:

Mrs. Henry W. Levinson, Executive Director of the educational council, Concern for Dying, suggests:

> Theoretically, the patient has the right to be wherever he or she wants to be. However in the case of incompetence of a patient, the institution can put up all kinds of roadblocks and often does. If the family is willing and able to stand firm on their right to make decisions for next of kin, one good position is, 'You required consent before you could treat this patient. We are now refusing that consent

367

and any further treatment of this patient will be without consent and will be considered assault and battery.'

If the hospital is not allowed to treat a patient generally the hospital utilization committee will say that the patient can no longer stay in the hospital. On occasion, a doctor or hospital lawyer will feel strongly about the patient's need for treatment or disagree so strongly with the family's decision that they will ask for a court order for the appointment of a guardian for the purpose of treating the patient without the consent of the next of kin. These cases are few and far between, however, and the majority of them involve minors.

The Society for the Right to Die (SRD) is also an educational council with legal advisors on its staff who sometimes act as patient advocates. It's executive director, Alice Mehling, very kindly said, "If you have difficulties, call SRD." (212) 246-6973.

APPENDIX H

THE BACH FLOWER REMEDIES

The basic cause of disease is due to disharmony between the personality and the Soul. The Bach Remedies help restore that harmony.

Dr. Edward Bach (1886–1936)

There are a number of ways to determine which flowers are needed. The simplest way, unless you know how to use a pendulum, is to talk with the person you're diagnosing. Then, using what she or he says and your own intuition, choose from the list below. If you use a pendulum, place the flower bottles close to the person, inside their auric field, and select the flowers that swing 'positive.'

To mix remedies use a ½ oz. or 1 oz. brown dropper bottle, fill it with spring water and add ¼ dropper of brandy. Add two drops from the stock flower bottles you've selected. Then shake the bottle 50 times. For chronic problems take about ¼ dropperful four times a day. For acute problems or crises, take a few drops every 10 or 15 minutes. You can also add drops to juice or water, bath water and massage lotions. Use in combinations of up to five remedies.

Rescue Remedy is a premixed composite remedy for all emergency or crisis situations. It's composed of Star of Bethlehem, Rock Rose, Impatiens, Cherry Plum and Clematis.

To order remedies, write:

The Secretary   Bach Center USA
The Dr. Edward Bach Centre   P.O. Box 320
Mounternon, Sotwill   Woodmere, NY 11598
Willingfor, Oxon
OX10 OPZ, England

The flowers cost approximately $108.00 and will last about ten years with regular use.

For those who have fear:

ROCK ROSE: For terror, panic, extreme fright. Give to the patient and to the people around him or her. Fear is conquered by a state of mind wherein the "small self" is forgotten in the need of the moment. Great courage, daring and compassion are the antidote for fear.

MIMULUS: For fear or anxiety of a known origin. Fears of everyday life. "All fear must be cast out: it should never exist in the human mind, and is only possible when we lose sight of Divinity." Positive qualities: understanding, courage, humor.

Appendix H

CHERRY PLUM: Desperation, fear of losing one's mind or of doing something dreadful. The positive Cherry Plum person has quiet, calm courage and endurance under stress.

ASPEN: Fears of unknown origin. Unexplained feeling of anxiety. Low pain threshold. The opposite virtue to cultivate is "fearlessness because of the knowledge that the universal power of love stands behind all. It makes the desire to invite experience and adventure because we know we can walk thru any danger unafraid."

RED CHESTNUT: Excessive fear and anxiety for others, especially those dear to us. Anticipating misfortune for others. Positive quality is the ability to send out thoughts of safety, health or courage to those who need them, especially if they're in danger or ill.

For those who suffer uncertainty:

CERATO: Distrust of self, doubt, foolishness, talkativeness. Saps other's vitality. Positive qualities: Quiet assurance, intuitive, sure of ability and judgment.

SCLERANTHUS: Undecided between two choices: imbalance. Difficulty in concentrating. Positive qualities: Calm, decisive people, poised and balanced.

GENTIAN: Doubt, depression and discouragement from a known cause. Failure, negative attitude. Positive qualities: Individuals who never let anything get them down. No failure when doing your best.

GORSE: Hopelessness, despair. "They are generally sallow and rather dark of complexion, often with dark lines beneath their eyes . . . Need sunshine to drive the clouds away." Strength may be gained in acceptance of suffering. Positive qualities, faith, hope.

371

HORNBEAM: Tiredness, weariness, mental and physical exhaustion. Auric contamination. Learn to coordinate time with effort, taking advantage of energy cycles and to use the energy of joy.

WILD OAT: Uncertainty in talented people who can't determine their course in life. Discovery of the Soul's purpose gives live direction. "If a case suggests that it needs many Remedies, or if the person does not respond to treatment, give either *Holly* or *Wild Oat*, and it will then be obvious which other Remedies may be required."

Not sufficient interest in present circumstances:

CLEMATIS: Dreamy, bored, unconscious, absent-minded, sensitive, mediumistic, poor memory. Positive qualities: Sensitive to inspiration and guidance from dreams. People who take a lively interest.

HONEYSUCKLE: Nostalgia, homesickness, dwelling upon thoughts of the past too much. Being able to use the past, with its emotional memories, but also being able to live now.

OLD ROSE: Resignation, apathy, passivity, boredom. "Let us turn life into an adventure of absorbing interest . . ." The joy of gaining experience and helping others.

OLIVE: Complete exhaustion, total fatigue of mind and body, especially after a long illness. Restores vitality, strength and an interest in life. Learn to pace yourself.

WHITE CHESTNUT: Persistent unwanted thoughts: mental arguments and conversations. Knows how to control thought and imagination and can use them creatively. Useful for sleeplessness.

MUSTARD: Black depression, gloom. "The Remedy dispels gloom and brings joy into life."

CHESTNUT BUD: Failure to learn by experience, hence repetition. Lack of observation. "This Remedy is to help us take full advantage of our daily experiences, and to see ourselves and our mistakes as others do." Keen observation, able to balance opposites.

Loneliness:

WATER VIOLET: Quiet, self-reliant people who are proud and aloof. Stiffness in mind and body. Positive: "Those who have great gentleness, are tranquil, sympathetic, wise, practical counselors, who have poise and dignity and pass gracefully through life."

IMPATIENS: Impatience, irritability, extreme mental tension. Makes quick decisions. For people quick in mind and action who can become exhausted through frustration when things don't move fast enough. Positive: Gentle and sympathetic, tolerant, considerate.

HEATHER: Self-centered, self-concerned, talks constantly. Saps others' energy. Understanding person who has suffered much and is willing to listen to and help others.

Over-sensitive to influences and ideas:

AGRIMONY: Mental torture, worry and fear concealed from others by a cheerful exterior. Peace-loving people who are distressed by quarrels. They can laugh at worries because they are aware of their unimportance. Helps transfer energy from lower centers to higher.

CENTAURY: Weak-willed; too easily influenced; willing servitors; submissive, timid. "We must earnestly learn to develop individuality according to the dictates of our own Soul." Positive: One who serves quietly and willingly, uninfluenced by others.

WALNUT: For people easily influenced by the strong opinions of others. The link-breaker. "Walnut is the Remedy of advancing stages, teething, puberty, change of life. For the big decisions made during life, such as change of religion, occupation or country."

HOLLY: Hatred, envy, jealousy, suspicion, anger. Active, intense types. "Holly protects us from everything that is not Universal Love."

For despondency or despair:

LARCH: Lack of confidence, anticipation of failure; inferiority complex; despondency. Positive Qualities: People who take the plunge into life; analytical and confident, sensitive.

PINE: Self-reproach, guilt, despondency. Blame themselves for everything that goes wrong. Of Pine, Willow, Rock Water and Larch, Dr. Bach said "(They need to realize that) one trace of condemnation against ourselves, or others, is a trace of condemnation against the Universal Creation of Love and restricts us and limits our power to allow Universal Love to flow through to others." These people will help others when needed, and persevere.

ELM: For those who are able and responsible, doing their life's work, but at times feel it is too much for them. Temporary faltering of self-confidence. Elm brings one back to earth. Helps materialize dearest hopes and wishes. Aligns centers.

Appendix H

SWEET CHESTNUT: Extreme mental anguish. For "The hopeless despair of those who feel they have reached the limit of their endurance." These are people of strong character. In the moment of anguish "the cry for help is heard and it is the moment when miracles are done."

STAR OF BETHLEHEM: For shock, after-effects of shock; refusal to be consoled. Restores balance. "The comforter and soother of pains and sorrows."

WILLOW: Resentment, bitterness, anger. Positive: Optimism and faith, accepting responsibility.

OAK: Despondency, despair, but unceasing effort. People who struggle on in the face of every difficulty. They never give up hope. "They are brave people, fighting against great difficulties without loss of hope or slackening of effort."

CRAB APPLE: Feel the need of cleansing of mind and body. Preoccupation with trivia. Restores us to our sense of proportion, singleness of purpose in creativity.

Over-care for the welfare of others:

CHICORY: Possessiveness, self-love, self-pity, perfectionism. "The cause of all our trouble is self and separateness, and this vanishes as soon as Love and the knowledge of the great Unit become part of our natures."

VERVAIN: Strain, stress, tension, over-enthusiasm. Tries to convert others. "It is the Remedy against over-effort. It teaches us that it is by *being* rather than doing that great things are accomplished."

VINE: Dominating, inflexible, ambitious, efficient, strong-willed. Positive: The wise, loving and understanding healer, leader or teacher who inspires others.

BEECH: Intolerant, critical, judgmental, lacking humility and compassion. Irritation with others comes out in rashes and allergies. "We need to be more tolerant, lenient and understanding of the different way each individual and all things are working toward their final perfection." Positive: Apply love wisely and wisdom lovingly.

ROCK WATER: Self-repression, self-denial, inflexibility. Hard masters on themselves. Positive: Reservoirs of energy. Emphasize the art of living. Love yourself.

APPENDIX I

GAMES

Dictionary Game

For four or more players. You'll need a dictionary, paper and pencils. One person (the starter) goes first and chooses a word from the dictionary whose meaning she or he doesn't think any other player knows. It can't be a word starting with a capital letter. The starter reads only the word and then writes down the dictionary definition in his or her own words. Each player writes a definition that seems right or invents one that's amusing. Then everyone passes in his or her definition to the starter, who reads all of them, not distinguishing between the dictionary definition and the rest (which means reading over them first in case someone's writing isn't clear). Everyone then guesses which is the "right" definition. Then the starter reads the dictionary definition. A player gets 10 points for writing the dictionary definition and 5 points if he or she guesses one someone else wrote. Play until you're tired of playing and add up the

Coming Home

points . . . if anyone cares. In my family we don't often bother to keep score. We just do it for the laughs.

Analogy

For as many players as you want. One person (the starter) secretly picks a person in the room. If there aren't many of you, include someone whom everyone knows. Each player uses an analogy to get clues about who this person is. The object, obviously, is to name the person. The player asks, "If she or he were a bird, what kind of bird would she or he be?" "If she or he were a flower, instrument, cloud, car, etc. . . .?" The starter answers with the kind of bird, etc. — "She'd be a seagull or a pelican." As soon as you have a feeling who it might be, guess!

APPENDIX J

REFLEXOLOGY FOOT & HAND CHARTS

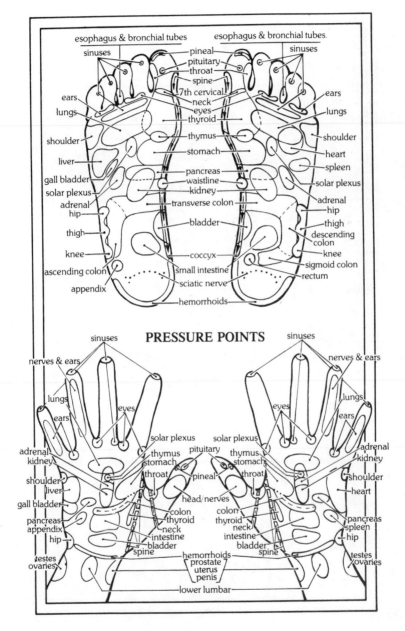

379

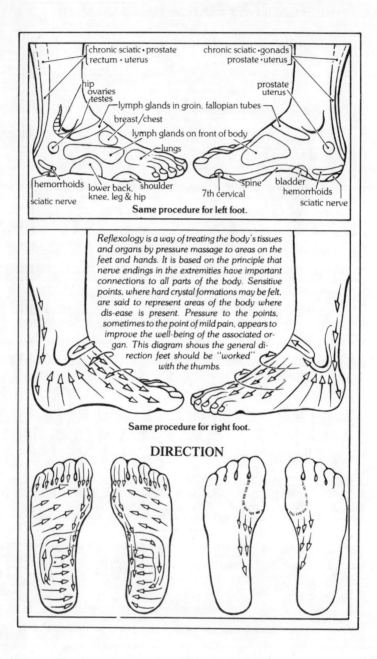

chronic sciatic • prostate
rectum • uterus

chronic sciatic • gonads
prostate • uterus

hip
ovaries
testes

prostate
uterus

lymph glands in groin, fallopian tubes

breast/chest

lymph glands on front of body

lungs

hemorrhoids

lower back,
knee, leg & hip

shoulder

spine

7th cervical

bladder
hemorrhoids

sciatic nerve

sciatic nerve

Same procedure for left foot.

Reflexology is a way of treating the body's tissues and organs by pressure massage to areas on the feet and hands. It is based on the principle that nerve endings in the extremities have important connections to all parts of the body. Sensitive points, where hard crystal formations may be felt, are said to represent areas of the body where dis-ease is present. Pressure to the points, sometimes to the point of mild pain, appears to improve the well-being of the associated organ. This diagram shows the general direction feet should be "worked" with the thumbs.

Same procedure for right foot.

DIRECTION

380

APPENDIX K

SOME HOLISTIC HEALING
TECHNIQUES AND TERMS

Acupressure: A finger pressure technique that breaks through energy flow blockages by releasing muscular tension. Acupressure uses the same system of points and meridians as acupuncture, but instead of placing needles through the skin, it works by manual pressure on tension blocks under the skin surface.*

Acupuncture: Therapy form developed in China which understands health and disease in terms of the balance or imbalance of energy flows *(chi)* within the body. These flows of energy are either stimulated or dispersed by inserting needles into specific points on the skin, by applying heat, by pressure, by massage, or by a combination of these. The system includes basic holistic principles

---

*Adapted from *The Holistic Health Handbook*, compiled by Berkeley Holistic Health Center. And/Or Press, 1978.

and practices including the five-elements theory, the cyclical laws of nature, dietary considerations, etc.*

Affirmations: Positive statements about oneself or one's situation, often used in creative visualization to focus one's attention and will on a desired result. Affirmations may be precisely specific or quite general.*

Aikido: In its purely practical application, an art of self-defense. However, aikido is more than a physical art. Its techniques are interwoven with elements of philosophy, psychology, and dynamics. It is a way of being that unites life energy *(ki)* into harmony with one's environment.*

Allopathy: Conventional systemic and symptomatic medicine as known and practiced by most physicians today. Deals generally with treatment and prevention of physical disease rather than with maintenance and improvement of health.*

Art Therapy: Free artistic expression used for diagnostic and therapeutic purposes, or as an objective means of following the progress of a particular therapy.*

Astrology: The science and art of astrology tells us precisely where the planets are at a given time and interprets the meaning of changing relationships between the planets. There is a meaningful correspondence, a 'synchronicity', between the outer worlds and earth which can facilitate understanding the patterns and possibilities in our everyday lives. A horoscope is a map of the positions of all the planets at the moment of birth, believed to be a pattern basic to understanding the personality, abilities and challenges of the individual.

Aura balancing: Process of realigning electromagnetic energy (the aura) to bring greater harmony among body, feelings, mind and soul. Based on view that human beings are inherently loving and have an inner reality more potent than any challenges.

Biofeedback: Technique by which one can learn conscious control of biological processes (especially those once thought to be involuntary by Western science) by means of subliminal information about the process that is obtained by electrical measuring instruments and fed back to the individual.*

Chiropractic: Based on theory that misalignment of vertebrae produces blockages of nerve function which causes unlimited symptoms and system malfunctions that can be cured by physical adjustments to the spine.

Color therapy: Use the light waves or energy of particular colors for healing purposes.

Dō-in: A technique for giving acupressure to oneself. It uses knowledge of the effects of specific points to obtain temporary relief.*

Dream Work: Techniques of using dreams as a means of bringing unconscious feelings, thoughts and patterns to conscious awareness.

Encounter: Approach to personality integration that encourages participants to be open and honest in a group setting, often eliciting emotions that lead to confrontation.

Feldenkrais exercises: Simple and often effective exercises developed by Moshe Feldenkrais to use body energy more naturally and efficiently to retrain the brain's habitual response patterns.

Gestalt therapy: Therapy and approach to personality integration originally developed by Fritz and Laura Perls that uses immediate excitement and awareness to develop personal responsibility.

Guided fantasy: Techniques where structured fantasy (stories, characters, situations) is used for the study of activation of subpersonalities, or personal archetypes, involving their attitudes toward a current problem or situation, and to obtain access to other contents of the unconscious mind.*

Herbs: Plants used for their medicinal qualities.

Homeopathy: A healing system based on the principle that "like cures like." Homeopathic physicians believe that a remedy has the potential to cure a disease if it produces symptoms (similar to those of the disease) in a healthy organism. Another basic premise of homeopathy is that there are no diseases as such, only 'diseased individuals.'*

Iridology: Diagnosis of health from markings that appear in close examination of the eye.

Martial arts: Oriental disciplines evolved from the path of the Warrior, which properly used can lead to spiritual and physical integration, **e.g.** Aikido, Karate, King Fu, T'ai Chi.*

Massage: A healing art that uses physical touch and manipulation to relax the body, balance and free energy, and soothe the mind and feelings.

Meditation: Quiet deep level awareness. Meditation is not a single practice, and thus not easily defined. It encompasses diverse methods such as formal sitting (as in *zazen* or Vipassana), in which the body is held immobile and the attention controlled; expressive practices (such as Siddha Yoga, the Latihan, or the chaotic meditation of Rajneesh), in which the body is set free and anything can happen; and even the practice of going about one's daily round of activities mindfully (as in Mahamudra, Shiken Taza, or Gurdjieff's "self-remembering").*

Movement therapy: The use of dance and other forms of directed physical movement for healing effects.*

Music therapy: Certain kinds of music employed to achieve specific health restoring and promoting goals, including heightened awareness and acceptance of all parts of the self.

Neoreichian therapy: A type of breathing activity developed from the work of Wilhelm Reich to release emotional patterns locked in the body. Yelling, crying, laughing, pounding, kicking, etc., are often used as part of the technique.

Polarity therapy: A science and practice of balancing the life energy in the human body. Objectives are to discover the anatomical relationship and function of the vital energy circuits and fields by which the body was built and continues to function, as "plus and minus" energy polarities, and to balance them by scientific skill rather than by force of mechanics. This is done through gentle hand contact, loving thought and attitude, exercise, and diet.*

Postural integratation: A form of deep connective tissue manipulation. Greater emphasis on the entire being, physical and emotional, distinguishes it from Rolfing. P.I. sessions often include Reichian breathing work and polarity manipulations.*

Psychosynthesis: An inclusive approach to growth developed by Roberto Assagioli that focuses on expressing the will of the Higher Self.

Psychic healing: Healing energy from universal sources is transmitted consciously by the practitioner (or the afflicted person) mentally, by laying on hands or by "absent healing" (from a distance).

Rebirthing: Practitioners guide a person to relive the birth process — thereby releasing the trauma of birth.

Reflexology: Foot zone therapy. Pressure and massage primarily to the toes and soles of the feet are used to stimulate nerve endings in the feet to promote healing in specific areas of the body.

Rolfing: A technique of deep manipulation of the musculoskeletal system to bring its major segments — head, shoulders, thorax and legs — toward a vertical alignment. The technique often stimulates painful areas which are thought to contain 'blockages' brought on by a person's past experiences and habits. Alignment relieves these patterns and allows the person to develop new ones. Developed by Ida P. Rolf.*

Shiatsu: A traditional form of Japanese finger-pressure massage used as a preventive health measure. Contact is made by slow, deep penetration of key points along acupuncture meridians.

T'ai chi ch'uan: Traditional series of movements that are intended to unite consciousness of body and mind. It is a form of spiritual and physical exercise and probably originated with the early Taoists.*

Tarot: An ancient set of 78 picture images representing fundamental human archetypal energy patterns. They have been found useful in a system in which the practitioner uses conscious and unconscious faculties to interpret the relationship of the Tarot symbols to an individual's life and unconscious knowing.

Appendix K

Visualization: Creative means for using imagination to positively transform any life situation. Visualization includes processes of forming images and thoughts in the mind, and then transmitting them to the body as signals or commands.*

Yoga: (Sanskrit — "to yoke, join, fasten or harness") Meditative work to concentrate and focus the mind in order to obtain union with universal spirit. Techniques and underlying philosophy which help to bring about a natural balance of body and mind in which the state of health can manifest itself. Yoga is an applied science of the mind and body stemming from the Indian philosophical system of Samkhva.*

APPENDIX L

WRITING YOUR CHILD'S STORY

This suggestion from the parent of a child who died, appeared in a Compassionate Friends' newsletter, St. Louis, Missiouri.

The possibility of forgetting even the smallest detail of our child's life is a fear most of us have. In truth, over the months and years many of these details do dim. Writing them down is a way to keep from losing these memories. This way we will not only have a permanent remembrance of our child for ourselves, but this will be a legacy for the other brothers and sisters. Here are some suggestions.

— Write in a spiral notebook.

— Begin at the beginning. Write all the details of your child's life from birth through the death day.

— Use your child's pictures to help remind you of occasions and happenings over the years. Ask friends and relatives to tell you anything they remember about your child. Also write any thoughts and feelings you remember having at the time.

— Record the 'bad' things your child said and did in his life, as well as the 'good' things, so you can remember him as a real person.

— Write about your child's death. Record as many details surrounding it as you care to retell. Write about the days before the burial, the funeral, the days after, two weeks, a month, and so on. Record how others helped.

Write a letter to your child, and include:

What I wish I had said to you.

What I wish I had done.

What I wish you would have done.

What I wish I could ask you.

What I wish I hadn't said to you.

What I wish I had not done.

What I wish you had not done.

What I would like to tell you.

Pour out your feelings to your child. Tell him of your anger, your guilts. Tell your child how you love her/him. Tell your child GOODBYE.

Don't worry about whether you write well or not. Don't worry about form or grammar. Just write.

Keep your notebook handy. Write any time you want to say something to him/her, or when you remember some detail that suddenly comes to mind. The times you have trouble sleeping write down the things that keep coming into your mind.

Appendix L

Writing about your child or to your child will be emotional. It will probably make you cry. Don't let this stop you. Crying can be extremely helpful in releasing your tensions and will help you with your grief work.

Remember, writing is just talking written down.

APPENDIX M

CONSUMER GUIDE
TO THE FTC FUNERAL RULE

Each year, Americans arrange more than two million funerals for family and friends. When arranging a funeral, consumers may not be initially concerned about cost. Still, many consumers may spend more for a funeral than for almost anything else they buy. In fact, at an average cost of $2,400, a funeral may be the third most expensive consumer purchase after a home and a car.

The Federal Trade Commission developed a trade regulation rule concerning funeral industry practices, which went into effect on April 30, 1984. It is called the Funeral Rule, and its purpose is to enable consumers to obtain information about funeral arrangements.

In general, the rule makes it easier for you to select only those goods and services you want or need and to pay for only those you select. Now, for example, you can find out the cost of individual items over the telephone. Also, when you inquire in person about funeral arrangements, the funeral home will give you a written price list of the goods and services available. When arranging a funeral, you can purchase individual items or buy an entire package of goods and services. If you want to purchase a casket, the funeral provider will supply a list that describes all the available selections and their prices. Thus, as described in greater detail in the following sections, the FTC's Funeral Rule helps you obtain information about the cost and availability of individual funeral goods and services.

TELEPHONE PRICE DISCLOSURES

When you call a funeral provider and ask about terms, conditions, or prices, of funeral goods or services, the funeral provider will:

- tell you that price information is available over the telephone.
- give you prices and other information from the price lists to reasonably answer your questions.
- give you any other information about prices or offerings that is readily available and reasonably answer your questions.

By using the telephone, you can compare prices among funeral providers. Getting price information over the telephone may thus help you select a funeral home and the arrangements you want.

Appendix M

GENERAL PRICE LIST

If you inquire in person about funeral arrangements, the funeral provider will give you a general price list. This list, which you can keep, contains the cost of each individual funeral item and service offered. As with telephone inquiries, you can use this information to help select the funeral provider and funeral items you want, need, and are able to afford.

The price list also discloses important legal rights and requirements regarding funeral arrangements. It must include information on embalming, cash advance sales (such as newspaper notices or flowers), caskets for cremation, and required purchases.

EMBALMING INFORMATION

The Funeral Rule requires providers to give consumers information about embalming that can help them decide whether to purchase this service. Under the Rule, a funeral provider:

- may not falsely state that embalming is required by law.

- must disclose in writing that, except in certain special cases, embalming is *not* required by law.

- may not charge a fee for unauthorized embalming unless it is required by state law.

- will disclose in writing that you usually have the right to choose a disposition such as direct cremation or immediate burial if you do not want embalming.

- will disclose to you in writing that certain funeral arrangements, such as a funeral with a viewing, may make embalming a practical necessity and, thus, a required purchase.

CASH ADVANCE SALES

The Funeral Rule requires funeral providers to disclose to you in writing if they charge a fee for buying cash advance items. Cash advance items are foods or services that are paid for by the funeral provider on your behalf. Some examples of cash advance items are flowers, obituary notices, pallbearers, and clergy honoraria. Some funeral providers charge you their cost for these items. Others add a service fee to their cost. The Funeral Rule requires the funeral provider to inform you when a service fee is added to the price of cash advance items, or if the provider gets a refund, discount, or rebate from the supplier of any cash advance item.

CASKETS FOR CREMATION

Some consumers may want to select direct cremation, which is cremation of the deceased without a viewing or other ceremony at which they body is present. If you choose a direct cremation, the funeral provider will offer you either an inexpensive alternative container or an unfinished wood box. An alternative container is a non-metal enclosure used to hold the deceased. These containers may be made of pressboard, cardboard, or canvas.

Because any container you buy will be destroyed during the cremation, you may wish to use an alternative container or an unfinished wood box for a direct cremation. These could lower your funeral cost since they are less expensive than traditional burial caskets.

Under the Funeral Rule, funeral directors who offer direct cremations:

- may not tell you that state or local law requires a casket for direct cremations.

- must disclose in writing your right to buy an unfinished wood box (a type of casket) or an alternative container for a direct cremation.

- must make an unfinished wood box or alternative container available for direct cremation.

REQUIRED PURCHASE

You do not have to purchase unwanted goods or services as a condition of obtaining those you do want unless you are required to do so by state law. Under the Funeral Rule:

- you have the right to choose only the funeral goods and services you want, with some disclosed exceptions.

- the funeral provider must disclose this right in writing on the general price list.

- the funeral provider must disclose on the statement of goods and services selected the specific law that requires you to purchase any particular item.

STATEMENT OF FUNERAL GOODS AND SERVICES SELECTED

The funeral provider will give you an itemized statement with the total cost of the funeral goods and services you select. This statement also will disclose any legal, cemetery, or crematory requirements that compel you to purchase any specific funeral goods or services.

The funeral provider must give you this statement after you select the funeral goods and services that you would like. The statement combines in one place the prices of the individual items you are considering for purchase, as well as the total price. Thus, you can decide whether to add or subtract items to get what you want. If the cost of cash advance items is not known at that time, the funeral provider must write down a "good faith estimate" of their cost. The rule does not require any specific form for this information. Therefore, funeral providers may include this information in any document they give you at the end of your discussion about funeral arrangements.

Appendix M

PRESERVATIVE AND PROTECTIVE CLAIMS

Under the Funeral Rule, funeral providers are prohibited from telling you a particular funeral item or service can indefinitely preserve the body of the deceased in the grave. The information gathered during the FTC's investigation indicated these claims are not true. For example, funeral providers may not claim embalming or a particular type of casket will indefinitely preserve the deceased's body.

The Rule also prohibits funeral providers from making claims that funeral goods, such as caskets or vaults, will keep out water, dirt, and other gravesite substances when that is not true.

OTHER CONSIDERATIONS

Most decisions about purchasing funeral goods and services are made by people when they are grieving and under time constraints. Thinking ahead may help you make informed and thoughtful decisions about funeral arrangements. In this way, you can carefully choose the specific items you want and need and can compare prices offered by one or more funeral providers.

If you decide to make advance plans about funeral arrangements either for yourself or a loved one, you can choose among several types of dispositions and ceremonies. The type of disposition you choose may affect the cost. Some people prefer a ceremonial service, religious or secular, with the body present. Others choose an immediate bur-

6666

66

ial and hold a memorial or other ceremony with no body present. Another service is cremation which may be performed either directly or after a ceremony. In addition, the deceased body may be donated (either directly or after a ceremony) to a medical or educational institution. To help ensure that your wishes are carried out, you may want to write down your preferences. It may also be helpful to tell relatives and other responsible persons what you have decided.

FOR MORE INFORMATION

Most states have a licensing board that regulates the funeral industry. You may contact the licensing board in your state for information or help. You may also contact the Conference of Funeral Service Examining Boards, 520 E. Van Trees Street, P.O. Box 497, Washington, Indiana 47501, (801) 254-7887. This association, which represents the licensing boards of 47 states, will provide information on the laws of the various states and will accept and respond to consumer inquiries or complaints about funeral providers.

FOR FURTHER HELP

If you have a problem concerning funeral matters, first attempt to resolve it with your funeral director. If you are dissatisfied, contact your federal, state, or local consumer protection agencies, the Conference of Funeral Service Examining Boards, or ThanaCAP. While the Federal Trade Commission does not resolve individual consumer or pri-

Appendix M

vate disputes, information about your experience may show a pattern of conduct or practice that the Commission may investigate to determine if any action is warranted. Write or call: Federal Trade Commission, Bureau of Consumer Protection, Division of Enforcement, Washington, D.C. 20580, 202/376-2891.

APPENDIX N

REFERENCES

About Dying. A Scriptographic Booklet. Channing L. Bete Co. New Haven CT, 1978.

Ars Moriendi (Dying Arts). Walter J. Johnson edition. (One of the world's first do-it-yourself books, it taught the art of dying. Original was published in Florence in 1488. A modern English edition was published by Arno Press. New York, 1977.)

Berkeley Holistic Health Center. *The Holistic Health Handbook*. And/Or Press, Berkeley, CA, 1978.

Blake, William, *Notebook*. Geoffrey Keynes, ed. Cooper Square, Totowa, NJ, 1971.

Boone, J. Allen, *Kinship with All Life*. Harper and Row, New York, 1976.

Bricklin, Mark, *The Practical Encyclopedia of Natural Healing*. Rodale Press, Emmaus, PA.

Caxton, William (translator). *Art and Craft to Knowe Ye Well to Dye*. William Caxton, Westminster, England, 1490. (This book includes instructions for everything from the art of blowing your nose to weeping well.)

Coughlin, George G. *Law for the Layman*. Harper and Row, New York, 1975.

Cousins, Norman. *Anatomy of an Illness as Perceived by the Patient: Reflections on Healing and Regeneration*. W. W. Norton and Co., New York, 1979.

Appendix N

Fortune, Dion, *Through the Gates of Death*. Samuel Weiser, York Beach, ME, 1968.

Frankl, Victor, *Man's Search for Meaning: An Introduction to Logotherapy*. Beacon Press, Boston, MA, 1959. (Victor Frankl is a psychiatrist who survived Auschwitz and Dachau. After his experiences there he would state, "The salvation of man is through love and in love.")

Fynn, *Mister God, This is Anna*. Ballantine Books, New York, 1974.

Gibran, Kahil, *The Prophet*. Alfred A. Knopf, New York, 1967.

The Gospel According to Thomas. (A. Guillaumont *et al*, translators of the apocryphal Coptic text.) Harper and Row, New York, 1957.

Gray, V. Ruth, *Dealing with Death and Dying, Some Physiological Needs*. Nursing 77 Books, Nursing Skill Book Service, Jenkintown, PA, 1976.

Grof, Stanislav, and Joan Halifax, *The Human Encounter with Death*. E. P. Dutton, New York, 1978.

Heline, Corinne, "Color and Music in the New Age," *New Age*, 1964.

Holland, Canon Scott, *Facts of Faith*.

Huxley, Laura, *This Timeless Moment*. Celestial Arts, Millbrae, CA. 1975. (Describes the death of Aldous Huxley, an innovative adventurer in the human mind. Huxley used LSD in his last days in order to experience his death as fully as possible.)

Illich, Ivan, *Medical Nemesis*. Pantheon, New York, 1976.

Internal Revenue Service
A Guide to Federal Estate and Gift Taxation (No. 448)
Tax Information to Survivors (No. 559)

Jampolsky, Gerald, *Love is Letting Go of Fear*. Celestial Arts, Millbrae, CA, 1979.

Khan, Hazrat Inayat, *The Purpose of Life*. The Rainbow Bridge Bookstore, San Francisco, CA. 1973.

Lack, Sylvia A., *Psychosocial Care of the Dying Patient*. Charles Garfield (ed.) McGraw Hill, New York, 1978. (Originally a paper given before the First National Training Conference for Physicians on Psychosocial Care of the Dying Patient, April 29, 1976. Sylvia A. Lack is a national hospice organizer.)

LeShan, Eda, *Learning to say Goodbye*. Macmillan, New York 1976. (Also available as an Avon paperback.)

Levine, Stephen, *The Gradual Awakening*. Doubleday, New York, 1979.

Lipnack, Jessica (ed.) "Dying: New Age Readers Respond," *New Age* magazine, March, 1978.

Lopez, Barry (ed.) "The American Indian Mind," *Omni* magazine. Sept.-Oct. 1978. (Section on "Knowing how to die," p. 113.)

Maclean, Dorothy, *To Hear the Angels Sing*. Findhorn Publications, 1980.

Marback, Ethel, *The Cabbage Moth and the Shamrock*. Star and Elephant Books, Green Tiger Press, La Jolla, CA. 1978.

Miriam, Satya, *Healing Is Transformation: The Opening of the Rose*. Baraka Books, New York, 1978.

Appendix N

Moody, Raymond, M.D., *Life After Life*, Stackpole Books, Harrisburg, PA, 1976.

Morgan, Ernest, *A Manual of Death Education and Simple Burial*. Celo Press, Route 5, Burnsville, NC 17814, 1977. (Available for $6.50 postpaid. Also available through memorial societies.)

Muggeridge, Malcolm, *Something Beautiful for God*. Doubleday, New York, 1977.

Muir, John, *The Velvet Monkey Wrench*. John Muir Publications, Santa Fe, NM, 1973.

Neihardt, John G., *Black Elk Speaks*. University of Nebraska Press, Lincoln, NB, 1961.

Osis, Dr. Karlis and Erlendur Haraldsson, "Deathbed Observations by Physicians and Nurses: A Cross-Cultural Survey," in *The Journal for the American Society of Psychical Research* and published as *Parapsychological Monograph No. 3*, Parapsychology Foundation, 1961.

Perry, Whitall N., *A Treasury of Traditional Wisdom*. Simon and Schuster, New York, 1971.

Rajneesh Foundation Newsletter, "Here Comes a Fresh Breeze of God," *Rajneesh Foundation Newsletter*, Volume III, No. 18, Sept. 16, 1977.

Seiver, George, *The Man and His Mind*. Harper and Row, New York, 1976.

Stern, Phillip, *Lawyers on Trial*, Times Books, New York, 1980.

Sultanoff, Barry, "Reflections," an article in *The Movement* newspaper, May 1986.

AURORA PRESS

Aurora Press is devoted to pioneering books that catalyze personal growth, balance and transformation. Aurora makes available in a digestible format, an innovative synthesis of ancient wisdom with twentieth century resources, integrating esoteric knowledge and daily life.

Recent titles include:

COMING HOME
Deborah Duda

CRYSTAL ENLIGHTENMENT
Katrina Raphaell

CRYSTAL HEALING
Katrina Raphaell

SILVER DENTAL FILLINGS • THE TOXIC TIMEBOMB
Sam Ziff

AWAKEN HEALING ENERGY THROUGH THE TAO
Mantak Chia

TAOIST SECRETS OF LOVE
Mantak Chia

THE LUNATION CYCLE
Dane Rudhyar

SELF HEALING, YOGA AND DESTINY
Elisabeth Haich

For a complete catalog write:

AURORA PRESS
P.O. BOX 573
SANTA FE NEW MEXICO 87504
(505) 989-9804